Praise for *The Promise of Proactive Parenting: Sea Change*...

The Promise of Proactive Parenting: Sea Change is a book that makes great sense. If your parenting is going to go the way you want it to, you need to have a plan for what to do. Lynne Griffin supplies such a plan. Her book gives very clear, highly usable recommendations that will work because they are based in a deep understanding of child development, as well as the differing needs of individual children. Lynne Griffin has written a wonderful, sensitive, very readable, and above all, very helpful parenting guide.

> Anthony E. Wolf
> Author of *Get out of my life, but first can you drive me and Cheryl to the mall?*

The Promise of Proactive Parenting has changed my life! This approach gave me realistic and practical tools for parenting. Lynne really cares about children and their families.

> Pam Millis
> Mother of two daughters

Finally, an approach that combines an understanding of children's development and temperamental differences with the knowledge that behavior occurs in the context of human relationships. Lynne's approach is generous and insightful. I really love this holistic and educational approach.

> Lois Haultain
> Director of The Positive Parenting
> Network of Australia

Lynne's approach has changed our whole method of parenting which has resulted in a significant boost in the quality of life for our entire family. *Proactive Parenting* has been the keystone to helping us gain control and manage the growing pains of our young family.

> Romalda and Peter Blanchard
> Parents of two young sons

The Promise of Proactive Parenting is an approach that respects parents' intelligence and demonstrates a real understanding of the challenges parents face today. The useful tools and case studies will be helpful to parents of children all ages. I really like this book!

> Sue Blaney
> Author of *Please Stop the Rollercoaster! How Parents of Teenagers Can Smooth Out the Ride.*

The Promise of
PROACTIVE PARENTING

7 April 04

Best Wishes —
Lynne
Griffin

susanemedici@yahoo.com

blank'sjamie@comcast.net

muhq5@comcast.net

mmkd@comcast.net

rosedmiller@me.com

nzappolo@comcast.net

kelly-donovan@comcast.net

The Promise of PROACTIVE PARENTING

Sea Change

Lynne Reeves Griffin RN, M.Ed.

cP

Aventine Press

Most of the case studies used in this book are composites of situations that the author has dealt with in private practice or in workshops. The names of actual parents and children have been changed to respect the confidentiality of specific individuals.

If you would like to contact the author about services such as workshops or consultation, you may email her at Lynne@eproactiveparenting.com

Published by Aventine Press, LLC
2208 Cabo Bahia
Chula Vista, CA 91914, USA
www.aventinepress.com

Library of Congress Cataloging-in-Publication Data
2004101326
ISBN: 1-59330-146-4
Printed in the United States of America

To Tom, Caitlin and Stephen
You are my most precious gifts from God
You have given me all the love and support
a person could ever hope for.

In Loving Memory of John and Patricia Reeves.

Acknowledgements

Where do I begin to thank the people who have made this book possible? I will begin by thanking all the parents and professionals that have shared their stories with me. Your anecdotes have given the book a richness that comes from real life struggles and successes.

To my friends and colleagues...Michele Brennion, Jeanne Crehan, Patti Donovan, Colleen Gibbons, Bruce Kerans. The support and encouragement you sent my way defines the word friendship.

To my editors....Julie Basque, Carolyn Hayes and Tom Griffin. I am so appreciative of the energy, enthusiasm and time you gave to make this book take shape.

To my Reeves and Griffin family members, especially Dianne Veale and Mary and Larry Griffin. How lucky I am to have such warm, loving people in my life.

To my dear family...Tom, Caitlin and Stephen. Words can not express the depth of my love and gratitude to you for believing in me and the message.

And last but in fact first to God. Prayers of thanksgiving to you for blessing me with family and work that bring great purpose to my life.

Success

To laugh often and much
To win the respect of intelligent people and the affection of children;
To earn the appreciation of honest critics and
endure the betrayal of false friends;
To appreciate beauty, to find the best in others;
To leave the world a bit better, whether by a healthy child, a garden
patch or a redeemed social condition; to know even one life has breathed
easier because you haved lived. That is to have succeeded.

Ralph Waldo Emerson

Table of Contents

ONE

Let's Sea Change

An Introduction to Proactive Parenting

Sex, drugs and school shootings are the makings of headlines all across the United States. How often do you hear that children today don't respect themselves or others? Newspapers and television abound with examples of disrespectful, violent and even criminal behavior and seem to suggest that nothing can be done to turn the tide. Today, your child is bombarded with sophisticated messages and exposed to situations that he is not yet developmentally able to handle. It isn't enough to tell your child to "just say no." You need to make good decisions for your child and then teach him the skills he needs to live with those decisions. From whether to teach your two-year-old not to kick like a cartoon character, let your ten-year-old surf the Internet, or let your thirteen-year-old see an R-rated movie, you probably feel overwhelmed. You might be asking, "Has parenting always been this hard?"

I think parenting has always been hard and will always be hard. Like your parents, you have to contend with teaching values, managing conflict and teaching your child to act in acceptable ways. But unlike your parents, you have to contend with new and pervasive societal influences. You need to work harder than ever to slow the pace of your child's life down while at the same time give her the skills she needs to think first and then make good decisions out in the world. The children you read about in newspapers or hear about on the news did not suddenly find themselves in situations beyond their emotional capabilities. More than likely these children were expected to act a lot older than their age for years before they found themselves the subject of a news story or an *Oprah* show. Everyday, you are besieged with information that influences your parenting and decision-making. Myth or fact..."Your child *needs* enrichment experiences such as sports and music." Myth or fact... "All brothers and sisters fight, you *shouldn't* interfere." Myth or fact... "A baby should sleep anywhere he likes as long as he sleeps." Myth or fact..."Long periods of time playing computer games isn't harmful to your child as long as the software is educational." Whether you get your parenting information from the media, other parents or just feel the pressure to follow the leader, these and other myths can mislead you into making decisions for your child that are counter productive to achieving family harmony.

Because of the new and more complicated societal influences, parenting is in fact harder today than it was even twenty years ago and if that weren't enough you have to do the job in less time than ever. Consider what is being expected of the child in this situation.

Emma

Emma is awakened at 5:45 a.m. She gets dressed and packs some food for the long day ahead. Emma's parents repeatedly nag her to gather the belongings she will need for the day. After an hour where emotions are running high for both Emma and her parents, she leaves the house at 7:00 a.m. Emma spends the early morning in the company of twenty children and one adult. During the day, she does her work in three separate locations under the direction of four different adults. She arrives home after her second enrichment activity and changes into comfortable clothes. The nighttime routine includes a new set of power struggles between Emma and her parents. "Sit down and eat." "Empty your backpack." "Finish your homework." At 6:45 p.m., bedtime is only a dream. At 7 o'clock, Emma finally sits down to do her homework. Emma is seven years old.

Throughout this book, I promise that you will learn practical strategies for facing today's parenting challenges.

Whether you are a new parent looking for a practical parenting approach or a parent of a teenager struggling with day to day conflict, this comprehensive approach has much to offer.

Developmental, behavioral and focused on temperament

Should you be discouraged with the affects of our changing society on discipline and parenting? Absolutely not! Adopting the common sense approach, Proactive Parenting will help you make sense of your challenges and help you to acquire the skills you need to take an active role in your parenting.

Proactive Parenting is a sensible, predictable, developmentally sound approach that teaches you how to parent effectively whether your child is a toddler or a teenager. The approach teaches you how to anticipate situations where your child may have difficulty and guides you in planning the right strategies based on your child's age. The approach is based on a framework of mutual respect between you and your child; it is developmental, behavioral and based on your child's specific temperament.

How old are you now?

At every age, your child is capable of new ways of moving, thinking, feeling and interacting with the world. Proactive Parenting is a developmental approach to parenting. The parenting strategies you use to teach your child how to play safely or clean her room will depend on her age and development. By knowing what your child is capable of at each developmental stage, you can have realistic expectations of her. The way your daughter thinks, socializes and copes with her feelings will change as she grows from an infant to a teenager. So as she grows, the discipline choices you make will need to adapt to fit her increasing capabilities.

Child development research universally suggests that the kind of experiences you give your growing child influence her physical and emotional growth and development.

There is a wide range of normal when it comes to reaching developmental milestones.   One child may walk at ten months, while another may not walk until age fifteen months. While each child develops at his own pace, it is important for you to provide age-appropriate discipline experiences. The parent of the "walker" will have to make different discipline choices than the parent of the "non-walker." The Proactive Parenting approach acknowledges that you are always teaching and your child is always learning as you parent. All the learning experiences you expose your child to, whether positive or negative, will affect development.

Tim

Your five-year-old son, Tim has been having some tough days lately. He melts down or gets angry if something doesn't go his way. He generally seems out of sorts. Yesterday he even said, "Why is everything going wrong?" Today, you decided to read your son the story by Judith Viorst called, *Alexander's Terrible, No Good, Very Bad Day*. After reading the story, you talk about your expectations for his behavior whether he is having a bad day or not. You say, "It is okay to have a bad day once in awhile, but you can't shout or hit people when things don't go your way. If you are upset, I want you to take a deep breath and tell me you are upset." Later that same day, Tim is coloring and gets upset because he doesn't like what he has colored. He takes a crayon, scribbles all over the paper and crumples it up. He bangs his fists on the table and shouts, "I hate this drawing!" You calmly walk over to the crayons and paper and begin to put the activity away. Tim starts to cry and says, "Don't put it away. I'm sorry, I'm sorry, I'm sorry!" You say, "If you can not color without losing your temper, then you will not color right now."

Reading the story to Tim was a proactive strategy for teaching him about behavior and expectations. New research confirms what experts and parents already knew; talking, singing, and reading enhance your child's development. And the time you spend reading and singing will create some of the closest moments you and your child will share. So, in the situation with Tim, the proactive strategy of sharing expectations about his behavior will positively influence his cognitive and social development. But so too will the actions you take when in conflict. The choices you make in handling misbehavior will influence development as well. If you spend most of your time reacting to misbehavior and losing control of your emotions, this too will affect your child's development. If Tim's mother repeatedly shouts or reacts negatively to his behavior, Tim's personality, his ability to learn and how he interacts with others will be negatively affected. In order to positively influence development, it becomes important to see interactions with your child as opportunities for teaching and learning. So let's say you agree that the discipline choices you make will influence your child's development. How do you know at what age certain strategies can and should be used? In Chapter 2, how your child thinks and learns at each age will be discussed in detail. Once you understand how your child thinks and learns you will be ready to learn how to choose strategies for discipline that are consistent with her age. In Chapter 7, I will discuss how Proactive Parenting works with children under age 3. In Chapter 8, I will discuss how Proactive Parenting works with children ages 3 to 9. In Chapter 9, I will discuss how Proactive Parenting works with children ages 10 to 18.

Show me the skills

Proactive Parenting is a behavioral approach to parenting. I believe that behavior can be modified through skill building. You can teach your child the appropriate ways to behave by refining skills he already has or by teaching him skills that he may not have. Like your child's development, skill building also occurs through an active process of teaching and learning. For example, your child may have some wonderful social skills but isn't able to be patient or share very well with friends. The good news is that the skills your child needs help with can be taught. For the child who has trouble speaking up for herself or would rather play alone, social skills can be taught. Proactive Parenting is a teaching, learning approach that can help you to modify, enhance, correct or refine behavior.

Caroline

Fourteen-month-old Caroline has a new habit.   She likes to stand up in her high chair.   You are becoming increasingly concerned for her safety.   Since she will do it whether you are right near her or not, you are afraid that she will fall.   Today, you decide to take her out of the high chair every time she stands up.   You will not reprimand or talk to Caroline, you will just repeatedly take her out. Whether she has just started to eat or she is done, you do it every time she stands up.   At first, Caroline thinks it is a game, but by the dinner hour, she is starting to get annoyed each time you take her out.   The next morning at breakfast, Caroline stands up in her high chair.   You get out of your seat and start to walk over to the high chair and Caroline quickly sits down.

In this situation, you matched an action to a behavior.   By not talking and simply being consistent, Caroline gets the message.   "If I stand up, I will be taken out of the high chair." She can not say this to you but she understands.   This is a good example of a behavioral technique called reinforcement. You discouraged her negative behavior...standing up in the high chair, by applying a consequence...taking her out. When I suggest to one of my clients to do something like this, I inevitably hear, "But if you take her out, you are just giving her what she wants."   To this I say, so what?   If your goal really is to keep Caroline safe...then you should take her out.   If she is done eating and goes to play...fine.   If she really wants to be in the high chair, she will quickly learn the way she must behave in order to stay there.   This behavioral approach takes patience and commitment; you can't get tired and give in.   You do invest time using this technique but you will also enjoy a positive outcome.   Did you notice in the situation with Caroline that the next day she tested her mother to see if she would still take her out?

I consider myself primarily a behaviorist.   I frequently coach parents, teachers, healthcare professionals and children in using techniques that will help them to modify or change behavior.   Discussing issues, choosing options and practicing strategies specific to the problem being addressed is integral to the Proactive Parenting approach.

Behavioral skills training has proven very successful in teaching or modifying behavior in children. I rely on a child's family and teachers in choosing specific techniques that will strengthen the behavioral process. While some of the techniques used in Proactive Parenting have their roots in cognitive and family therapy, most of the techniques or strategies used in Proactive Parenting have their roots in behavioral research. Using verbal or written agreements between you and your child is called contingency contracting. Practicing what you preach is called role modeling. Letting your child practice situations in which he might have difficulty is called role-playing. Regardless of the technical term, Proactive Parenting will teach you how to be an effective coach. By using these behavioral techniques, your child will acquire the social, cognitive, self-control, stress management and problem-solving skills she needs to make responsible decisions about her behavior. Throughout the book, but specifically in Chapter 2, the fine points of behavioral skill building will be outlined.

It's not how you start, it's how you finish

The temperament of every child is unique. If you have more than one child, you know that no two children are exactly alike. In fact, if you have more than one child, you may be reading this book with one particular child in mind. Your child may learn the skills she needs to behave in acceptable ways very easily. Or your child may find learning certain skills more difficult. It isn't uncommon to hear a parent say, "I've tried different parenting strategies, but they don't work with *my child*." Because each child has different strengths and different needs related to temperament, each will require an individualized approach to skill development. The discipline strategies you use with one child may not be effective with another child.

Maya and Nico

Maya and Nico are eleven-year-old twins. It is their first day of middle school and you are getting ready for work. Nico has been up since six o'clock eager to start the new year. With just ten minutes until the bus comes, he shouts, "Did someone move my school supplies? Where is my jacket?" While you try to help Nico get organized, you realize Maya is still upstairs. You call out to your daughter; "The bus comes in five minutes." When she doesn't come down, you walk upstairs and say, "Maya, what are you doing, it is almost time to leave." While her room is as neat as a pin, she sits down on her bed, and starts to cry. "I don't want to be in middle school. I'm not going!" Looking at the clock, you sigh, knowing that everyone will be late.

Will the strategies you choose to get Maya and Nico successfully off to school be the same? The answer is no. While Nico's enthusiasm about starting the new school year is great, he needs to work on becoming more organized. While Maya is organized by nature, she is struggling with what the new year might bring. She needs to learn how to cope with transition. Proactive Parenting encourages you to think about the specific temperament of each child, in advance. By age eleven, you know that Nico and Maya's temperaments are different.   They each have different strengths.   Nico accepts change in stride and Maya is orderly and prepared. Yet, in order to make the transition to middle school successful, each child must strengthen different skills.   The coaching you do will be aimed at helping each child to strengthen different skills. Proactive Parenting recognizes that the specific temperament of your child will affect the discipline strategies you choose. The plan you need to help Maya will be unique and not the same plan you will use to help Nico. Whether your child is sensitive, persistent, intense or moody, you can factor these elements of temperament into your Proactive Parenting. The challenging traits your child is born with can be refined, making it easier for him to get along in the world. In Chapter 2, you will learn about the different elements of temperament as well as how to maximize the positive. Using behavioral techniques, you will learn to minimize the challenging aspects of temperament and effectively teach your child the skills he needs to handle any situation.

Three kinds of discipline

In our society, the word discipline is associated with punishment. When you think of the word discipline, do you envision your child doing something he is not supposed to be doing while you debate whether or not to step in? I believe that discipline is so much more than that. The word discipline means to teach and learn. Teaching and learning, therefore, discipline, takes place all the time. With ever-increasing stress in your life, are you spending more time reacting to your child's behavior and less time anticipating the ways in which you can teach your child to behave well? Actively teaching your child about values, acceptable behavior and good decision-making is a proactive, not reactive approach to parenting.

In Proactive Parenting, there are three kinds of discipline and each is interrelated to the other two. Proactive Parenting is an approach that includes proactive discipline, conflict discipline and societal discipline.

Proactive discipline

Proactive discipline teaches your child values, responsibility and good decision making. It takes place when "discipline" is the farthest thing from your mind or your child's. Whether you realize it or not, this is the type of discipline that you should do most of the time. It is the kind of discipline that is the most effective in changing your child's behavior. Proactive discipline takes place when your child is not doing anything you object to. I bet when your child is behaving well, you would just as soon leave well enough alone, but this is a perfect time to actively teach your child what you expect of him. It is the time you spend talking about feelings, ideas, opinions and expectations.

Lila

Lila is a four-year-old who is bright, funny and full of energy. You have just arrived home with your new baby and Lila is very excited about her new sister. Your relatives are focused on the new baby, so you ask your sister to hold the baby while you spend some time with Lila. You and Lila find a quiet place to sit. As you snuggle and talk, you explain to her what the day might look like. "We might have lots of company because everyone wants to see the baby and her new big sister. I am a very tired mommy and I will have to lie down and feed the baby a lot. A very little baby eats just a little bit at a time, but she will want to eat often. I will need you to be patient when I am feeding the baby. When I am done we can read a book or play a quiet game. Can you help me to make our new baby part of our great family?" Lila enthusiastically responds, "Yes, I can help you. I want to hold her, when can I hold her?" As you give Lila her baby doll, you tell her, "You can hold her only when I say you can. Never pick her up without asking me. Most of the time, I want you to take care of "your baby" while I take care of your sister."

In proactive discipline, you expect cooperation and recognize that your child is an important part of your family dynamics. Lila's mother took the time to set the tone of the day for Lila. Setting the stage for what to expect will help Lila to begin the adjustment to having a new sibling...a process that will take time.

Conflict discipline

On the other hand, conflict discipline is the kind of teaching and learning that takes place when your child *is* doing something you object to. What you do during conflict teaches your child how to accept limits and act in acceptable ways.

Lila

Several hours later when all but your own mother has left, the baby is asleep in a carrier seat and Lila is watching TV. You step out of the room to wash your hands. When you return, you see Lila trying to pick up the baby. The baby starts to cry. You go over to the children and make certain that the baby is safely in the seat. You take Lila by the hand and walk her to the next room and say; "You cannot pick up the baby without asking me. Sit here until I come back." Lila starts to shout, "I want to watch my show." She gets up to follow you. You say, "If you don't get yourself under control, you will not continue to watch the show." Lila sits down and starts to cry.

You might be saying to yourself, "My child would just keep on struggling with me, she would never sit down." If you aren't always consistent in your follow through, if your child has a challenging temperament or if you fail to make expectations known in advance, your child may not accept your limits. In upcoming chapters, I promise to show you how to use conflict discipline in any number of difficult circumstances. For the purpose of this example, I want you to see the difference between how Lila's mother used proactive discipline and then conflict discipline to teach Lila the rule about picking up her sister. In proactive discipline, she shared the expectation about not picking up her sister. In conflict discipline, she provided an action that sent the message that the rule *will* be enforced.

Societal discipline

The third aspect of discipline described in Proactive Parenting is societal discipline. In order to parent in our complex society, you need specific strategies for teaching your child how society influences her behavior. This kind of discipline gives your child the skills she needs to make the right decisions in complex situations. By becoming more proactive and less reactive, you can combat the influences of our complicated society. Your child can learn to develop the skills necessary to make good age-appropriate decisions.

Lila

As you walk back into the TV room, you notice the show that Lila has been watching is not one of your favorites. You have always felt that the characters are disrespectful and often hit each other when they are angry. As your mother comes in from the kitchen, she says to you, "What just happened with Lila?" After you explain, she says loud enough for Lila to overhear, "I don't know why you won't let her hold the baby more, I let your brother hold you and nothing terrible happened."

Lila's mother will be more successful over time if she factors into her parenting the influences affecting her discipline of Lila in every situation. Whether it is a TV show that sanctions aggressive and disrespectful behavior or family members that don't support your discipline choices, you need to reflect on additional influences that affect your parenting.

In Chapters 3, 4, and 5, each type of discipline will be explained in detail. You will learn why each type is important in its own right as well as specific strategies to use in certain circumstances. In Chapter 6, you will learn how proactive, conflict and societal discipline can be combined to make your discipline plans more effective. I will describe for you the practical ways to incorporate proactive, conflict and societal strategies into every day parenting dilemmas you face. You will learn how to use all the time you spend with your child wisely.

Benefits of Proactive Parenting for you

If you are reading this book, then you are one of many parents searching for the information you need to parent well. But before you spend the necessary time and energy adopting a new way to approach your parenting, you want to know if it will work for you, right? Proactive Parenting was developed several years ago, and has been shared with thousands of parents, teachers and health care professionals through workshops, private consultation, media appearances and via my web site, eproactiveparenting.com. The focus of my work is to help parents, teachers and health professionals understand child development and behavior management of children from birth to young adulthood. In my private practice, and through my lecturing and writing, I assist parents and teachers to incorporate Proactive Parenting into their discipline styles. The feedback I receive from those that have adopted the approach is overwhelmingly positive. I know that Proactive Parenting will change the way you think about your parenting because it is a common sense approach and you won't need another expert to decipher it. Here are the benefits you will acquire as you use the Proactive Parenting approach.

* By being proactive instead of reactive, you will increase harmony in your family and have a relationship that is more meaningful with your child.

* By anticipating the situations that your child will have difficulty with and planning ahead, you will reduce the conflict between you and your child.

* By having age-appropriate plans for managing conflict, you will feel empowered to follow through on the expectations you have for your child.

* By providing discipline to your child that is developmental, behavioral and focused on your child's specific temperament, your child will feel loved, nurtured and protected from unhealthy influences in society... by you.

When you spend time setting expectations, eliciting cooperation, teaching responsibility, talking about values, and creating special times together, your family will be strengthened. You can learn to be proactive, while still managing the complexities of daily living.

While becoming proactive will increase family harmony, there will always be some degree of conflict in the parent/child relationship. However, you will begin to see those times of conflict as opportunities for learning. You will no longer dread those times of conflict with your child because you will view them as natural and necessary to your child's learning. Using the approach will build your confidence and make you feel supported as you make the tough decisions you need to make, to keep your child, a child. While some parenting approaches focus on proactive aspects of child rearing apart from limit setting and monitoring the influences of society, this approach combines the three types of discipline. The Proactive Parenting approach offers you a sensible way to provide comprehensive teaching and learning experiences for your child.

Benefits of Proactive Parenting for your child

Sometimes it's hard to be a kid. I'm sure you want your child to have an easier time accepting limits and doing what is right. While society at large has greater and greater expectations of your child, you can provide a shelter from these expectations by embracing a proactive approach. Proactive Parenting will benefit your child in the following ways.

❋ By using a plan for discipline that is individual to your child's age, development and temperament, your child will learn to accept his own feelings and act in responsible ways.

❋ By skill building and showing your child that his actions have consequences, your child will be motivated to do the right thing, even when you're not around.

❋ By giving your child opportunities to make mistakes and change behavior, your child will learn to make good decisions at every age.

❋ By maximizing strengths and refining certain elements of temperament, your child will have a positive self-esteem.

Your child wants to make good decisions and do the right thing at the right time. But she needs you to show her the way. Proactive Parenting is a practical method of raising respectful children who are capable of making good decisions in complex times.

Why adopt Proactive Parenting?

Let's go back to the situation described at the beginning of the chapter. Emma and her parents face the same struggles day in and day out. Stop for a moment and think about your typical day. How do you get everyone off to work and school in the morning? How do you handle the evening hours where activities, dinner, and homework issues create stress? What time does your child go to bed? Emma and her parents are not the only ones feeling the pressure to do it all. Are you feeling overwhelmed by the fast pace of your busy life? Do you feel isolated from other parents? You are not alone; many parents are learning how to parent without the help of their own parents or other relatives. With the pressure to do more in less time and often without support from family and friends, you need to work smarter not harder and for that Proactive Parenting offers you proactive discipline.

When I ask parents to name the two toughest tasks of parenting, most put setting limits and following through at the top of their list. Have you ever been that parent trying to manage a tantrum in the candy aisle of the supermarket? Do you dread trying to get your daughter to finish her homework? Setting limits and following through doesn't have to be exhausting and for that Proactive Parenting offers you conflict discipline.

Influences that undermine your parenting abound. Through television, via the Internet and from friends, your child is getting messages that encourage him to mature before he is developmentally ready to do so. Your child is growing up faster than ever, sometimes facing challenges formerly faced by an older child. Think for a minute about some of the challenges you faced in high school. Do you realize that today, those same challenges are being faced by the middle school age child? You need to slow down the pace of your child's life and help him make good age-appropriate decisions and for that Proactive Parenting offers you societal discipline.

As the situation with Emma highlights, there are challenges to being a proactive parent. In Chapter 10, you will learn how to recognize these challenges, set limits on inappropriate influences and help your child accept those limits. Chapter 10 will help you face the challenges head on, with clear cut strategies for dealing with the pressures of parenting today.

You will sea change

Throughout this book, you will acquire the ability to assess your child's development, specific temperament and situations that produce conflict in your family before you are actually in that conflict. Once you understand how development, temperament and specific situations impact your child, you can parent towards temperament and development, not against it. You will learn how to blend your parenting style with your child's style of behaving. With this new perspective, you will start parenting with a plan. The plan will be individualized to your child and includes proactive, conflict and societal strategies. You will learn how to incorporate age-appropriate expectations into your parenting and how to choose strategies that will help your child develop the skills he needs to be capable, responsible and cooperative. By using a *planned* approach to problem solving, you will see a major transformation in how your family operates. You will create a sea change.

Questions and Answers
Chapter 1

Let's Sea Change

An Introduction To Proactive Parenting

Q: My mother had five children and I only have two. Why does it seem that I am having a more difficult time parenting than she did?

A: We live in complex times. More parents than ever are working outside their home. You may be learning your parenting in isolation of other parents. There is enormous societal pressure to have more and do more with our children. By using the Proactive Parenting approach, you will learn how to make the tough job of parenting easier. You will learn how to be proactive instead of reactive and you will learn how to make the right choices for your family regardless of what others say and do.

Q: My children are two and ten years old and are like night and day. How can one approach work for both my children?

A: One approach to parenting can work, if the individual differences of your children are respected. Proactive Parenting is an approach that factors in the age, development and the specific temperament of each of your children. You will learn how to maximize your children's strengths and develop the necessary skills that each of your children needs to be more effective in the world.

Q: How can I parent effectively when everyone around me and the popular culture constantly promote ideas that are counter to my own?

A: You have taken the first step by recognizing that there are a number of additional influences to your par-

enting.   When you become aware of what your child is
exposed to, when you set limits on negative influences and
when you teach your child the skills he needs to handle
those influences, you will be parenting very effectively.
Your child can learn to make good decisions in complex
times, no matter what his age.

TWO

It's In The Bag

The Way Children Think and Learn

Kelly is stepmother to four-year-old Evan and seven-year-old Madeline. She has had a role in parenting the children for over a year. As she sits in my office, she expresses the following concern. "I still don't know if my expectations of the children are too high or too low. Am I right in thinking that Madeline should be able to remember to bring her library book to school on Wednesdays? Should Evan still need me to lie down with him at night until he falls asleep?" Kelly struggles with having age-appropriate expectations of the children because she isn't familiar with development. Her expectations for Madeline may be too high. Most seven-year-olds are still learning to plan ahead and be responsible for their belongings. Remembering the days of the week is one skill but remembering to do something unique each day is an advanced skill. For Evan, however her expectations may be too low. Evan should be able to fall asleep on his own after a simple bedtime ritual.

Do you struggle with having the right expectations for your child? Are you unsure of what you can expect of your three-year-old or your thirteen-year-old? Does your child have elements of temperament that make parenting a challenge? Do you feel your child just doesn't know how to get what he needs without engaging in conflict?

Three factors that most influence effective parenting are your child's development, temperament and behavioral skills. Development refers to your child's *capabilities* to behave. Temperament refers to your child's *style* of behavior.

And behavioral skills refer to *how well* your child can behave. In this chapter, I will highlight how understanding these three factors will help you to make the right discipline decisions for your child. Let's start with how your child thinks and learns based on his developmental age.

Thinking and learning

Most of your child's skills, values, attitudes, and desires are learned. But at each age, your child is capable of learning in new ways. Learning takes place when a connection or association is made between a stimulus and a response, where prior to learning no such association existed. Simply put, if an event occurs and there is a response to it, in any way, some kind of learning takes place. Let's say that every time your newborn baby cries you feed her. Your baby will soon learn that crying and feeding go together. What is learned can be good or not so good. In this example, if your baby really is hungry, then the response fits the stimulus or event. But if your baby is crying for another reason and is always faced with feeding, this can cause your baby to become increasingly frustrated and maybe even overweight. The responses your child can have to learning may be thinking, feeling or action responses. In fact, thinking, feeling and certain actions can be the stimulus or the response. Here are some examples.

Thinking stimulus...feeling response
• No one is going to pick me for the game in gym...I feel left out

Action stimulus...thinking response
• I hit my brother...I'm going to get in trouble

Feeling stimulus...action response
• I'm afraid of the dark...I run to mommy

Whether the situations above happen once or several times, your child is learning something that will affect future behavior. I've tried to explain learning theory so that you can see how easily connections and therefore learning can take place. Remember, any learning that takes place involves a complex and continuous series of stimuli and responses.

There are two reasons why it is important to understand how your child thinks and learns. The first is that the Proactive Parenting approach was created based on the belief that you can influence this thinking and learning by manipulating the stimulus and/or the response. Don't worry, throughout the book, I will show you how. It is easier than you might think. And the second reason it is important to understand learning theory is because if you know what your child is capable of learning at different developmental ages, you will be able to choose appropriate discipline strategies. Proactive Parenting considers thinking and learning from a developmental perspective. In each of the following descriptions of development, I will discuss how the way your child thinks and learns influences your parenting.

Infants

Your baby was born ready to learn. She has the ability to notice the world around her and as her brain and body grow she can interact with people and objects. While you can enhance your baby's learning by providing a trusting, loving, nurturing and safe environment, you can not teach your baby certain skills before she is physically ready. No matter how hard you try, you will not be able to teach your one-week-old baby to sleep through the night or teach your three-month-old child to hold a pencil. This concept of physical readiness is true for your child at each developmental stage. There are just some physical abilities that come with age.

Jean Piaget, renowned Swiss psychologist, described developmental stages of thinking and learning that are somewhat similar to the idea of physical readiness. He believed that each child has the capability to think and learn only when he reaches a certain intellectual stage. Your infant is in what Piaget called the sensorimotor stage. She learns about her world through people and objects.

You will see your baby react to you and to her toys based on physical characteristics. She responds to your smile or the bright and moving mobile. At first, she enjoys repetitive acts for their own sake but later uses repetition for results. The four-month-old boy drops the rattle just to drop the rattle but the six-month-old boy drops the ball because he knows you will pick it up. This repetitive act becomes a game. By between seven and ten months of age, your child learns about the permanence of objects. She understands that whether you hide a stuffed animal or leave the room, both the toy and you still exist. Your child gets more and more social during the first year of life. He enjoys social interaction and learns so much through play. The more you talk, laugh and sing with your baby the more you encourage your baby to make the necessary connections to learn about the world he lives in. His brain development is stimulated by how much you encourage the building of these connections.

Olivia

Olivia is an eight-month-old girl who has just learned to crawl. She is overjoyed with her newfound ability to explore her world. At first, her mother was thrilled with her new skill too, but soon realized how this changed her parenting of Olivia. Today, Olivia discovered the VCR. She reaches into it and finds it fascinating. Mom tells her, "No" and she continues to go straight to it. For the hour before her nap, her mother calmly kept saying, "No" while moving Olivia away from the entertainment cabinet. During her nap, she moved the VCR to a higher location in the cabinet and closed the doors.

We often don't give much thought to discipline for the infant, yet if discipline means to teach and learn then your baby needs discipline too. Of course, the way you discipline a baby is different from the way you discipline an older child. In Chapter 7, I will give specific examples of how to apply Proactive Parenting to the child under age three. But here are some keys to parenting the infant that are in keeping with the way she is able to think and learn.

- Be repetitive when you want your child to understand a connection between an action and a consequence.
- Supervise your baby closely because your physical intervention will be needed often.
- Use play as the way to teach your child to make connections about expectations.
- Sing, talk, and laugh with your baby to enhance her brain's ability to learn now and later.
- Modify your environment with safety in mind.

Toddlers

Toddlers have been labeled terrible and terrific. And indeed if you have a toddler, you probably think he is both. The energy and enthusiasm for learning that your toddler shows can be both contagious and exhausting. A major developmental task of this age is language development. Language is the essential ingredient your child needs for learning all the higher order mental processes such as thinking, planning, reasoning, judgment, attention and memory. While physical development is still rapid, your child is beginning to problem solve in new ways. He can not consistently understand that his actions have consequences but he is beginning to understand that he has influence over what happens to him. He is learning what is called cause and effect thinking, through his never-ending exploration. Your toddler will begin to develop his vocabulary; this is called expressive language. But he will know so much more than he can communicate back to you; this is called receptive language. In fact, I tell most of my clients who have toddlers that their child probably understands three times what they think he is able to understand. Your toddler loves to play and play is the major way your child learns about the world. Through play, your child begins to use symbolic thinking, another major developmental change that occurs to how the toddler learns. To the infant an egg and a ball are the same; to your toddler they are not. Your toddler imitates to learn; this copycat behavior can drive older siblings crazy. Your toddler learns very concretely, without thought to the consequences of his behavior. He acts first and thinks about it later. Often, only after he has done something wrong does he realize that he made a mistake. Your toddler has limited ability for distal communication or to respond to your directions from a distance. This is partly because he is impulsive by nature and partly because of language development.

Jake

Jake is a two-year-old, doing what toddlers love to do... striving for independence. He is sitting in his booster seat at the kitchen table eating his lunch while his Dad finishes preparations on his own lunch. Jake's milk is in a sippy cup and he has cleverly learned how to get the top off. Dad notices him playing with the lid and says, "Jake, don't take that lid off, leave it on." Jake continues to play with it and Dad continues to give him directions to leave it alone. Just seconds later, the milk spills on the table and Jake says, "uh-oh!"

This is an example of the kind of learning that takes place many times a day for your toddler. Only after the milk has spilled, does Jake understand the consequences of his actions. Jake's "uh-oh" is his realization of what happens when you play with the sippy cup lid. As he continues to explore his world, he will learn more consistently that his actions can change the outcome of events.

Here are some parenting tips for your toddler based on his ability to think and learn.

- Balance your toddler's exploration with safety, structure and boundaries.
- Continue to be repetitive in your discipline because your child is not consistently able to understand the connection between actions and consequences.
- Discipline with more action and less words. Your toddler isn't able to stop doing something simply because you tell him to from a distance.
- Be discriminating about using the word, "No." For the impulsive toddler that word almost encourages her to complete what she started.

- Continue to supervise your child closely. Her newfound mobility makes this a high parenting priority.
- Childproof your home and other environments your child spends time in. This attention to safety will decrease your conflicts over what your child can and cannot do.

Preschoolers

The child, age three to six, is delightful. Often the temperament of your child is coming into full view; more on how temperament influences parenting later in this chapter. Your child still thinks and learns very concretely. A client of mine once explained death to her three-year-old son by saying that, "Grandma is in Heaven and Heaven is in the clouds." The next time the family took a plane ride her son said, "I don't see Grandma anywhere!" Language development continues but the emphasis shifts to abstract words having to do with emotions. Objects now have meaning and represent other things. A doll is a baby and baskets can be hats. Your child plays out roles, she identifies with what Mommy and Daddy do for work and with their chores around the house. She can begin to generalize yet, sees things as good/bad, black/white and happy/sad.

Your child is beginning to develop a conscience but still believes that if he doesn't admit he did something wrong, he didn't really do it. Saying it out loud would make it real. It is hard for the three to six-year-old to see another person's point of view, which is why when he says he is "sorry" it can seem false.

While starting preschool and making friends, your child is fully engaged in learning cause and effect. Your child understands more consistently that her actions have both positive and negative consequences and is beginning to internalize feelings of wrongdoing. In fact, your child may imagine that she has influenced events that she has not; this is called magical thinking. Learning self-control is another major developmental challenge of this age. Self-control is a mental process of regulating emotion and behavior. You will know your child has self-control when you don't intervene as much in her troubles and when you notice less intense reactions from your child. So, while your child has a growing ability to delay gratification and is starting to think first before she acts, she will struggle with self-control issues during this period.

Serena

Serena is a five-year-old sitting at the table having breakfast. Her mother is scurrying around the kitchen getting ready for work. Serena is playing with her milk, which is in a regular cup. She carefully tips the cup, swirling the milk around the rim. She knows that the milk will spill if she is not careful. She also knows that she will get attention from her mother if she spills it. Serena is capable of understanding in a more complex way that her actions have varied consequences.

This example shows you the difference between the toddler who acts first and thinks later and the preschooler who is able to think first and then act. While the exact age at which your child consistently understands cause and effect will be individual, you can expect this understanding to kick in anytime between two and a half and three and a half. Since your child is ready to learn this at any time within that range, it is important to use the following discipline strategies with your preschooler.

* Balance your preschooler's emerging independence with safety rules, structure and boundaries.
* Respond in cause and effect ways to your child. "If you throw the blocks, you can not play with them." (Information on choosing the right consequences will be discussed in Chapter 4)
* Ask your child to repeat back to you, the rule. If your child can say what the rule is, she is more likely to do what is expected. It also allows you to clarify any misunderstandings.
* Discipline with more action and less words. While your child is better able to understand directions from a distance, if he is stressed he will have more difficulty following the rules.

- Help your child attach feeling language to her actions. It is important for your child to begin to understand how her feelings affect her behavior.

School age children

Your school age child is independent in many ways, yet this independence may lull you into believing that he needs less attention and direction from you. Yet, the child, age 6 to age 10, still requires lots of coaching. But clearly, the kind of parenting you provide does change. Instead of being physically dependent on you, your child requires more social and emotional coaching during the school age period. I believe that the school age child can sometimes get lost in the shuffle. Your daughter can take care of her basic needs like dressing and eating so you might expect her to do more for herself than she actually can.

Understanding how the school age child thinks and learns will help you to provide the best coaching. There are big differences between the thinking of a child at the beginning of the school age period and the end. Your six-year-old is becoming somewhat consistent with his understanding that his actions have consequences and by the age of ten can predict what will happen given a certain set of circumstances.

In fact, your school age child uses his understanding of rules and consequences to make decisions. He has the ability to reflect on the implications of his actions...think first and then act. Learning self-control is still a focus for the school age child but more often than not, your child is able to make good decisions that are safe and socially acceptable. But like the preschool age child, he can still be impulsive when he is stressed or tired. One of my clients describes her son this way. "He can follow any directions I give him when he is rested, but he just can't follow directions at bedtime. He is 8 and I still have to walk him through brushing his teeth and getting into his pajamas." You might find this to be true for your child, too. Again, it is important to know how your child thinks and learns to then be able to choose the right discipline strategies. Would it surprise you to know that your child still thinks very concretely at the early part of this stage of development? Do you rattle off five or six commands only to find that your daughter hasn't even completed one? "Change your clothes, start your homework, don't eat that snack in the family room, put away your backpack..." Does that sound familiar? The school age child is better able to complete multi-task directions than the younger child but may still have difficulty when tired, hungry, distracted or disinterested.

Other major developmental challenges for the school age child include developing complex friendships and nurturing their relationships with other adults. Friendships are now based on mutual interests and identification begins to include your child's peer group.

The term identification simply means that your child forms judgments about herself by comparing herself to others. While your child can start to see other people's point of view, she is still very self-centered. Her ability to reason is still concrete in many ways and her judgments are focused on fairness.

Noah

Noah, a seven-year-old boy comes home from school announcing, "I am not doing my homework today!" His mother asks him to explain why. As they talk, his mother finds out the classroom homework policy. Each day that all the children complete and bring in their homework, the class is allowed to put a marble into a jar. When the jar is filled, the class gets to enjoy an extra recess period. Noah's class had finally filled the jar and today was the day for the extra recess period. Right before the children were to go outside, a boy in Noah's class misbehaved and the entire class was not able to go out. "It isn't fair, I didn't do anything. Why did Miss Johnson make everyone stay in? Now, I don't feel like doing my homework." Later Noah asks, "Do you think that if I don't do my homework, we won't get to go out for the extra recess tomorrow?"

Noah is thinking about the rules and consequences in terms of fairness. This situation also demonstrates Noah's newfound ability to examine how changing certain actions can change the results. He is capable of considering the consequences to his actions in advance. This will allow him to make choices about his behavior based on what he predicts will happen next.

Parenting tips for the school age child are based on your child's more advanced thinking skills and your child's specific motivations.

- Continue to provide your child with age-appropriate structure and boundaries. Your child still needs the security and supervision that you have been providing.
- See yourself as your child's coach as you shape behavior. Although your child is more independent in some ways, she still needs the perfect blend of repetition and emphasis on social and emotional skill building.
- Ask your child to participate in problem solving complex situations. This strategy respects your child's developing reasoning skills.
- Respond in cause and effect ways to your child. Your child can consistently understand that his actions have consequences and he needs you to reinforce this understanding.
- Create a low stress home environment. Your child has so much to learn during the school age period and has little experience managing stress. High levels of stress make achieving developmental milestones that much more challenging.

Adolescents

Your adolescent is facing tough academic and social pressures formerly faced by young adults. Society's high expectations coupled with rapid changes in physical, cognitive and emotional growth and development make these years perhaps the most difficult years of your child's life. As with the school age period, you will see big differences between younger adolescent and older adolescent thinking. Early adolescents can begin to reason abstractly. Your child's thinking is not bound by concrete information, your child can speculate about what events will take place in the future. The adolescent begins to be able to evaluate his thoughts and the ideas of others. It is an exciting time because your child is able to form opinions and discuss them in new ways. He can analyze information and support his positions on topics important to him.

Your child is becoming a unique individual. He is beginning to define himself based on his own strengths, interests, goals and plans for the future. Friendships during adolescence are based on mutual goals and interests. Identification shifts from parents to the peer group. It is common to hear a parent talk about how their adolescent doesn't want them involved in their life. I think nothing is further from the truth. While your child will strongly identify with his friends' issues and concerns, he still cares about what you think and wants you involved in what interests and excites him. He wants you to relate to him more as a peer than an authority figure. Your adolescent wants you involved in his life but perhaps in different ways than in the past. Understanding and respecting the way in which he wants you involved in his life will be the challenge.

Our society gives both parents and adolescents messages about independence that can be dangerous. Although during adolescence, your child is capable of abstract thinking and complex decision making, he is still not capable of adult thinking. The adolescent with too much free time and inadequate adult interaction and supervision can find himself in situations beyond his emotional capabilities.

In adolescence, your child can consistently understand and even predict the consequences to his behavior. Unfortunately, because he may feel infallible and independent he may disregard the consequences of certain actions even knowing what they are. Acting in the moment and thinking that, "bad things happen to other people, not me" is common thinking at this age. Unfortunately, the consequences of certain risky behaviors may last a lifetime.

Jackie

Jackie is a thirteen-year-old who loves to shop. She is always asking to go to the mall. This morning, after several phone calls to her three closest friends she tells her Mom that she is going shopping at a mall twenty minutes from home. Mom asks her, "Who is going? Is a parent staying at the mall while you shop?" All of her answers are in conflict with the established rules. She is going with a large group of kids and no parent intends on staying while they shop. After she is told she is not going to be able to go, she says, "I don't understand what you are worried about. What could possibly happen to me at the mall? I can take care of myself. Why don't you trust me?"

This situation illustrates Jackie's ability to form her own opinions about decisions and how she identifies with her friends. There are two reasons why discipline at this age can be difficult. First, because your parenting style and your child's behavioral style have been learned over time. And second, because your child is capable of thinking in abstract ways and has her own opinions. She has a stronger desire to have her thoughts and ideas respected.

Remember, it is never too late to learn to parent more effectively. Here are some tips for parenting the adolescent.

- Continue to provide your child with age-appropriate structure and boundaries. Too many adolescents have too little supervision. Without proper supervision, your adolescent may be faced with situations beyond her capabilities.
- Respect your child's ideas, feelings and opinions. You don't have to agree on everything but it is important to respect your child's point of view.
- Talk with your child...don't lecture. Conversations in times of peace go a long way in forming a respectful parent/adolescent relationship.
- Continue to coach your child as she develops social and emotional skills. With society's high expectations, your child will still need your assistance.
- Involve your child in problem solving complex situations. Your child's mature reasoning skills will be invaluable as you solve problems that affect you both.
- Continue to respond in cause and effect ways to your child's misbehavior. Your child still needs you to demonstrate that his actions have consequences no matter how old he is.

What's temperament got to do with it?

Your child's style of behaving is evident early on. The way your baby sleeps and eats and the way she reacts to new people and situations begins to tell you about her style. By preschool age, you know your child's temperament well. You know how your child will make the transition from playtime to bedtime. You know if he can take life's ups and downs in stride. A major strength of this approach is that temperament is factored into creating proactive plans for discipline geared to each child's specific style of behaving. In order to create this individualized plan, you need to know what the elements of temperament are and how to strategize keeping them in mind.

Elements of temperament

Vincent, father of four children shares this with me after a workshop. "I've read a lot of books and tried a lot of parenting strategies but they just don't work with Claire. I have four children and three of them are so easy. Nothing I do with Claire seems to get the same results." Vincent is one of many parents that tell me about the very real temperamental differences between their children and the enormous impact this has on their parenting. What he needs is an approach that helps him to examine the specific temperament of each child and then use behavioral techniques to effectively teach each child the skills he or she needs to behave well.

When I conduct an observation of a specific child at home or at school, I look at nine elements of temperament. Once I get a sense of the child's behavioral style, I can then recommend to parents and teachers the best strategies for shaping behavior.

Here are the nine elements of temperament described by numerous experts.

1. Activity...your child's level of activity or liveliness.

2. Adaptability...your child's ability to adjust to change or transitions.

3. Distractibility...your child's ability to stay focused and not get distracted.

4. Intensity...your child's pattern of reacting to everyday situations.

5. Mood...your child's basic nature, optimistic or pessimistic.

6. Persistence...your child's ability to persevere in order to accomplish a task or meet a goal.

7. Physical regularity...your child's patterns of eating, sleeping and eliminating.

8. Reactions...your child's ability to warm up to something or someone new.

9. Sensitivity...your child's ability to feel both physically and emotionally.

Each child has all nine elements of temperament but in varying degrees. Your child may have a temperament that makes it easy to parent him. Or your child may have a temperament that makes parenting very challenging. More often than not a child has some elements of temperament that are stronger than others and some elements that don't interfere with getting on with others at all.

Each element of temperament can be plotted on a continuum. Let's take sensitivity for example. Looking at Figure I, you can see that if I observed 100 children for the element of sensitivity, most would fall into the realm of normal with a predictable variation. Some children wouldn't be very sensitive, some children would be very sensitive and most children would fall somewhere in the middle of each extreme.

Figure 1

The Bell Curve of Temperament
Continuum of Sensitivity in One Hundred Children

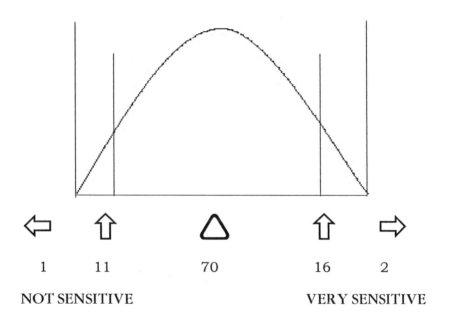

| | 11 | 70 | 16 | 2 |

1   11   70   16   2

NOT SENSITIVE   VERY SENSITIVE

- One hundred children observed for sensitivity.
- Numbers above indicate degree to which children were sensitive.
- The solid triangle indicates most children's degree of sensitivity.
- The vertical arrows indicate numbers of children with extremes of sensitivity.
- The horizontal arrows indicate numbers of children that fell out of the standard deviation or out of the realm of normal on the bell curve.

A few children, however, would be considered out of the realm of normal. Those children would be considered to have some type of dysfunction or disorder. The child who is unable to manage sensory information effectively may have the diagnosis of Sensory Integration Dysfunction. A word of caution is appropriate here. If your child has an element of temperament on the extreme end of the continuum for sensitivity or distractibility for example, this doesn't mean she is a candidate for a diagnosis of Sensory Integration Dysfunction or Attention Deficit Disorder. It may simply mean that your child has some challenging elements of temperament that could benefit from a strong behavioral plan.

Before you conclude that your child's behavior is out of the realm of normal, institute a good behavioral plan. Once you have a solid plan that you consistently follow, you will have a better sense of the scope of your child's behavioral issues. Often when a client comes to me believing that their child has an extreme element or elements of temperament, out of the realm of normal, we discover that a good behavioral plan solves a great deal. In Chapter 10, I discuss the benefits of using Proactive Parenting for your child should she have special needs.

Your child might be slow to warm to new people and have difficulty adjusting to transitions yet none of the other elements of temperament stand out as problematic. Once you become aware of how your child reacts and adapts, you can plan accordingly. Perhaps you forewarn your daughter of the company you have coming to the house or maybe you prepare her for the transition from your neighbor's house to your home. Choosing strategies based on the unique temperament of your child is the key to a good behavioral plan. In the behavioral skill building section of this chapter, I will show you how to maximize positive elements of temperament and minimize the not so positive elements of temperament. In order to do this you need to have a better sense of your child's specific temperament. Take the *Discovering your Child's Style* quiz to gain a better understanding of your child's specific temperament.

Discovering Your Child's Style

The *Discovering Your Child's Style* quiz will help you learn more about your child's temperament in two ways. First, by taking this quiz, you will raise your awareness about your child's way of reacting to the world he lives in. Second, you will be better able to choose appropriate discipline strategies if you factor your child's style into your proactive plan for parenting.

The Quiz

For each element of temperament, circle the statement that best describes your child.

Keep in mind, it is best to take this quiz for one child at a time.

Activity

My child...

a. is very active and always busy doing something
b. is as active as other children her age
c. sits still and is very seldom active
d. is extremely inactive

Adaptability

My child...

a. is often upset when met with the unexpected
b. can go with the flow or get upset; it depends on the particular situation
c. easily adjusts to transitions and change
d. transitions too quickly from activity to activity, adapts almost too readily to change

Distractibility

My child...

a. often appears not to be listening, and is easily distracted by other details that have caught his attention
b. can get distracted if something he is interested in presents itself, but is often able to pay attention to what is being asked of him

C + O   c. can pay attention and follow multi-task directions
      d. has an attention span so long that it interferes with necessary transitions

Intensity
My child...
a. has emotional reactions that are like peaks and valleys, one minute high and the next low
b. has emotional reactions that are varied but appropriate to the situation

C+C̄
Both   c. has the ability to tolerate frustration and rarely reacts in dramatic ways
d. rarely reacts even to situations that warrant an emotional reaction

Mood
My child...
a. is often in a negative mood, she really sees the glass half empty
b. has difficulty seeing the bright side when a situation is challenging
c. is even tempered and usually in a good mood

C + O   d. is always in a good mood even when a situation is challenging

Persistence
My child...
a. is rarely able to let go of a desire to do something or of an issue if it bothers him
b. will be persistent if he is doing something he enjoys but not so if he is doing something he doesn't enjoy

C   c. knows when to be persistent and when to go with the flow
O   d. goes with the flow at his own expense

Physical Regularity
My child...
a. has an erratic schedule of eating and sleeping
b. has patterns that are mostly predictable with some limited variation

C +O   c. eats, sleeps, and eliminates at predictable times
        d. physical regularity is rigid, physical needs must be met
           on schedule or issues arise

Reactions

My child...

a. rarely tries new things or meets new people without a
   lot of coaxing and preparation
C + O b. will try something new if the circumstances are right
   and the activity is something she is comfortable with
c. enjoys trying new things and meeting new people
d. rarely reacts to new situations and new people

Sensitivity

My child...

a. is extremely sensitive both physically and emotionally
b. is sensitive physically and emotionally only in situations where he is really engaged
C + O c. is sensitive only when he is tired or someone clearly
   hurts his feelings
d. is rarely sensitive to his own physical and emotional
   pain or that of others

The Results

Now add up how many A's, B's C's and D's you circled.
Identify the letter you chose most often and then look
at the corresponding description below. The description
will highlight how much your child's temperament should
factor into your parenting. Remember, your child will
require individualized discipline strategies based on his
unique temperament.

Mostly A's   **The Dynamic Style**
Your child has a number of strong elements of temperament. In light of this, you definitely need to strategize
with temperament in mind. Your child will benefit from

discipline that factors in how he reacts to the people and events around him. You play a key role in maximizing your child's strengths and teaching him the skills he needs to get along in the world in ways that are less stressful for both of you. Being proactive is critical to your parenting success.

Mostly B's   **The Situational Style**
Your child has some strong elements of temperament and some elements that don't impact the people around him. You will need to strategize with temperament in mind, when certain situations in which your child has difficulty present themselves. It will be important for you to consider how temperament and situations come together to prove challenging for your child. Being proactive will be beneficial to you as you anticipate where and when your child will need your coaching.

Mostly C's   **The Agreeable Style**
Your child has few elements of temperament that could be considered strong. You probably find this child easy to parent because of her ability to adapt easily to change. Factoring temperament into your parenting may be less crucial, but it is always important to be proactive. Every child deserves a parent that is as involved as the proactive parent.

Mostly D's   **The Compliant Style**
Your child may have elements of temperament that could be considered strong but these strong elements don't stand out. You may find that your child's temperament is so yielding that he sometimes gets lost in the shuffle. While your child may be easy to parent because of his ability to go with flow, he may be lacking important skills that could benefit him and help him get his needs met. Your child's behavior doesn't have to be disruptive for him to benefit from the proactive strategies found in this approach.

What kind of temperament does your child have? Is his a dynamic style, powerful and impacting other people often throughout a given day? Or did you find that your child's style is one dependent on specific circumstances and is only challenging under certain conditions? Do you find parenting your child to be challenging? You may classify your child's temperament as challenging for any of the following reasons.

- Your child has numerous strong elements of temperament.
- Your child's elements of temperament interfere with the functioning of your family.
- Your child's elements of temperament are different from yours.
- Your child's elements of temperament are the same as yours.
- Your child's elements of temperament remind you of someone you have difficulty interacting with.

Whatever style your child has, she will benefit from behavior skill building that is proactive and geared to her specific style of interacting with the world she lives in. Now that you have new ways to describe your child's temperament, you can teach skills and refine behavior with a skill building approach.

Behavioral skill building

Every child is born with some skills that make it easier to live in the world. Does your child have regular patterns of eating and sleeping? Does she have an optimistic outlook on life? You know better than anyone what your child's strengths are. However, your child was probably born lacking some skills for making life a little easier. Does your son get easily frustrated if he is unable to accomplish a certain task? Does your daughter get easily hurt by the insensitivity of others? Whether your child is missing certain skills because of her developmental age or her temperament, your child needs the right coaching to develop skills that will make her more successful in life.

You can teach your child the appropriate ways to behave by refining skills she already has and by teaching her skills that she may not have.

Owen

Owen's mother describes him as a feisty, persistent and intense fourteen-year-old. She struggles daily with his intense reactions and stubbornness. "Everyday I wake up hoping that things will go more smoothly. But an hour into our day and we are struggling over something new." Do you clash with your child on a daily basis? Are you *hoping* he will change rather than *actively changing* the dynamic between you and your child? Do you sometimes feel angry or sad that this is the temperament of your child? Like Owen's mother, you need help adopting a parenting strategy that will build skills and therefore minimize the strongest elements of temperament.

Before you can begin to modify challenging elements of temperament, you must take into account your child's strengths. Behavioral skill building starts with identifying your child's most positive qualities. Take a moment now to answer the following questions.

1. What capabilities and qualities make your child special and unique?

2. List the aspects of your child's temperament that you love?

3. What skills does your child have for getting along with others both in and out of your home?

Once you have identified your child's strengths... celebrate them! It is just as important to focus on what is remarkable about your child as it is to focus on what issues still need your attention. The next step in behavioral skill building is to identify the areas of temperament your child needs to refine or the skills your child needs to learn to minimize her strong elements of temperament. It is time now to accept the temperament your child was born with, knowing that behavioral skill building can help you and your child to modify, enhance, correct or refine challenging aspects of temperament.

Here is how I explain a child's balance of positive and not so positive attributes and how skill building can make a positive difference. Imagine your child with an invisible bag by his side. In the bag, your child holds his strengths for getting along in the world. Each child has a different set of skills in his bag. The shy child may play well alone but have difficulty playing with other children; he has self-entertaining skills in his bag but lacks social skills. The outgoing child may play well with others but have difficulty sharing toys; he has social skills in his bag, but is missing cooperation skills. Your job as a parent is to identify your child's strengths and determine what skills your child still needs to learn. Identifying what skills your child needs to develop is the first step in helping him put the needed skills..."in the bag."

Jessie

Jessie's parents have always considered her to be strong willed. But at age five, Jessie's intensity and persistence are becoming a problem in social situations. Her parents are noticing that the neighborhood children rarely want to play with her because she bosses them around and dictates what they will and will not play. In one of our sessions, Jessie's mother tearfully reveals, "Of course I love Jessie, but sometimes it is hard to like her. If I am feeling this way, I don't want to know what other people are thinking."

Jessie's parents were able to say what many parents might be feeling about their child. Yet, the reason this feeling persists is because parents rarely feel that there is anything they can do to change their predicament. While you can not change your child's temperament, you can build skills through an active process of discipline. For Jessie's parents, the first step toward behavioral skill building was identifying Jessie's strengths as a person. What talents and attributes does she already have "in her bag"? Here is what they came up with.

- Jessie can speak up for herself and get her needs met.
- Jessie can focus on what she wants and will do what it takes to achieve her goals.
- Jessie can make transitions smoothly and is not phased by meeting new people or trying new things.
- Jessie can learn quickly and stay interested when learning is challenging.

The next step in behavioral skill building is to acknowledge that Jessie has some strong elements of temperament that need to be refined and lacks some skills that would help her to function more effectively. Here is what her parents identified.

- Jessie has intense reactions to situations not going her way.
- Jessie lacks effective social skills.
- Jessie isn't as sensitive to other peoples needs and feelings as she could be.

Jessie is not choosing inappropriate ways of playing with other children over ways that are more effective. She simply knows no other way of getting her needs met. If she had the right skills in her bag, she would use them. Once the aspects of Jessie's temperament that need to be refined are identified, teaching new skills can begin. But how do you get new skills in the bag? I believe that temperament is what you are born with and personality is what is crafted. It is through the three kinds of discipline (proactive, conflict and societal) that Jessie will learn the necessary skills to become less intense, more sensitive and to develop supportive friendships. Jessie's parents were taught specific ways to help Jessie learn new ways of socializing. They utilized behavioral strategies related to each type of discipline. Here is the behavioral plan Jessie's parents and I developed.

Proactive strategies

- Talk to Jessie about how she plays with other children. It should be a teaching time not a lecturing time and it should happen when she is in control.

- Tell Jessie how you want her to change her behavior. Again, do this when everyone is under control. She will not be able to recreate the appropriate behavior if she is never taught what appropriate behavior looks and feels like.
- Talk to Jessie about situations when being a good friend will be important. Share with her the can do's not just the can't do's. Telling her what she shouldn't do in a situation isn't enough.
- Give her some alternatives to her present behavior. She may need specific language she can use in future situations.
- Role-play a typical situation so that Jessie can practice influencing the other children in ways that are more positive.
- Be available in social situations. If Jessie is trying new skills, she may need your help or role modeling.
- Tell Jessie what will happen in social situations if she can not behave in acceptable ways. Making clear the consequences to her behavior, in advance, is critical.
- Be patient. Learning social skills is a process. Try to notice her attempts and be sure to compliment her on her efforts.

Conflict strategies

- Be the authority that Jessie needs. If after you have shared expectations with her, she can not socialize in respectful ways, be prepared to step in.
- Be direct and specific about what you expect her to do. You may need to provide a consequence to the behavior such as taking her out of the situation.
- Be sure you make an impact. If the consequences to her behavior don't make impact, learning won't take place.
- Remain calm. Remember, Jessie needs you to be her coach and ally so that she can learn the right skills for the right situations. These skills don't come naturally to her. She needs you to help her to learn better ways of getting what she needs.

Societal strategies

- Look at the influences in Jessie's life. Is she playing with children that are a good deal younger or older than she is? Do you have a new baby in the family? Is either parent out of the home more than usual? What happens in a child's life does affect her ability to behave appropriately.
- Modify or limit the influences. Whenever possible take charge of the influences contributing to the problem. You can't change the fact that you have a new baby but you can give Jessie more one-on-one time with you. You don't need to stop Jessie from playing with younger or older children but you could balance it with playing with same age peers.
- Help Jessie develop the skills she needs to get along with other children. The behavior she is presently exhibiting will ultimately affect friendships. Role-play how to be a friend in challenging situations.
- Recognize and be active in your role in helping Jessie to develop the skills she will need to "fit in" with other children. Supervising and later giving Jessie feedback on what went well will be important.

Over time, Jessie will develop new ways of interacting with friends. These successes will positively reinforce the way in which Jessie socializes. The benefit of behavioral skill building is that once the skills are learned, Jessie will be able to rely on them for a lifetime.

Chapter summary

Your child's learning is influenced by his development, temperament and through the quality of his experiences. Understanding how your child thinks and learns as well as knowing his unique temperament is critical to being able to develop the right discipline plan. Behavioral skill building is an active process of shaping behavior. It includes techniques aimed at modifying, enhancing, correcting or refining behavior. Through actions and words matching actions, your child gets the necessary skills "in the bag". In proactive discipline, you will express expectations and teach your child effective ways of behaving. In conflict discipline, you will make expectations real by providing incentives for positive behavior and consequences to unacceptable behavior. In societal discipline, you will acknowledge influences and set limits on inappropriate influences while still helping your child to fit in with friends. Both in times of peace and in times of conflict, you will make expectations clear. The next three chapters will examine each type of discipline in detail. For each aspect of discipline, you will learn how to model, teach, train, coach and provide constructive feedback to your child about behavior.

Questions and Answers
Chapter 2

It's In The Bag

The Way Children Think And Learn

Q: I have three children, their ages are 10, 4 and 1. Sometimes, I feel like it is impossible to have the same expectations of them. Do I really need to have different rules for each child?

A: Discipline strategies are most successful when they are based on developmental age and specific temperament. So, I am certain you will need to have different expectations for each of your children. The good news is that you can establish some basic safety and respect rules that apply to everyone in your family. Then you will need to factor into your discipline plans the unique ways each of your children thinks and learns.

Q: My child is easy going when she is alone with me and her father. But in social situations, she is timid, shy and refuses to talk to or play with other kids. I can understand setting limits with an aggressive or feisty child but how do you set limits on shyness?

A: Just because you are able to empathize with your daughter's temperament doesn't mean she wouldn't benefit from behavioral skill building. In fact, if your daughter is going to be able to socialize with others, and be able to speak up for herself, she needs exactly the kind of coaching Proactive Parenting suggests. Embrace your daughter's strengths but help her to build the skills she will need to be successful in life.

Q: I understand that my child is born with certain strengths and that if I want to refine or help him get new skills, I have to teach them to him. But how will I know he has them "in the bag?"

A: You will know that your child has the new skills he needs "in the bag" when you don't have to intervene as much in his troubles, and when you notice less whining, tantrums, catastrophes or power struggles. The ultimate goal is for your child to make decisions that don't create conflict or result in actions that require imposed consequences.

THREE

The Calm Before The Storm

Proactive Discipline

When Sean describes his son Aiden's behavior in the supermarket, it is as if he were talking about a television situation comedy. Sean and Aiden, age two and a half, shop every Tuesday at four o'clock. Aiden almost always tries to climb in and out of the carriage. In reaching for things on the shelves, he knocks products to the floor and then cries loudly. Other shoppers give disgusted looks to Sean, making him feel inadequate at caring for his young son. Sean feels like he is being firm by telling Aiden, "If you don't stop misbehaving...we will leave this market and you will not get the treat I promised you." To this Aiden grabs the grapes in the back of the carriage and throws them on the floor.

Can you relate to Sean's supermarket nightmare? Most parents can, in fact the supermarket situation described above is a very common parenting experience. When shopping with young children, is it possible to grocery shop and parent simultaneously? Well of course, the answer is yes. But the trick is to rethink how you do it. The key is to anticipate situations that you know your child will have difficulty with and plan accordingly. This kind of parenting approach assumes that a lot of work is done before the conflict arises. It assumes that you will think about potential problems in advance rather than waiting until problems occur.

Proactive discipline

Proactive discipline teaches your child values. It instills a sense of cooperation, responsibility, self-control and good decision-making. It is the discipline that takes place most of the time. Proactive discipline happens constantly. It is both active and passive; it is what your child learns just by being with you. By watching you and talking to you, in times of peace, your child learns what is expected of her.

In proactive discipline, you decide what the family rules are regarding safety and respect. Sean will be more successful when he tells Aiden in advance, what he expects of him in the supermarket. Once clearly shared, in ways that your child can understand, these rules become non-negotiable. In other words, these rules must be followed. In proactive discipline, you openly and calmly communicate these rules. The conversations you have with your child about non-negotiable rules set the stage for expected behavior and remind your child that there are consequences to his actions.

Although expectations are shared in advance, it doesn't guarantee that your child will make the best choices in the situation. It is in conflict discipline, that you enforce these rules by allowing natural consequences and providing logical consequences to unacceptable behavior. Conflict discipline is spelled out in detail in Chapter 4. And in Chapter 6, I will discuss how to put all the aspects of discipline together. In order to put it all together, it is important to understand each aspect of discipline on its own. In this chapter, proactive discipline will be highlighted.

Principles of proactive discipline

A principle is a fundamental assumption or rule that guides your actions. Each of the three aspects of discipline has principles that point out how you can provide this kind of discipline. Here are the principles of proactive discipline....

* Anticipation
* Clarity
* Communication
* Role-modeling
* Respect

Anticipation

The hallmark of proactive discipline is anticipation. In Chapter 2, I reviewed development and temperament. Now that you understand development a bit better and have new ways of thinking about your child's temperament, you will be better able to anticipate situations that are difficult for your child. Because you can foresee potentially problematic situations, you can plan ahead and make better parenting choices than in the past.

Rose

Nadia and Ben have been going out to dinner once a week since they met. Since the birth of their daughter, Rose, they have continued their ritual. When Rose was a newborn, it was relatively easy to take her out. Yet, now that she is seven months old it has become harder. Rose is active and doesn't want to stay in the high chair. Once out of the high chair, it is impossible to get her back in, quietly. She is not easily entertained with toys especially later in the day. Whenever Rose's naptimes or bedtimes are altered, she is very cranky the next day. Given this situation and the principle of anticipation that is essential to proactive discipline, Nadia and Ben should be thinking about the following options. Given Rose's developmental age and temperament, Nadia and Ben might...

• Go to the restaurant prepared with foods and toys that Rose can't resist.

- Supply Rose with her favorite toys...but only give them to her one at a time and delay this for as long as possible.
- Ask for quick service from the waitress.
- Go to the restaurant for lunch when Rose will be better able to cope with the expectations.
- Go to the restaurant for just an appetizer, giving Rose limited exposure to expectations and increased likelihood of success.
- Engage Rose while she is in her high chair.
- Be prepared to leave if the situation gets unbearable for Rose, the other patrons of the restaurant or themselves.
- Not take Rose to the restaurant.

In the situation with Rose, Nadia and Ben sometimes choose to forego the restaurant ritual for now in favor of a more relaxed meal in their own home. Is this a sacrifice for Nadia and Ben? Yes, it may be. But resisting what they know about Rose's age and temperament just wouldn't make sense. Their frustration would only grow if they ignored what they know about their child in favor of having expectations that are going to be met with conflict. Will Rose ever learn how to behave in a restaurant? Of course, she will. Can you use a behavioral skill building approach in this situation to teach Rose how to behave in the restaurant? Yes, but given her developmental age and temperament, it might be a long and tedious process. Nadia and Ben chose to wait until she is older to expect this of her. As a parent, you get to decide if this lesson is important enough to do the required skill building.

Clarity

Have you ever let your child know what is expected of him at the precise moment that you expect him to do something? This usually meets with resistance and conflict, am I right? The principle of clarity suggests you be clear about expectations, preferably in advance. But how do you know what your expectations should be? Remember, use what you know about development and your child's temperament to decide. In proactive discipline, some expectations for behavior may be negotiable such as *what coat you wear* in winter. But certain rules in your family will be non-negotiable such as *wearing a coat* in winter. Non-negotiables fall into two categories. Those non-negotiable rules related to safety and those non-negotiable rules related to respect. In my workshops, I ask participants, "Would you ever let a two-year-old walk in a busy mall parking lot without holding your hand?" Everyone says emphatically, "No." Most agree that you would do whatever it takes to get the message across to your child that walking without holding your hand is unacceptable. Whether you took the child's hand firmly or picked her up, you wouldn't let her walk alone. You would make it clear that holding your hand is non-negotiable. What other non-negotiables do you have? I would argue that many parents aren't clear about what they consider non-negotiable. Ambivalence is the enemy of effective parenting. Proactive discipline suggests you get some clarity around the non-negotiables that are right for your family. Remember, it is critical to factor in development. While the non-negotiables for a three-year-old might be different than the non-negotiables for a thirteen-year-old, some non-negotiables are the same regardless of age.

Here are some examples of how non-negotiables change with age...

Safety non-negotiables...

- Two-year-olds and car seat safety
- Ten-year-olds and bicycle safety
- Seventeen-year-olds and driving safety

Here are some examples of how non-negotiables remain the same regardless of age...

Respect non-negotiables...

- Talking back
- Disobeying
- Being aggressive

Do you know what your non-negotiables are? In order to make them clear to your child, you must first make them clear to yourself. Both parents should sit down together and discuss what the rules are in the car, at the dinner table and out in public. At every age, you will have nuances to development that require you to know what your expectations are no matter where you are. Each time your child reaches a new developmental stage, I recommend you have this discussion. Ideally, both parents agree to the non-negotiables that matter most to one another. While parenting together can be challenging given individual parenting styles, you know it is in the best interest of your child for him to see a unified front. For parents that are separated or divorced, parenting together is just as important, perhaps more so. In Chapter 10, I will discuss this challenge to the proactive parent.

Communication

Now that you are clear on what your non-negotiable rules are, you can communicate them to your child. There is a time and place for communication in parenting and it is during proactive discipline. It is when your child *is not* doing anything you object to that you want to communicate both your expectations for behavior as well as the consequences of certain actions. It is during conflict, that your actions speak louder than words. A lengthy discussion of how to effectively apply conflict discipline can be found in Chapter 4. In proactive discipline, you set expectations and state clear consequences to unacceptable behavior. In conflict discipline, you follow through on the established limits and provide consequences to inappropriate behavior.

Communication is a critical aspect of proactive discipline. It sets the stage for the behavioral skill building you will do with your child and it allows you to follow through in conflict discipline, if your child chooses not to meet expectations. Telling your child, in advance, what your expectations are is a positive step in providing the structure and boundaries your child needs to behave.

Joaquim

Joaquim is a ten-year-old boy who has difficulty adapting to the unexpected. Since he was a young boy, Joaquim has had outbursts that involve crying, talking back or getting very angry, when met with the unforeseen. Joaquim's father learned early on that the more he told Joaquim about what the day would bring, the better able Joaquim was at handling inevitable ups and downs. From when he would pick him up from the afterschool program to what they would have for dinner, Joaquim's father would communicate what he knew of the day's events. Did Joaquim's father still have to help him build skills to handle the unexpected? Of course! The first step in proactive discipline is for Joaquim's father to communicate the expectations for the end of day routine. The second step is to communicate to Joaquim what will happen if he has difficulty adapting to the expectations.

Communication functions to get your child's attention, share information, comment on behavior and express feelings. Your child best accepts all of these purposes of communication when it is done in times of peace.

Role modeling

You are your child's first and best teacher. No matter what other influences your child is exposed to, your influence has the greatest impact. The influences of the world at large are enormous for your child and I will discuss how to cope with all of that when I discuss societal discipline in Chapter 5. But remember, what you do and what you say still carries the greatest weight regardless of your child's developmental age and temperament. Sure there are times when your child may seem to prefer getting his teeth pulled to acknowledging that you are important in his life, but don't be fooled. The structure you provide, the limits that you set and your ideas and opinions matter to him.

At a workshop, Susan asks how she can get her eleven-year-old to stop swearing. She says, "He swears constantly. It has really become part of his every day conversation.

Damn it, I want it to stop and I don't know what to do about it." To that, members of the audience chuckled. Susan was role-modeling the exact behavior she wanted to set limits on and she was oblivious to the impact her behavior had on her son.

If you yell at your daughter, is it any surprise that she will yell at you? If you spank your son, are you surprised when he hits his sister? Looking at your own behavior may shed some light on the particular challenges you face with your child.

Here are some tips for effective role modeling that are part of proactive discipline.

- Think about the role models in your child's life. Which ones have a positive impact on your child and which ones have a negative impact?
- Discuss what makes a good role model with your child. Ask her what qualities she thinks a good teacher, coach or neighbor should possess.
- Examine your own behavior. Consider the messages you might be sending to your child about certain behaviors.
- Set a good example. When you are expecting your child to behave in a particular manner, hold yourself to the same standard.

Respect

Respect is probably the most important guiding principle in parenting. Respect defined means "to show consideration to, to value or honor." If you want your child to respect you, then certainly you must extend respect to your child. Respect is truly a two-way street. If you embrace respectful parenting, then you will raise a respectful child.

Teaching respect is an active process and it begins with believing that respect is a right, not a privilege. When your two-year-old screams for juice, this is an opportunity to teach respectful behavior. You don't have to have a power struggle over how to ask for juice, but this situation is telling you it's time to describe what respect is and what it is not. Your child must be taught very specifically, what respectful behavior looks and feels like. So too, your child needs you to concretely describe what disrespectful behavior looks and feels like. Your child will internalize respect when he is shown that it is only the respectful behavior that gets him what he needs.

Extend respect to your child and to people in general. Remember the effect good role modeling has on your child. Your child is watching you and will imitate your behavior. It is not only respectful but also essential to provide structure and boundaries in proactive discipline. Everyone wants to know what is expected of him. You wouldn't think it was very respectful for your boss to spring a new project deadline on you, would you? No matter how old your child is, she needs clear boundaries and structure to be successful. It is tempting to think that an older child can manage without structure and boundaries. But in reality, too much independence can be stressful and it can place your child in situations that she is emotionally unable to handle. I will discuss the importance of supervision in the societal discipline chapter.

To understand the importance of structure and boundaries, I use the following visual image. I'd like you to imagine two backyards. In the first backyard, there is a fence. The fence is new and has a gate with a solid latch. There are no holes under the fence for the dog to crawl through and all the slats are intact. There are toys of all varieties in this backyard...a swingset, sports equipment and a sandbox. In this yard, your child can play with anything he wants...he has freedom within structure. In the second backyard, there is a fence. This fence is old and has an open gate with a broken latch. There is a hole under the fence for the dog to crawl through and there are a number of missing slats. This backyard has all the same toys...but where do you think your child will play? In the yard or out the gate? The structure and boundaries you provide is the fence. If your child is young, the backyard is small and the freedoms are few. If your child is older, the backyard is bigger and there is perhaps more freedom. At each developmental age, you revisit the size of the yard and its contents. But you never remove the fence! Now image the fence you currently provide for your child. Is your fence intact...are you providing solid structure and clear boundaries? This visual image and what it represents will become very important as I continue to describe Proactive Parenting. Finding respectful ways of providing the fence to your child regardless of his age or temperament will be the key to creating a balance between expecting too little of your child and expecting too much. If you want your child to enjoy freedom within structure, you must maintain the fence. To do so is proactive and it is respectful.

The proactive strategies

A strategy is a careful plan or method of action. Each of the three aspects of discipline has strategies that you use to provide this kind of discipline. Proactive discipline is about planning ahead. Proactive parents anticipate problems or difficult situations and use proactive strategies to guide their child's behavior. When you identify a behavior or situation that requires shaping, you will use all of these proactive strategies to correct, refine and change your child's behavior. If a particular behavior happens once, it happened once. If a particular behavior happens twice, be assured it will happen again.

Here are the proactive strategies used in proactive discipline.

• Have proactive conversations
• Set expectations and discuss consequences
• Explore other factors affecting behavior
• Provide emotional coaching and problem solving
• Spend time together

Have proactive conversations

If your child is going to be expected to change behavior and learn new ways of coping with his temperament, he must first understand your desire for things to change. You know your child better than anyone and you know what situations he finds challenging. You also know in what situations he needs more skills to be effective in getting what he needs. In proactive discipline, you are his teacher and the teaching begins with a proactive conversation. Of course, the conversation must be age-appropriate. If your child is young, the conversation will be brief and simple. If your child is older, the conversation will be longer and will have more depth.

Charlie

Charlie has difficulty sitting at the table during mealtimes. He is an active five-year-old and finds it hard to sit still. If you're like most parents, you will only talk to Charlie about sitting still at the table, when you're at the table. When you have a proactive conversation, you are talking about the situation at any other time but in the situation that creates conflict. When Charlie's mom talked to him about sitting still at the table she did it when she was tucking him in one night. It sounded something like this, "Charlie, I want to talk to you about mealtime. In our family, I want everyone to come to the table, sit down for the whole meal and then ask to be excused. You are a boy who has lots of energy and you have trouble sitting down sometimes, don't you?" During this conversation, Charlie had the chance to share his point of view. "I don't like sitting for so long and my chair is uncomfortable." His mother went on to say, "I know it is hard but I am going to help you. You are a big boy now and I know you can do this." It is important to make your communication a conversation not a lecture. It should be positive and allow both you and your child the opportunity to share your unique perspectives. During this conversation, be sure to tell your child why this is important to you. In Charlie's situation, his mother said, "You will be starting kindergarten soon and I know learning how to sit still at dinner will help you to sit still in class. Let's work on this now." The proactive conversation is just the first step in helping Charlie gain the skills he needs to follow the dinner rules.

Proactive conversations should always include clearly stated expectations for future behavior as well as what the consequences will be if your child can't meet those expectations. I will talk about setting expectations in detail in the next strategy, *Set expectations and discuss consequences.*

Proactive conversations are very important in behavioral skill building. Many parents already have these kinds of conversations with their child. Unfortunately, they have them in conflict. They are, in effect, having the *right conversation* at the *wrong time.* Do you talk a lot in conflict? Can you envision Charlie's mother talking to him at the table saying, "Charlie, you need to sit still. Why can't you sit still? If you don't sit still, I will..." Your child is less able to hear you and respond to you when you talk in conflict. Conflict is a time of action and I will discuss that kind of discipline in Chapter 4. Proactive conversations deserve their own space and time.

Here are some tips for having proactive conversations.

- Converse in age-appropriate ways.
- Be positive.
- Be clear and specific.
- Be realistic and reasonable.
- Know how your child's temperament and development affect the length of the conversation.
- Allow for differing points of view.
- Talk...don't preach.
- Listen to your child's ideas, feelings and opinions.
- Converse in times of peace.

Set expectations and discuss consequences

It is during your proactive conversation, that I want you to set expectations and discuss consequences. Most parents share their expectations in conflict situations. But you can only be clear about your expectations when you have thought about them in advance. Stop for a moment and ask yourself the following questions. What situations produce the most conflict in my family? Is it getting out of the house in the morning or getting your child to bed at night? Is it when your child plays with the next door neighbor's child or when your son is working on a school project? Next ask yourself what behaviors does my child exhibit that I think are unacceptable? The final and critical question is...What are the appropriate consequences to this particular behavior that will encourage my child to make different choices? I'm going to stop right here and tell you, that if I had the answer to this question I would undoubtedly be a millionaire. You see, choosing the right consequences for particular behaviors depends on your child's development and temperament. No two children will respond to the same consequences in the same way. In Chapter 4, I will discuss how you choose appropriate consequences that will make an impact on your individual child. I will teach you how to know when a consequence will change behavior or have no impact at all. This approach takes into account your individual child and what it will take to help her make choices about behavior that fit your values and expectations.

Proactive discipline is not about being in a situation and "winging it," it is about having a plan. Maybe your daughter won't say hello when she goes to her grandmother's or maybe your son is a poor sport when he plays Monopoly. Whatever the situation, you need to use some strategies in advance...proactive strategies and some strategies in the conflict...conflict strategies. Do you want to see these situations played out differently? If so, then setting expectations and discussing consequences during your proactive conversations should be your game plan.

Addy

Addy is an intense and persistent twelve-year-old. She has a habit of asking her mom if her friend can stay for dinner or sleep over right in front of her friend. If the answer is yes, then all is right with the world. But if the answer is no, Addy gets angry, begging and pleading with her mom to change her mind. It is to the point where her mother is embarrassed about Addy's behavior and feels she must answer yes, to keep the peace. Here is a situation that has already happened repeatedly. Do you think it will happen again? Of course, it will. In fact, Addy has no real reason to change her behavior because Mom either engages in the pleading or backs down. If Addy is to behave differently in this situation then she must learn what the expectations are and what will happen if she is unable to rise to the occasion. This is done by having a proactive conversation with Addy *before* her friend arrives. She should be told that her friend may not stay for dinner today. She should be told not to ask in front of her friend. And she must be told what will happen if she does, "your friend will have to go home early if you ask me if she can stay in front of her." The first step is to anticipate the situation your child is having difficulty with. The second step is to establish your non-negotiables limits. The third step will be to follow through...and that I will discuss with you in Chapter 4.

Here are some tips to help you set expectations and discuss consequences.

* Set expectations and discuss consequences during proactive conversations.
* Be direct and specific when sharing expectations and potential consequences.
* Tell your child why you have particular expectations.
* Focus on the behavior not the child.
* Know how your child's temperament and development affect the expectations and consequences.

Explore other factors affecting behavior

From the temperament of your child's playmates to the rules at your child's school, many factors can affect your child's behavior. Remember, the three primary factors affecting behavior are development, temperament and behavioral skills. We discussed those at length in Chapter 2. But there are additional factors that will influence your child's behavior. Examining what other factors may be contributing to your child's difficulty in certain situations is a valuable proactive strategy. Many factors can complicate your child's behavior. But repeatedly, I see three factors that consistently contribute to a child's difficult behavior. They are a child's sleep pattern, stress tolerance and peer relationships. I'd like to discuss each of these factors as they relate to proactive discipline. If you factor them into your parenting, you can often make dramatic progress shaping your child's behavior. And often that progress comes quickly.

Sleep patterns

Everyone has had a bad night sleep at one time or another. And when you do, the next day you probably tell anyone who will listen about it. You tell them how you looked at the clock at 1:00am and 2:00am and 3:00am. You may even tell them how you're dragging your body through the day. When you have a poor night sleep, you have less energy the next day. And you know the only way to feel better is to take an afternoon rest or go to bed early the next night. Not so, for your child! While your child's behavior during the day is affected by a poor night sleep or not getting enough sleep over time, his behavior looks very different from yours.

Your child may experience any or all of the following as a result of being sleep deprived.

• Irritability, crankiness or more tears
• Impatience with you, his siblings or his friends
• Hyperactivity, restlessness, fidgety
• Overly excited, jittery, nervous
• Stomachaches and headaches
• Lack of appetite

If you aren't thinking that sleep deprivation is a factor contributing to your child's behavior, you may be mistakenly thinking that his behavior is related to his challenging temperament or even to a disorder such as Attention Deficit Disorder (ADD) or Attention Deficit Hyperactivity Disorder (ADHD).

So, how much sleep should your child be getting? Experts suggest the following.

- Infants...14 to 16 hours of sleep per day including naps.
- Toddlers...13 hours of sleep per day including naps.
- Preschoolers...12 hours of sleep per day including naps.
- School age children...10 hours of sleep per night.
- Teenagers...8 ½ hours of sleep per night.

Most parents tell me their child sleeps far less than these recommendations. I've heard many parents say, "My child just doesn't need that much sleep." Not so, according to the abundance of research on sleep and children. Your child's behavior during the day is a direct result of his nighttime sleep. Making sleep a high priority in your family is critical to increasing your child's reserve energy, flexibility, good decision-making and general happiness. With those guarantees, I think getting everyone to bed is worth the effort.

Here are some tips for making sleep a priority in your family.

- Use lights to make distinctions between day and night.
- Be more playful during the day, and less so at night.
- Create nighttime rules for the household, this is especially important for adolescents.
- Keep your child calm in the evening to avoid overstimulation.
- Limit television, video games and the Internet right before bed.
- Restrict sugary snacks or those containing caffeine such as soda and chocolate before bed.
- Avoid having your child get overtired, watch for signs that your child is ready, and then put her to bed.
- Keep the bedtime routine simple.
- Parent together to establish routines that both parents can follow consistently.
- Talk to other parents about their experiences.
- Learn what you can expect of your child, based on her age.

Of course, even the best sleep habits on your part won't guarantee success. So, what do you do if sleep becomes a struggle? Start by keeping a journal of bedtime routines and your child's sleep patterns. The problem may reveal itself to you if you can observe patterns in behavior. In Chapter 7, I will give an example of how you might solve a typical sleep issue in a young child. Contrary to popular belief, the sleep issues you and your child struggle with are generally easy to correct, and the sleep patterns you establish now set the stage for sleep patterns later in life. Regulating sleep patterns now is worth the effort.

Stress tolerance

Everyone experiences it. The media talks a lot about it. But does stress really affect your child? The answer is absolutely, yes! With busy schedules, high academic expectations and the changing structure of families, your child is experiencing stress. All stress, however, isn't necessarily bad. Stress and anxiety *can be* great motivators. If other four-year-olds can write their name, then your son might work really hard to learn to write his name. If your daughter's mid-term exam is tomorrow; she might be studying right now. But stress and anxiety *can be* immobilizers. Given your child's temperament, stress may interfere with her ability to behave well day-to-day. If your child is more reactive and intense or less adaptable, he may be more sensitive to stress.

Family dynamics also play a role in the stress your child must cope with. Losing a grandparent, coping with a parent's chronic illness, being overscheduled with after-school activities or moving to a new school will contribute to how well your child can use the skills he has learned to behave well. Some stress is unavoidable and your child must learn to cope with certain amounts of it. But excessive stress and needless stress should be kept to a minimum because your child doesn't have the same experience you have managing it.

In proactive discipline, this valuable strategy of examining other factors contributing to challenging behaviors should include assessing your child's level of stress.

Here are just some of the questions you might ask yourself about your child's level of stress.

- Does my child's temperament make her more likely to have difficulty managing stress?
- Is our family adjusting to new situations, people or circumstances that are more stressful than usual?
- Is our family schedule busier than it should be, busier than usual or busier than my child can tolerate?
- Does my child exhibit any physical or behavioral symptoms that could be stress related?

Again you see the importance of understanding development and knowing your child, in order to make the best parenting decisions. I can't tell you what the "right" amount of stress is for your family, because there is a fine line between the motivating kind of stress and the immobilizing kind of stress for each child and each family. What I can tell you is that you need to *constantly* be assessing the level of stress your child is exposed to as well as take steps to minimize it when you can.

Here are some of the symptoms of stress and some strategies for keeping stress to a minimum.

Symptoms of stress

Physical symptoms can include...

- headaches
- stomachaches
- changes in appetite
- sleep disturbances or nightmares
- elimination problems such as bedwetting, constipation, regressed toilet training

Behavioral symptoms can include...

- aggressive behavior
- oppositional behavior
- anxiety, fear or separation issues
- regression to earlier developmental behaviors
- withdrawn behavior

Looking at this partial list of symptoms of stress, it is easy to see the importance of recognizing stress as a factor affecting behavior. Now here are some of the strategies you can use to manage stress on behalf of your child.

Stress management strategies

- Assess your child's level of stress and his ability to tolerate it.
- Educate your child about the circumstances that can cause stress and the symptoms of stress.
- Provide a safe, secure and predictable "fence".
- Simplify schedules, activities and life in general whenever possible.
- Give your child productive outlets for stress such as journaling, physical activities or drawing.
- Utilize the other proactive discipline strategies described in this chapter...have proactive conversations, set expectations and discuss consequences, provide emotional coaching and spend time with your child.

Peer relationships

Learning to relate to people other than your immediate family is important for success in life. The role of friendship in your child's life is both complicated and essential. In the neighborhood, at childcare or at school, your child must interact with other children. And at every developmental age, your child is capable of learning a new set of skills to do so effectively. Yet, your child may find that play is hard work because she doesn't find interacting with friends easy to do. Whether it is the inevitable acquisition of social skills or coping with challenging friendships, peer relationships can affect your child's behavior.

Spencer

When Spencer was a young boy, other parents used to comment on his ability to get along with anyone. He was even tempered, social and always able to find a way to include everyone. Now at age fourteen, Spencer has only one close friend and is often content to spend time by himself on the computer. He enjoys chatting with friends he has made online. Yet, he is getting increasingly reluctant to accept invitations to go places when he is invited. Spencer's father, Ted, attributes this change in Spencer this way. "Don't all teenagers withdraw like this? I've talked to friends who say that their teenagers never come out of their rooms. Things could be worse, I could be arguing with him over the places he goes or the friends he hangs with."

Ted makes some interesting points about the change in Spencer's social behavior. The first point he makes is questionable though. While privacy is important, all adolescents don't withdraw socially. Of course, it is important to think about development and how that impacts behavior. However, what I saw in this situation was that Spencer's temperament and what was required of him socially might be more responsible for his change in behavior. The second point Ted makes is that he would rather contend with Spencer's social isolation than arguing over Spencer's social life. While I won't disagree with Ted's preference, I think both situations are problematic in unique ways. Whether your child is isolating himself socially or spending time with friends that negatively influence him, proactive discipline is still required. Each situation described here is an extreme in the spectrum of learning how to have successful peer relationships. Again, assessing your child's ability to form and maintain healthy peer relationships is the first step in being proactive about friendship and social skills.

Here are some additional strategies for supporting your child as he strengthens his relationships with friends.

- Talk with your child about what makes a good friend.
- Ask your child if he is having any difficulties with particular friendships or with other children at school.
- Make sure your child has the skills needed to stay safe emotionally and physical among peers.
- Help your child take steps to encourage new friendships while still maintaining his current successful friendships.
- Share with your child that some friendships will feel comfortable and some will not, and that it is okay to encourage some friendships and not others.
- Role-play with your child how to join into peer groups, how to share and how to compromise.
- Give your child the language he needs to use when spending time with friends. The child that finds social skills challenging often doesn't have the appropriate scripts.
- Supervise social experiences so that you can intervene on your child's behalf. This is especially important for younger children but equally important for the older child with social difficulties.
- Take your child's social concerns seriously. If your child brings his worries to your attention, he is telling you he doesn't have the skills he needs "in the bag" and he needs help getting them there.

These are just a few general suggestions for encourage positive social skills. In Chapter 8, I will share with you a specific example of how to use Proactive Parenting to teach effective social skills to a school age child.

Provide emotional coaching and help with problem solving

Those parents that are most successful using Proactive Parenting, see themselves as their child's teacher or coach. The proactive parent comes to see those difficult or challenging behaviors and situations as opportunities for learning. Remember, no matter what situation or behavior presents itself you can teach your child a better way of handling it. All skills can be taught. Emotional coaching and problem solving are very proactive strategies. Emotional coaching is the kind of teaching and learning that is based on guidance, feedback, trial and error, and support. The parent who understands that it is a process to learn how to wait for dessert or get used to going to the doctor, is a parent who will ultimately see their child's success when it comes to doing these simple yet necessary things. Many specific strategies fall into the category of emotional coaching and problem solving. I will share with you the ones that I think make proactive discipline come alive.

- **Active listening**

Notice the word *active*. The words you use are only part of effective communication. Your ability to really listen to your child's ideas, feelings and opinions is critical to emotional coaching. Acknowledge your child's feelings, validate his difficulty with a certain situation and let him know you respect his opinion. This doesn't mean you always give in to non-negotiable limits...it simply means you hear his point of view.

- **Books**

This is probably my favorite way to provide emotional coaching. Reading to your child is a great proactive strategy used to shape behavior. You can influence behavior and provide opportunities for discussion by choosing a book with just the right story line. Some aspects of growing up are universal, and you can bet there is a book about it. Conversations about expectations are not effective during conflict but are best discussed during times of peace. Even your older child can benefit from reading the same book that you do and then discussing it with you. As you talk about the character's struggles, you can share your values and discuss life choices.

- **Can do's and can't do's**

In behavioral terms, this is referred to as behavioral substitution. An effective emotional coach tells a child not only what she *can't* do but what she *can* do. Remember that your child sometimes behaves inappropriately because she either doesn't have the skills or doesn't know her options. Share with your child options for behavior before she does something you object to. When visiting friends for dinner recently, I noticed Anna's mother matching can do's with can't do's with ease. "You can eat the cookie with your hands but you need to use a spoon for your ice cream." Or "You can stay up a bit later but you can't spend that time watching TV."

- **Feedback**
  True behavioral feedback is positive and constructive, not negative. Studies show that in order to change behavior, people respond best to 80% positive feedback and 20% constructive feedback. The positive feedback encourages us to keep trying and the constructive feedback allows room for improvement. Negative feedback is just that. It demeans and does not encourage. In Proactive Parenting, feedback is best given after your child has demonstrated success or effort in achieving a new skill. Let's say your child struggles with handling disappointment and something doesn't go his way. When he demonstrates self-control, be sure and give him specific praise about what he did that was effective. Remember, don't share this on the heels of the episode...wait. You will have time later to tell him exactly what you liked about how he handled the situation. And won't he be encouraged to try the same strategies in the future?

- **Goal setting**
  If your child needs to learn a new set of skills or face a new challenge, he needs to set goals. Goals keep you focused on where you are going not where you have been. They help you to measure progress and stay motivated. Most of all, with a goal in mind, you will be able to choose other proactive strategies to help you reach your end.
  Goals should be realistic and achievable. You wouldn't expect the sensitive, withdrawn child to have a birthday party with 30 guests. But you might set a goal that includes calling up one friend and inviting him over for cake.

Remember to factor in development and temperament as you set goals and never forget to include the child. Your child knows best what her hopes and dreams are for the future.

- **Journaling**
   The behavioral process of writing or drawing in a journal allows your child an outlet for intense, sometimes overwhelming feelings that he may have difficulty verbalizing. The beauty of a journal is that not only does it give your child an active way to capture feelings but it also provides an opportunity to reflect on previous thoughts and feelings. Other creative expressions such as artistic or physical outlets can also be helpful given a child's specific temperament.

- **Physical action**
   In behavioral work, there is a belief that action comes first and feelings follow. Physical action as a discipline strategy can be used in proactive discipline and in conflict discipline. I will describe two ways to use it in proactive discipline. In Chapter 4, I will discuss a third way to use it in conflict. The first way to use physical action as a proactive discipline strategy is simply to have your child do something to see how it feels. The thought being that comfort with it will follow. An example of this is letting a child get on a bus in August before he will have to get on it for real in September. This exposure alone may instill feelings of comfort with the process. The second kind of physical action that works behaviorally involves using action as an outlet. For the active child or the child with sensory issues, some physical actions actually make it easier for the child to integrate sensory information better, later in the day. Swinging, twirling and running may be ways to help the child who needs to get some energy out in appropriate places at appropriate times.

- **Projecting**
   This term refers to what I call, "what's the worst case scenario?" Here you ask your child to play out, in conversation, what his worst fears are about a situation and

what he will do should any of these scenarios actually occur. This technique actually has its roots in cognitive therapy. It is a reframing strategy as well. As a coach, you help your child see that what he fears isn't so bad and that many situations can be seen from a variety of perspectives. Ask questions like, "do you really think that will happen?" Or "how will you handle that if it does happen?" Projecting helps both you and your child have realistic expectations for situations and it allows you an opportunity to separate anxiety from reality. When five-year-old, Dania was asked what her biggest concern was about going to kindergarten, she replied. "I'm afraid you will forget to pick me up for the weekend." Dania thought that she stayed at school Monday through Friday. This conversation allowed Dania's dad a chance to allay her fears...she would come home from school everyday. Imagine Dania's relief to learn this.

- **Role-playing**

This important behavioral strategy has already been mentioned in some of the case studies I shared with you so far. Role-playing is an extremely effective strategy that helps your child get concrete experience, "in the bag." Sure she might just be practicing what she will say when a friend asks her to smoke a cigarette, but this practice makes being able to say the right thing in the real situation much more likely. Since your child won't feel the same pressure practicing that he would in the real situation, he can get lots of experience trying new skills out. Playing school, post office and restaurant with your child may feel natural and fun. Sharing expectations while you play may feel clever. But it is important to remember that your school age child, your adolescent and even you can benefit from the kind of repetition role-playing allows. Keep in mind your child learns in concrete ways right up through adolescence. Role-playing is a concrete way to practice new skills and get positive and constructive feedback, all without the stress of doing something the first time for real.

- **Scripting**

If it came naturally to your child to do and say the right thing at the right time, I believe she would do it. But remember certain behaviors and conversations may not come easily to your child. Your child may benefit from the behavioral strategy known as scripting. Scripting involves giving your child some words or phrases to use in situations where knowing the right thing to say is challenging. For the child who finds social work difficult, conversing is a two step process. The first step is thinking up what to say and the second step is saying it. With scripting, you have made your child's job 50% easier by giving him some standard phrases to use. When you are going to a party and you expect your child to say hello to the adults, give her three different things to say. Let her practice saying them and let her choose whether to use any of the three or come up with one on her own. Again, your child is more likely to meet with success partly because you have shared your expectations in advance and partly because you provided appropriate scripts for your child to use. Just a footnote here. If your child has lots of difficulty socially, scripting will be important but it won't be the only proactive strategy you use to help your child be successful.

Emotional coaching and problem solving will include other proactive strategies as well. However, the ten I've highlighted here will be discussed often in the situations I share with you in this book. Proactive discipline is about building skills in your child through active teaching and coaching.

Spend time together

By far, the most important proactive strategy is to spend time with your child. By providing proactive discipline, you invariably spend more time with your child. You spend that time having proactive conversations, setting expectations and providing emotional coaching. And while those strategies are critical to the success of the approach, so is spending time with your child without any agenda. Find a shared interest, take them for a long drive, or just be sure to "tuck" your child in each night. You will be amazed at what your child will share with you.

When you increase the amount of peaceful time you spend with your child, conflict is reduced. Talking, laughing and sharing your lives with each other builds a connection between you and your child that is harder to break when you do find yourself in conflict. Statistics that say how small the average amount of time a parent spends per day talking with their child is not only disturbing but sad. Think about the time you spend with your child. Is your communication mostly about what your child is doing wrong or doing right? Your child cares so much about what you think of her. Like a mirror, you reflect back to her, her worth as a person. The time you spend with her should be about building her up not breaking her down.

Not enough time in the day, parents claim is the number one reason they don't spend time together. I'm not asking you to make this complicated. In fact, here are some simple ways to build this one-on-one time into your already existing routines.

- Read to your child everyday. If your child is older, take turns reading aloud an exciting story.
- Teach your child how to cook. You have to make dinner anyway, why not get your child to help.
- Do chores together. It is tempting to ask your child to do one thing while you do another, but if you fold the laundry together, you get the opportunity to talk.
- Take a walk together. Fitness is important for both of you and here you get the benefit of spending time together.
- Ask for company. When you drive one child to an activity, ask another child to come along for the ride. Share a soft drink while you wait and focus on what your child wants to talk about.

These simple ways of spending time together are just examples of what you might choose to do. Think about your daily routines and build in uncomplicated ways of learning about your child's life.

Sean and Aiden

Back to the grocery store. Remember how difficult the shopping experience was for both Sean and two-year-old, Aiden? Now that you know more about proactive discipline, things can look quite different. What proactive strategies can Sean use with Aiden to make the trip to the market more successful? Here are my suggestions...

Have proactive conversations
- Tell Aiden you are going to the market today and let him know you expect cooperation.
- Remind him a few times that you are going and he is expected to behave.

Set expectations and discuss consequences
- Tell Aiden exactly what your expectations for successful shopping are. "Aiden, I need you to be safe and respectful at the store and I need to get our food. Being safe in the store means staying in the carriage. Being respectful means no yelling or throwing things."
- Tell him what the consequences to certain behaviors will be. "Every time you stand up, I will make you sit down. If you scream, throw things and I can't do our shopping, we will have to go home and come back another time."
- Tell Aiden exactly what you will do to help him such as getting a planned snack.

Explore other factors affecting behavior
- Aiden is probably stressed in the market because he lacks boundaries.
- Create the "fence" by keeping Aiden in the carriage. At two and one half, he doesn't have the self-discipline to stay with you.
- Shop earlier or when Aiden is well rested. At four o'clock, Aiden doesn't have the reserve energy he needs to be successful especially if he is missing the "fence".

Provide emotional coaching and problem solving
- Give Aiden can do's and can't do's. "You can have grapes when we start and a bagel at the end but you cannot

have candy. You can put the things I give you in the carriage but you can't take things off the shelves."
- Role-play going shopping keeping expectations and consequences in mind.
- Remember emotional coaching is best done in advance.
- Let Aiden get some of his energy out before you shop. If Aiden is an active boy and he has been sitting for awhile in the car, then sitting in the carriage will be hard for him.

Spend time together
- Spend time playing with Aiden before and after the shopping trip. Because you are making the "fence" more secure, Aiden will benefit from feeling a continued connection with you.
- Engage Aiden in the shopping experience. Point things out to him; teach him what you are doing, but find a way to include him in the process. If engaged in shopping, he will be more focused on positive behaviors.

So, now you fully expect Aiden to cooperate in the market, right? Well he is certainly more likely to, given all the proactive strategies Sean has put into place. Yet, proactive discipline is no guarantee for success nor should it always be. That's where conflict discipline comes in. Your child learns a great deal by experiencing the consequences of his actions. Now that you know your proactive discipline strategies for this situation, you need to provide the follow through. Sean has to be fully prepared to take Aiden out of the market. When he does, Aiden gets the message that Sean was serious about the expectations. Maybe the first time a trip to the parking lot will suffice. After that, the trip home and the return later will enhance Sean's credibility. Don't fall into the habit of hollow threats...Aiden is smarter than you think.

Chapter Summary

Proactive discipline is the most important discipline you provide for your child. Its guiding principles are anticipation, clarity, communication, role modeling, and respect.

The proactive strategies include having proactive conversations; setting expectations and discussing consequences; exploring other factors affecting behavior; providing emotional coaching and problem solving; and spending time together.

When providing proactive discipline the proactive parent remembers that...

- The best teaching you do is proactive discipline.
- Proactive discipline builds self-esteem.
- Proactive discipline is about good communication.
- Proactive discipline is about aligning yourself with your child.
- Proactive discipline must be combined with a good conflict discipline plan.
- Proactive discipline includes societal discipline strategies.
- Proactive discipline takes time...but reaps rewards.

Questions and Answers
Chapter 3

The Calm Before The Storm

Proactive Discipline

Q: Whenever I try to have a proactive conversation with my son it deteriorates into conflict. Should I continue talking even though the spirit of what I was trying to do has been lost?

A: No, when proactive conversations turn into conflict... now you are in conflict and you need to stop talking. I have two suggestions to remedy this dilemma. First, spend time with your child with no agenda. If the only time you spend with him is about your expectations for behavior, he will quickly become defensive around you. Second, when you must set expectations about something and your child rebuffs you, tell him you will wait until he can calmly discuss the situation. Let him know that you will not discuss expectations with raised voices or disrespectful body language.

Q: After I have had a proactive conversation with my daughter about what I expect, do I ever bring it up again or do I just expect her to do what I have suggested?

A: Remember, in proactive discipline you are your child's coach. You will need to remind your daughter of your conversation often and of course, in advance of the situations she has difficulty with. A baseball coach would never show a child how to swing a baseball bat and consider his job done. He would reinforce good skills during practice and intervene far less during the game. The same is true of behavioral skill building and Proactive Parenting.

Q: Why do I discuss my expectations with a two-year-old? Can she really understand the purpose of a proactive conversation?

A: Remember, the proactive conversation is to be done in age-appropriate ways. The conversation you have with a two-year-old will be brief. Yet, there are a number of important reasons not to skip this important proactive strategy with a young child.

Proactive conversations...
* are respectful at any age.
* help you to have a game plan for age appropriate discipline.
* set the stage for the action you will take in conflict.
* demonstrate parenting that is based on cause and effect learning.

FOUR

The Perfect Storm

Conflict Discipline

Micah, like many mothers, struggles with creating a balance between her work life and her home life. That struggle literally begins every morning at six when she tries to get Luke, her eight-year-old son, up and ready for school. Her morning is filled with phrases like, "Hurry up". "You're going to make me late." "Did you eat yet?" "Why aren't you dressed yet?" Luke has been pushing the limits of the morning routine since the first day of school in September. The fall has come and gone and Micah is at her wit's end. She shares with me her desire to make some changes in the pattern she and Luke have established. "He dawdles every morning with the things I ask him to do. Yet, he makes sure he watches his morning show and gets the nice breakfast he likes. He used to know just how far to push me and still get us both out of the house in time. Now he makes his bus, usually just in the nick of time, because it's important for him to ride with his friends. But his lack of cooperation and disrespect for my job has escalated, to the point where I am late every day now."

For many parents, this situation sounds all too familiar. Yet, this is an example of parenting in conflict. The morning routine doesn't have to look like this for Micah or for anyone. When you parent in conflict, rarely will your child hear what you have to say. That is because conflict situations are more about power and control than they are about problem solving and skill building. In this situation, there seems to be no reason for Luke to make the effort to change behavior. Micah talks a great deal, but there are no consequences associated with Luke's inability to be respectful about getting off to school each day. In fact, it doesn't surprise me that Luke's pushing of the limits has escalated. As Micah continues to share expectations in conflict, with no real follow through, Luke pushes the boundaries never finding "the fence." Micah and I created a proactive plan for this conflict situation. Of course, it included proactive and conflict discipline strategies. In helping Micah, it was important to describe to her the principles and strategies for conflict discipline. I will share with you her discipline plan for conflict at the end of this chapter.

Conflict discipline

Conflict discipline teaches your child to accept limits and act in acceptable ways. It is the discipline that takes place during conflict. When you and your child are in a power struggle over bedtime or arguing over homework, your child is learning what behavior you will accept. How you set limits and more importantly, how you follow through on the limits you have established, make up conflict discipline. With each situation in which you provide conflict discipline, your child will learn what is expected of her and she will learn how to make decisions differently next time based on how this conflict is managed. The key to conflict discipline is to develop a plan for typical disciplinary situations, in advance. You know your child's temperament. You know if your daughter is going to have issues when you drop her off at preschool. You know if your son will get overwhelmed at a family cookout if it starts at six o'clock. Having a plan for the foreseeable conflict will allow you to act with authority and be the proactive parent your child needs. Having the right strategies lets you remain calm when those situations arise and helps you to teach your child how to behave in these situations.

Principles of conflict discipline

Remember, principles are guiding ideas that support your actions. Each of the three kinds of discipline has guiding principles.

Here are the principles of conflict discipline....
* Action
* Authority
* Consistency
* Emotional Integrity
* Predictability

Action

In proactive discipline, words are so important. What you say and how you communicate with your child is central to the success of proactive discipline. In conflict discipline, however, actions speak louder than words. Remember, all discipline is about learning to function more effectively in everyday life. Learning is a very concrete process for your child. Talking, skill building and feedback take place in proactive discipline. Action takes place in conflict discipline. In order for your child to get certain learning experiences "in the bag", the actions you take in conflict must support the words you shared before conflict. Messages about how to behave well are received more quickly when the actions fit or match the misbehavior.

Sophie

Two-year-old Sophie is an active, happy and persistent little girl. Her mother loves the end of the day when Sophie spends some time before dinner in a warm tub. This routine seems to calm her daughter, making the rest of the evening routine a little easier on everyone. Lately however, Sophie's love of independence is making her unsafe in the tub. Even though her mother is right in the room, Sophie has taken to standing up in the tub to reach her toys, the towel or to get out on her own. It is tempting in this situation to tell

Sophie, "sit down or I will have to take you out." But the power of conflict discipline lies in the action conveying the message more effectively than your words ever could. The talking... "You must sit in the tub or I will have to take you out," is a proactive discipline strategy. This proactive conversation that describes the expectation and the consequence, belongs before Sophie comes anywhere near the tub. Once you've shared the expectation in advance, there is no further need for talking. The action of taking her out is the only piece that belongs in conflict. Will Sophie be unhappy with this action? Probably, she will be. But this action delivers a message and Sophie's reaction clearly tells you that the message was received. I will share more with you about making impact later in this chapter.

Another specific way to use action to teach your child how to behave appropriately is called overcorrection behavior. If your child throws his backpack down on the floor when he comes home from school, having him place it down in the right place five times will remind him of this expectation. Be sure and warn your child proactively if you are going to use this strategy. It should not be done in a sarcastic or angry way but in a teaching manner. If you spring it on him in the conflict you will inevitably create a power struggle.

Authority

When you think of the ideal parent/child relationship, do you see yourself as your child's friend? If so, that is fine, as long as you are providing proactive discipline. Remember, proactive discipline is where the talking and sharing of ideas, opinions and values lie. You align yourself with your child during proactive conversations. But there is a time and place for you to be the authority figure your child needs. An authority is someone with the power to enforce rules and guide behavior. An authority is a person with the ability to gain respect because he has the power to influence the actions of others. You may really believe that your child wants to be the authority in your family, yet having all that control and power is a scary place for your child to be. When your child pushes the limits and boundaries, what looks like a play for power is really an attempt to find the structure and boundaries that make her feel safe. She *needs* you to step in and demonstrate through action, the knowledge, skill and experience she doesn't have to handle a particular situation. The trick is to learn when to align yourself with your child; proactive discipline...and when to be an authority figure to your child; conflict discipline.

Barrett

Bedtime for five-year-old Barrett has always been a challenge for his Mom. Barrett's Dad works late each evening, so the bedtime routine falls to his tired mother. Barrett's Mom describes him as an independent, persistent child always looking for ways to be in charge. She describes herself as a mother with lots of patience until the end of the day when she is exhausted. The bedtime routine that begins the almost nightly power struggle between Barrett and his mother looks like this. Barrett knows his bedtime is 8 o'clock but does everything in his power to push it off as late as possible. "I need another drink. I didn't have enough to eat, I'm hungry. I forgot to brush my teeth." After all the gyrations downstairs, a new set of delaying activities happen upstairs. "I want two stories tonight. That's not the stuffed animal I want to bring to bed. Stay with me until I fall asleep." You can call it looking for control over bedtime, but what I see is a boy who needs an authority figure to step in and provide age appropriate boundaries to this obvious testing of limits.

When Barrett's mother and I talked about how to set the stage for this conflict by providing proactive discipline, she never thought Barrett would accept limits at bedtime. Her proactive strategies involved sharing with Barrett how the new bedtime routine would look. She did this at lunchtime and reminded him at dinnertime. She also shared with him that if he pushed the limits, she would not remind him again, she would just leave his room. If he got out of bed and followed her, she would walk him back in as many times as it took for him to get the message...It is time for bed. She let Barrett know that she was doing this for him. He needed to go to bed without all the fuss and she was going to help him. Barrett's mother shared all of this with him in a confident, positive manner. To me she said, "He will never go for this. He will make my life miserable. I will probably get him to bed around midnight. But I am willing to try anything." Well, after losing the bedtime story and Barrett's mother leaving the room three times, Barrett went to bed. Of course, Barrett didn't cheerfully accept his mother's new persona, but one week later his mother describes her evenings this way. "Barrett seems to be so much happier at bedtime. Our time together at the end of the day is so special. I never would have thought that he would do so much better with fewer options around the bedtime routine."

Consistency

Some of the biggest misconceptions in parenting have to do with consistency. Look at the following two statements and decide whether each is true or false.

True or False

a. Consistency means I must do the same thing each time my child misbehaves.

True or False

b. I'm not being consistent if I don't follow through on the limits I set, even if I realize that a limit isn't that important.

If you are like many parents, you might think both statements are true. Yet in fact, both statements are false. Let's examine each statement separately. *Consistency means I must do the same thing each time my child misbehaves.* No, consistency means you must do *something* each time your child misbehaves. Realistically speaking, you won't be able to do the same thing each time your child behaves inappropriately.   But if you have decided a particular behavior is non-negotiable, then you must act on it each and every time your child chooses to do it. Four-year-old Tessie hits other children when she is frustrated. There are many proactive strategies that must be used to improve her frustration tolerance and give her the skills she needs to make different choices in conflict. But every time she hits, something must happen to deliver the message to Tessie that hitting is never acceptable. You might make her leave the room or you might have her friend go home, but every time she hits, something must happen. If you respond with action each and every time, she will get the message. If you act five times and then on the sixth time, you do nothing, Tessie learns that sometimes hitting is acceptable.

Here's the second statement. *I'm not being consistent if I don't follow through on the limits I set, even if I realize that a limit isn't that important.* Common sense should tell you this statement is false. Doesn't it sound like the perfect set up for a power struggle? Will you really follow through with something that is unimportant for consistency sake? This is where the old phrase, "pick your battles" fits into parenting skill building. If you find that you have set a limit and it is not in the non-negotiable categories of either safety or respect, let it go. And let it go as quickly as you realize it. The sooner you get out of a power struggle, the sooner you can recover the peace between you and your child. Taylor, a mother of four children under the age of ten, found herself one day arguing with her six-year-old over whether or not he should wear brown socks or blue socks to a friend's house. Here's what she said to me, "I suddenly thought...with all I have to do today, why am I arguing with this little boy over socks. But I also thought...well, I set the limit now I must follow through." This is a popular misconception that I run into in my work. What I recommend in this kind of situation is to make the conscious choice to give in. Once you realize that following through with the limit isn't worth your energy...let your child win one. Your child won't suddenly think you are going to abandon all the limits. In fact, your child might see you as a reasonable person willing to compromise if you present it the right way. Wouldn't Taylor's child be surprised to hear her say, "You know what? You're right, the color of your socks doesn't really matter. You may choose your socks today."

Emotional integrity

Have you ever gotten angry with your child? Have you ever yelled at or diminished your child? While all feelings are acceptable, all actions based on feelings are not. Emotional integrity is about acting on your feelings in appropriate ways. Is it okay for you to be angry with your child? Yes, anger is a normal emotion. Yet, what you do with that anger matters a great deal. Yelling and diminishing your child is never an appropriate way to handle your feelings. In Proactive Parenting, emotional integrity is easier to maintain than you might think.

When you have a plan for managing conflict, keeping your cool is easier because...

1. You have anticipated your child's difficulty in a particular situation so you're not taken by surprise when she behaves in a particular way.
2. You have a chance to avoid or correct behavior before it reaches the point where it frustrates or angers you.
3. You have decided on the strategies you will use to teach appropriate behavior so you don't need to feel the stress of thinking on your feet.
4. You have made the commitment to see conflict as a learning opportunity so you don't need to be upset.

Mothers and fathers set the emotional tone in a family. If you are upset, angry and frustrated a lot of the time, your child will be too. Remember the information I shared with you in Chapter 3 about role modeling? If what you are role modeling for your child is emotional intensity, your child learns that this is the way to express yourself. How would he know any differently? If you feel like you're on an emotional roller coaster when parenting your child, then most of your parenting is probably being done in conflict. Having emotional integrity will show your child that you have a course of action planned to teach appropriate behavior. When you enact your plan, messages are conveyed in convincing and matter of fact ways, not emotionally. You role model rational behavior not behavior that is reactive.

Bridgett

Twelve-year-old Bridgett listens to the radio in her room before dinner. Proactively, it has been shared with her that she will only be called once for dinner. Coming the first time she is called is the respectful thing to do. She is told that no one will yell and carry on. Mom or Dad will simply come and shut off the radio or begin dinner without her. The first night she doesn't come when called, without talking her Mom goes to her room and shuts off the radio. The second night she doesn't come when called; the family begins eating without her. Bridgett doesn't like either of these actions and loudly says so. Bridgett is reminded of the new expectation. This is the new plan. On night three, Bridgett comes to the table the first time she is called.

Predictability

Have you ever volunteered in a preschool or elementary school? Have you noticed how each day looks the same? Outdoor activities, snack time and circle time happen at the same time every day. In fact, in the event that a teacher changes the schedule even slightly, every student seems to notice and comment on it. That is because children love predictability. Being able to predict what will happen next and when, gives your child a sense of security and clearly provides structure and boundaries..."the fence". Remember in Chapter 2, I shared with your how your child thinks and learns? As early as one year of age, your child is learning through cause and effect. Concrete experiences that your child can predict enhance all kinds of learning. Predictability is achieved in proactive discipline through the provision of structure and routines. But predictability is also achieved in conflict discipline through consistently providing action for non-negotiable behaviors related to safety and respect. In behavioral work, when a consequence matches a behavior each and every time the behavior surfaces, over time there is a change in behavior.

Every time seven-year-old Luther eats his dinner with his hands, his father gets out of his chair and takes his plate.

After the third meal, Luther begins to eat with his hands, looks at his father and says, "Sorry, sorry I forgot." Luther's father hadn't even gotten out of his chair, yet because his father has been consistent in matching a consequence to an inappropriate behavior, Luther can predict what will come next. This ability to predict allows Luther the opportunity to make a new choice.

Because of this principle of predictability, parents that provide consistent limit setting and follow through see changes in behavior very quickly. Often a difficult behavior can be modified in a few days to a week. But sometimes things get worse before they get better.

Mairead

Mairead's mother came to Proactive Parenting with the same problem that Barrett's mother had. Her five-year-old, Mairead was also having difficulty at bedtime. As we talked, Mairead's mother said she was fearful that the tighter bedtime routine I was suggesting would make Mairead angry. She fully expected her to get very upset when faced with the new boundaries. We did however create a proactive plan that included lots of talking about the new routine, long before bedtime, so that Mairead would be fully prepared. I also shared with Mairead's mother how to handle the situation should Mairead become angry about the new routine. The first day, Mairead's mother shared the new bedtime routine with her daughter several times. It included brushing her teeth, getting into her pajamas and having one story. After the story, Mairead's mother would leave the room and Mairead was to stay in bed. If she got out of bed, her mother would walk her back to her room as many times as it took for her to get the message that it was time for bed. The first night, Mairead did get angry with her mother for following through on the limits that had been established. She threw toys around her room and loudly said, "Why are you doing this. I hate this new bedtime thing you are doing to me." Although Mairead's mother, felt vulnerable to this kind of emotional outburst from Mairead, she stuck to the plan. She walked Mairead back to bed ten times. Finally, a tired, emotional Mairead went to bed. The next day Mairead and her mother talked about the previous night. Mairead was given the opportunity to say she didn't like the routine but her mother said the next night would look the same. And that night, Mairead's mother followed through with the same routine. Mairead got angry again, but her mother only had to walk her back to bed six times. The following night the situation looked less intense and Mairead's mother only walked her back once.

Does your child get angry when faced with your follow through on a limit? There are two common reasons for your child's anger. The first is related to temperament. Your child may have intense reactions to his feelings. When met with things that don't go his way or when disappointed, he may react strongly. The second reason for the anger is that your child's idea of predictability is that you *won't* follow through on the limits that were set. When you continually don't follow through on the limits and then all of a sudden you do, your child is taken by surprise. Although you have shared with him proactively that you will follow through, it has not been his experience that you will do so.

The behavior Mairead displayed of throwing toys, making a mess of her room and shouting to her mother is called retaliation behavior. This behavior is seen when a child is met with structure and boundaries and isn't used to how it feels. The good news is that when you demonstrate consistent follow through, retaliation behavior goes away very quickly. Be sure not to take this angry, sometimes out of control behavior as an indication that you should back down. In fact, it tells you to do just the opposite. Your child needs you to follow through now more than ever. Remember, establishing routines, sharing expectations and discussing consequences are done in proactive discipline.

Here are some tips for demonstrating predictability to your child in conflict.

- Know your child. If you suspect your child will get angry about new limits, be prepared.
- Stay close. If you believe your child will exhibit retaliation behavior, you will need to intervene.
- Keep your child safe. Intense feelings are scary to you and your child and safety must be the priority.

I'm not sharing this information to frighten you. In fact, more than likely your child will take to the new limits surprisingly effortlessly. But for some children this resistance to accepting limits is a reality. I want you to feel certain that even when met with behavior like Mairead's, following through with established limits is exactly what you must do. I am confident that no matter how intense the reaction is from your child, she still wants predictable boundaries...a solid fence.

The conflict strategies

Remember, a strategy is a careful plan or method of action. Each of the three aspects of discipline has strategies that you use to provide this kind of discipline. Conflict discipline is about action. Proactive parents have a plan for conflict and use conflict strategies to guide their child's behavior. In proactive discipline, talking delivers messages about behavior. In conflict discipline, action delivers messages about behavior.

Here are the conflict strategies used in conflict discipline.

- Establish authority
- Be direct and specific about non-negotiables
- Remain calm
- Provide consequences
- Make an impact

Establish authority

The concept of authority is both a principle and a strategy. Adopting a philosophy, that sometimes your child requires rules to be enforced, makes authority a guiding principle for conflict discipline. Establishing authority is also an active step you take in difficult situations making it the first strategy you use for providing conflict discipline. In proactive discipline, imagine the body language and tone of voice you might use with your child. It should be friendly, supportive and engaging. When you establish authority in conflict discipline, your demeanor should become all business. By this I mean, your posture is straight and tall. If you do any talking, which as you know by now should be limited; your tone of voice may be lower and more serious. Your facial expressions should not be angry but should be serious. This persona you take on, establishes authority because your child starts to see that this body language and tone of voice belongs to the mother or father that does not negotiate with the established limits.

The trouble with time out

Some parenting experts recommend establishing authority by using "time out". Yet, with all the parents I meet through my work, I rarely find parents that say "time out" works for them.

Reflect on the following statements to see if "time out" works for you.

1. I am always calm and in control when I use "time out".
   Yes or No

2. My child stays in the "time out" chair until the timer goes off.   *Yes or No*

3. Sitting in the "time out" chair changes my child's later behavior.   *Yes or No*

4. My child is able to explain later why he was in "time out".   *Yes or No*

If you answered yes to all of these questions, then "time out" is working for you. You might ask, "If it works for me, is there any reason why I should stop using it?" The answer is no. There is no reason to stop using it, if it works for you. But I'll bet most of you answered "no" to all the questions. I believe that is because the "time out" that involves a chair, a timer and a corner is ineffective. More often then not, it sets up a power struggle between you and your child.

Here are the reasons why I think this kind of time out is ineffective.

- The child most in need of gaining self-control is the child most likely to react strongly to being placed in a chair and waiting for a timer to go off.
- Once a power struggle begins over sitting in a chair for a certain period of time, the child forgets what brought him to the chair in the first place.
- Sitting in a chair and waiting for a timer to go off is a consequence that is usually not related to the child's misbehavior.
- Providing action in conflict discipline should be done right on the spot. Moving a child to a "time out" location is unnecessary.
- Both the parent and the child may get hurt if a parent tries to get a child to sit or stay in the "time out" chair.

So what should I do instead, you might ask? In the next few pages, I will share with you the five strategies for using conflict discipline. You begin to manage misbehavior by establishing authority.

Here are some tips for establishing authority.

- Make certain you know what your non-negotiable rules for behavior are. Ambivalence is the enemy of effective parenting.
- Step in with simple actions. I will share more about this when I discuss providing consequences.
- Take on a no-nonsense persona. Remember to use body language and tone of voice to show that you mean business.
- Don't use distal communication. Giving orders from a distance usually results in a power struggle and your important messages will not be received through talking in conflict.
- Only use the kind of "time out" that means you and your child get some distance from each…but be sure your child is safe.

Be direct and specific about non-negotiables

To negotiate or not to negotiate...that is the question. In proactive discipline, many issues are negotiable. You might compromise on how long your child stays at a friend's or whether homework is done before or after dinner. But once you have established a non-negotiable rule...the negotiations are over. Negotiations in conflict turn into power struggles. In Chapter 3, I discussed the principle of clarity around non-negotiable limits. Limit setting is most effective when limits are clear and established in advance. When you know what the rules are and you convey them to your child before conflict, you will have great success. But what parents often ask me is, "But what if I'm in a situation and my child does something I object to and I haven't been able to prepare her in advance?" This parenting approach wouldn't be very practical if it didn't have provisions for the reality of parenting, now would it? Of course, there are times when you haven't foreseen that a particular situation or behavior would be challenging. And I would never suggest that if you haven't prepared your child you are out of luck. In fact, in conflict discipline there are a number of choices you have for handling the unexpected.

Here are two options for being direct and specific about non-negotiable limits in conflict.

1. Step in with simple action. Sometimes there will be no need for talking or for making a big fuss over a limit. Two-year-old, Collin heads straight for the flowers on the coffee table. Each time he heads in that direction, his mother without talking points him in the other direction. After four times, Collin groans and goes off to play with the trucks in the corner.

2. Get out of the situation making certain to create your proactive plan for when this happens again. Remember if a situation happens once, then twice, it is very likely to happen again. Have your proactive plan ready to go for the future. Six-year-old, Jade is playing at a friend's house and you arrive on time to pick her up. She hides

from you and makes an embarrassing scene of leaving. Without adding to the scene, you make your apologies to her friend's father and firmly guide Jade to the car. You do not share with Jade all the things she did "wrong" in this situation because you know she will be unable to hear you. This has happened before and you know Jade does not have the skills she needs to make transitions smoothly. You know you must develop a proactive plan for building skills once this conflict is over but before Jade goes to a friend's house again.

In the examples above, did you notice how each parent limited the talking they did with their child in conflict? You can be direct and specific with your child about non-negotiable limits with little or no talking. If you talk at all, you do so with authority. And be sure the words match your actions. But remember, action imparts your message in conflict. While it is best to make decisions about your non-negotiables in advance, like the mothers in these examples, you will be faced with situations that require you to take charge. So how do you decide whether to step in with simple action, develop a proactive plan for the next time or both?

Here are some guidelines for being direct and specific about non-negotiables in conflict that might guide your choice.

Choose simple action when...

- the behavior you object to is related to safety.
- the simple action is obvious to you.
- the simple action makes sense to you and your child.

Choose to create a proactive plan when...

- the behavior is related to bigger issues such as respect or temperament.
- it is clear to you that your child doesn't have the necessary skills to behave differently.
- the situation has happened before and you realize it will happen again.

Remain calm

It is no small task to remain calm in conflict. Yet, many of the parents I work with tell me that with a pro-active plan for discipline, keeping their cool is so much easier. When I say remain calm, I don't mean you can't have real feelings such as sadness, anger, frustration or disappointment when your child behaves inappropriately. It just means that you maintain your credibility as an authority figure by staying in control emotionally.

Antonio

Fourteen-year-old, Antonio comes to his parent's bedroom Saturday morning at 8 am and says, "I'm going to the skate park with Mike. I'll be back later." His Dad says, "Antonio, I told you yesterday that I would need your help with yard work today. You will have to call Mike and let him know you won't be able to go until this afternoon." Antonio unhappy to hear he won't be going, rants and raves about his father's unfairness. He follows his Dad from room to room complaining about having to help. He is desperate to engage his Dad in conflict. Antonio's father stops the conflict by saying, "I'm disappointed you made plans knowing you had a commitment. I won't talk to you when you are this upset. Cool down and then we can discuss what is and what is not negotiable." Antonio's Dad goes out to the porch, to have his coffee.

Antonio's Dad resisted the urge to argue with his son. By remaining calm and putting some distance between himself and his son, he demonstrated his authority. He referred to the need to be direct and specific about what was non-ne-gotiable in the situation. He easily could have debated the issue with his son through a lot of talking. But if he did, he would have been putting a log on an emotional fire.

Imagine you have a precious jar of energy located in the center of your being. In this precious jar, you have all the energy you need to parent each day. If you parent wisely, you will use a lot of this energy each day but energy will be replaced each day, too. When you have a proactive plan for discipline and your child accepts your limits, energy goes back into the precious jar. Sadie, mother of three says, "Some days I wake up and I can visualize the jar as full, but by nine o'clock, it is empty! If you feel this way, it may be because you are parenting in ways that deplete your energy quickly.

Here are some energy wasters...

- Talking too much in conflict
- Yelling and shouting
- Giving directions at a distance...distal communication
- Expecting too much of your child developmentally
- Not factoring in temperament to your discipline plan

Are you engaging in any of the energy wasters? Any of them will deplete the energy you have to parent. But there are energy builders in parenting, too. I highly recommend using these, because they will add energy to your precious jar.

Here are some energy builders...

- Use action, not talking, in conflict.
- Share your feelings in a calm, controlled manner with your child.
- Avoid power struggles with your child unless it relates to a non-negotiable limit.
- Use the kind of "time out" that means you and your child get some distance from one another...but be sure your child is safe.
- Have a proactive plan that includes conflict discipline strategies.
- Recognize and celebrate your child's success in skill building.

Remaining calm in conflict teaches your child how tough situations are managed and how hurt feelings are repaired. Whether you are an adult or a child, conflict in life is inevitable. The conflict discipline strategy, *remain calm* is important because it role models for your child healthy conflict resolution.

Provide consequences

For some parents, providing consequences is easier said than done. Do you find you are willing to provide a consequence that changes behavior, only to wonder what the action or consequence should be? You are not alone. Many parents struggle with this aspect of discipline. But the strategy of providing consequences is critical to the success of conflict discipline. Once your child is consistently exposed to the experience that his actions have consequences, he is in a position to make different choices. Even as an adult, you are exposed to this idea that your actions have consequences. If you hit the snooze button on your alarm twice this morning, you may have missed your bus to work. If you speed in view of a police officer, you will get a ticket. Each of these consequences to your actions sends a message that the behavior was inappropriate. And the goal is that each consequence will encourage you to change your behavior. Sometimes consequences to behavior happen naturally like missing the bus. Other times consequences are imposed, like the police officer giving you a ticket.

Anya

A bright and energetic fifteen-year-old, Anya is learning the complexities of balancing school life with social life. She has shared with her mother that she has a big test tomorrow but she also has tryouts for the school play in the afternoon. Both doing well on the test and trying out for the play are important to her so she is going to try to balance both after school today. She arrives home at six o'clock. She eats a quick dinner and hits the books. At ten o'clock, Mom checks in with her and she is in tears. "There is so much more information here than I thought. I can't keep my eyes open." Mom resists the urge to point out that if she hadn't waited until the last minute, she might not be so overwhelmed. Two days later, Anya finds out that she got a D on the test.

Anya's situation is a typical learning experience for the young adolescent. Learning to organize, prioritize, balance school and fun are the challenges of this developmental period. Anya's behavior in this situation isn't bad or wrong, its just behavior that won't get her what she needs. You can tell her all you want to plan ahead and study further in advance, but the D on the test drove that message home better than your talking ever could. It was the natural consequence to cramming for a big test.

Natural Consequences...
- occur as a direct or indirect result of a behavioral choice your child has made.
- are not imposed on your child by you.
- send a message to your child that certain behaviors have certain consequences.
- may change future behavior.

William

Ten-year-old, William has been putting off his homework until the last minute, everyday this week. It will be especially important for him to get his homework done quickly and efficiently today because he has a late soccer practice. Since William has even more difficulty getting homework done after dinner, his mom reminds him of his afternoon schedule over breakfast. Proactively she said, "William, when you come home today you can have a snack and relax for one half hour. After that, you must get your homework done because you have soccer practice today. I will not be able to take you to practice until the homework is finished." Now here comes the conflict... Although he was reminded about the expectation, right before the time he should be leaving for practice, Mom finds out that his homework is not done. William says, "Mom, lets go. I'm going to be late." Mom replies, "I will be happy to drive you, when your homework is finished." While he tries to engage in an argument, Mom says, "I'm finished talking. Finish your homework and I will take you to practice."

This example shows that being proactive won't always guarantee that your child will make the right choices.

William was clearly told what the expectation and the consequences would be, should he choose not to get his homework done in a timely fashion. He either chose to test the limit or he really forgot. Either way he learns that his action...putting off the homework, had consequences...he would be late for practice. In any situation like this, it is very important not to be drawn into emotional conversations. When you engage in the talking and explaining, you join in a struggle that looks like a game of tug of war between you and your child. Often your child might start the struggle by picking up his end of the rope. But you must resist the invitation to pick up your end of the rope. Remember, talking in conflict doesn't deliver the message as powerfully as action can. The logical consequence to William not doing his homework was not going to practice on time.

Logical consequences...
- are directly related to a behavioral choice your child has made.
- are imposed on your child by others.
- send a message to your child that certain behaviors are not negotiable.
- may change future behavior.

Did you notice when I describe natural and logical consequences I said that they *may* change behavior. That's because for consequences to change behavior they need to fit the misbehavior and make an impact on your child. I will describe how to choose consequences that impact behavior, later in this chapter. But first I want to share with you how to know if the consequences to certain actions are "RITE".

Choosing the RITE consequences

So how do you know if the consequences or actions you take in conflict are correct? After you have clarity about whether the behavior your child is engaging in is nonnegotiable, think about the actions you take in conflict. Here is a tool you can use to think about whether the consequence fits the misbehavior.

Is the consequence...?

R espectful
I nfraction based
T imely
E ffective

Let me explain each point. When you choose **respectful** consequences, you consider your child's age and temperament. The consequences you choose are never meant to demean or humiliate your child but instead are well thought out. Remember, you want your child to make a more positive choice in the future. You don't want your child to become angrier and make a similar choice in the future because his feelings are continually hurt. Consequences are used to teach not to punish. Consequences that are **infraction based** are established to fit the misbehavior. A common error you might make in providing consequences is to use an action or take something away from your child that has nothing to do with what your child did. Be sure the actions you take in conflict are related to your child's misbehavior. When you provide consequences to your child make certain the action is **timely**. When your child is fighting over the rules of Monopoly, having him stop the game until he can get under control emotionally has a greater impact than taking away a TV show that comes on in four hours. For consequences to be **effective**, they must in some way make an impact on your child. Making an impact on your child is a conflict discipline strategy in its own right. I will spend the next few pages sharing how to do this.

Choosing the RITE consequences is important to the success of conflict discipline. Thinking about providing consequences in advance will make you most successful at choosing the RITE ones.

Make an impact

The word impact means to have an immediate and strong effect on someone. In conflict discipline, if behavior is to change positively, the consequences you choose must have an immediate and strong impact on your child. Without impact, your child doesn't get the right messages about behavior. Without receiving clear messages about inappropriate behavior, the idea that actions have consequences doesn't get "in the bag." As I have mentioned before, your child may not be impacted by the same consequences as another child. This is because each child is motivated to make behavioral choices for different reasons. Based on your child's age, certain motives exist and shape behavior. Every child is motivated to behave for fun and attention. And *sometimes* these developmental motives will influence how you choose consequences for behavior.

Here are some of the developmental motives behind the way your child behaves.

Infants are motivated by...
• feeling connected

Toddlers are motivated by...
• avoiding anxiety
• mastery or learning new things

Preschoolers are motivated by...
• mastery
• being in control

School age children are motivated by...
• mastery
• social connections
• independence

Adolescents are motivated by...
• social connections
• independence
• recognition

You might be asking yourself, "Why is it important to understand age-related motives?" Understanding age-related motives is important because if you want to make an impact on your child, you must effect her in an age appropriate way. I am not suggesting you withhold love and attention to get your child to behave. What I am saying is that there are certain situations where your child's motives will enhance the power of the consequences you choose. Did you notice how social relationships become important for your school age child? Because this is a strong motive for behavior in many children, it becomes a strong motive for changing behavior. If your child is disrespectful to you when a friend is over, having his friend go home is a logical consequence to his behavior, right? This action will make an impact on your child if he is motivated socially. But if your child is not very social, having his friend go home may not make an impact on your child at all. This example shows how development plays a role in the consequences you choose to make an impact on your child's behavior.

The second factor that affects your ability to make an impact on your child's behavior is temperament. The consequences you choose to shape behavior will be different based on each individual child. The sensitive child may simply need to sit apart from his brother to get the message that it isn't okay to color on his paper, while the persistent child may need to leave the room entirely.

Temperament is also the most significant factor effecting how quickly your child gets messages about behavior. Remember, how I mentioned earlier the importance of using simple actions when providing consequences? Did you think to yourself, "She doesn't know my child...simple action will never work?" In conflict discipline, finding the consequences that make impact can be challenging. But I still want you to start with simple action. Here's why. If you always react to your child by choosing consequences that are dramatic, over the top or highly emotional...you are adding to the escalation of the situation. In order for your child to be persistent or continue to test the limit...he has to do something even more dramatic than you did. But if you start with simple action and it doesn't make an impact, you will be able to "raise the bar" so to speak. Each time your child matches you with continued misbehavior you will continue to "raise the bar". At some point, your child understands, "my actions have consequences and I better stop the misbehavior here or the consequences will be bigger." If you "shoot the moon" by going to the most dramatic consequence you can think of, you leave yourself no room to move if that consequence doesn't make impact. "By shooting the moon", you can frustrate your child showing her that you handle situations by making emotional decisions. It lessens your credibility and teaches your child that she must behave in dramatic ways to find "the fence".

Lori

Seven-year-old, Lori loves to play outdoor games when she visits her cousins. Before going to the cousins' house, Dad reviews with Lori the rules for playing fair and being a good sport. He tells her how he will respond to her if she has difficulty playing. He says, "First, I will go over and put my hand on your shoulder to remind you to get it together. If you can't, you will need to take a break for two minutes. If after that you aren't under control, you will have to go into the house. If after all these reminders to behave, you can't seem to make good choices, I will take you home." Lori arrives and the games begin.

As Dad listens to the children play, he can hear in Lori's voice that she is getting agitated with her younger cousin. This behavior usually leads to bigger more unacceptable behaviors such as yelling and sometimes hitting. Dad walks over to Lori and puts a hand on her shoulder, reminding her of the expectations. He tells her if she can't manage to play well, the next step is for her to sit out for a couple of minutes. As she continues to play, she is getting more upset with the way the game is going. He walks over and guides her to a step to sit on until she can get it together. She assures him that she will be fine and pleads to go back and play. Dad tells her she can go back and play in one minute but if she can't get it together, the next step will be to go inside and sit with him. If she can't get it together after that, he will have to take her home.

Do you see the progression of actions attached to the misbehavior? Have you ever been tempted to say to your child, "If you don't get under control, we are going home?" By "shooting the moon," your child never misbehaves without getting consequences imposed that are extreme. Starting with the lowest level action teaches your child so much more. There are some benefits to making impact on your child by "raising the bar."

Raising the bar teaches your child that...

- you are the authority in conflict.
- you have a plan for stopping misbehavior.
- non-negotiable actions have consequences.
- stopping the misbehavior early lessens the impact.
- boundaries exist and your child doesn't have to escalate behavior to find "the fence".

Micah and Luke

Back to the morning routine. Remember how challenging it is for Micah and Luke to get to work and school? Now that you know more about conflict discipline, things can look quite different. While I'm happy to share Micah's plan for conflict discipline with you, I want you to be sure that Micah and I developed a proactive discipline plan for this never-ending conflict. Micah had proactive conversations with Luke, in advance of the conflict. Together they discussed the problem, the expectations and the consequences should the situation happen again. And of course, it did. So what conflict strategies did Micah use with Luke to make the morning routine more successful? Here's what I recommended...

Establish authority
- Go to where Luke is, stand tall and make eye contact with him.
- Use a firm voice to tell him he must begin getting ready for school.
- Stay physically close to Luke as he gets ready. Each time he gets distracted, you will be able to step in with small actions.

Be direct and specific about non-negotiables
- Deliver your message using one sentence, "Please get up, I will not be late for work today."
- Use simple action such as, raising the shades, turning off the TV or packing up his breakfast.

Remain calm
- Adopt a matter of fact tone of voice.
- Don't yell or raise your voice. In fact, don't talk much at all.

Provide consequences and make an impact
- Limit the breakfast options to only those foods that can be taken on the go. Don't make available the big breakfast Luke enjoys. Or if he begins the big breakfast and time is running short, pack it up for him to take on the bus.
- Turn off the TV when Luke hasn't done what he needs to do or if the time is running short.
- Let Luke miss the bus. He prefers to ride the bus over being driven to school...this becomes a motivator.
- Call the school to let them know Luke will be late. ·
- Take your time getting him to school so that he feels the impact of being late, not just getting there in the nick of time. (Micah needed to prepare her boss for her need to do this. Yes, it required sacrifice on her part but she was late for work everyday with her old style of trying to get Luke to school. With this plan, Luke's behavior will change and Micah will be on time for work.)
- Go into the school to explain why Luke is late, with Luke standing by your side.

Note these consequences were discussed with Luke in advance. Micah shared these with Luke and she knows these will make impact on him. Remember the consequences you choose for your child may look different based on his age and temperament.

When the consequences are imposed in a matter of fact way, the message is delivered to Luke that his actions affect himself and others. When the expectations and consequences are shared in advance...proactive discipline, your child knows what is coming and can make better choices. Micah needed to use all the consequences she established including going into the school to explain why Luke was late. But she only had to do this once. Every other day that Micah used this plan, Luke began to cooperate at a much earlier stage in the progression. And after four days, he cooperated fully. You too, can change the dynamics in your family using a behavioral plan for conflict that includes proactive discipline.

Chapter summary

Conflict discipline is the critical follow through necessary to reinforce all of your proactive discipline strategies. Its guiding principles are action, authority, consistency, emotional integrity, and predictability.

The conflict strategies include establishing authority; being direct and specific about non-negotiables; providing consequences; remaining calm and making an impact.

When providing conflict discipline the proactive parent remembers that...

- Setting the stage for conflict happens when providing proactive discipline.
- Conflict discipline teaches responsibility and internal motivation.
- Conflict discipline is about action not talking.
- Conflict discipline is about being the authority your child needs.
- Conflict discipline must be combined with a good proactive discipline plan.
- Conflict discipline includes societal discipline strategies.
- Conflict discipline takes time...but reaps rewards.

Questions and Answers
Chapter 4

The Perfect Storm

Conflict Discipline

Q: When we are in a restaurant and my child is acting up, I repeatedly tell him that we will leave. Why doesn't he take me seriously?

A: He doesn't take you seriously because he knows you won't leave the restaurant. It's good that you established the limit, "if you don't stop the misbehavior...we will leave the restaurant". However, you must follow through on the consequence if you are to have any credibility. The talking occurs when you set the limit, the action must occur if your child is to understand that the limit is non-negotiable. Just think of the impact leaving a restaurant would have on future behavior. Don't ever choose a consequence that you do not intend to follow through with... your child knows you better than you think.

Q: How much talking do I do in conflict discipline?

A: If I challenged you not to talk at all in conflict, teaching and learning would still take place through action. You may talk during conflict as long as you remember these important points.

1. Keep talking to a minimum.
2. Only restate the rule and the consequence.
3. Keep emotional dialogue out of conflict...save it for later.
4. Be certain your actions match the few words you choose to say.

Q: If I just use small actions in conflict, does my child really know the rule and why it exists?

A: Yes, because your actions deliver your message. Remember, the time to share what the rules are and why they exist happens before or after conflict, not during. If the best talking we do is in conflict, unfortunately your child cannot hear it or learn from it.

Q: My child is so persistent, that I know small actions in conflict are not going to work. What should my plan be?

A: Small actions in conflict may work better for you than you think. They work because by acting and not talking, your child gets your message without the challenge of starting a struggle for power and control. Small actions also work because when you start with them and then "raise the bar" as needed, your child gets the message that you are willing to continue to provide consequences until she gets the message to change behavior. Over time your child will choose to behave, rather than choose to experience consequences that gradually have greater impact on her.

FIVE

Turn The Tide

Societal Discipline

Nicole describes her new feeling as a sinking feeling in the pit of her stomach. As the mother of twelve-year-old Eve, the feeling comes whenever Eve asks to join a new social situation. "Can I go to the mall? Can I go to a concert?" The feeling comes because Nicole is unsure of what Eve will face in these situations. Last night, Eve asked her mother if she could go with her new friend and his family to an amusement park. Immediately, Nicole gets the uncomfortable feeling. She has never heard of this new friend. Is he a friend or does Eve see him as a boyfriend? Are the parents going to stay at the park with Eve and her friend? Does Eve have the skills she needs to stay safe regardless of what presents itself in this situation? To Nicole these are just the first questions that come to her mind. She begins to feel overwhelmed by what she doesn't know about the situation and about what she should do in response to Eve's question. She describes her feelings this way. "I feel like every day I am faced with her growing independence. I know she wants to enjoy her friends but I feel like I am constantly faced with making decisions that I don't feel prepared to make. I am not sure adolescence is about her changing as much as it is about me not being able to let go. Will she be safe? Is this a reasonable request from a twelve-year-old? I don't want to be overprotective but I need some help making these decisions."

Have you ever felt like Nicole? I know I have. But there are tools available through Proactive Parenting that can help Nicole answer these and many other questions. For

Nicole and Eve to feel better prepared to cope with the power of our society on them, they both have some work to do. You, too can take an active role in shaping how the world at large influences the relationship between you and your child. The critical aspect of discipline that guides you is societal discipline.

Societal discipline

Societal discipline teaches your child how society influences his behavior and gives him the skills he needs to make the right decisions in complex situations. Increasingly, your job as a parent involves being aware of the influences on your child as well as helping him accept your limits. Whether your toddler should watch action hero movies or your sixth grader should go to a formal dance, you need to make decisions that are in your child's best interest.

As soon as your child is out in the world, others influence her. When your infant is in childcare, her behavior is shaped by other adults. When your child is in school, her behavior is shaped by other children. Your child is influenced by toys, TV and media messages. I will discuss how these particular influences challenge the proactive parent in Chapter 10. Societal discipline begins so much earlier than you might think. And certainly as your child gets older, the power of the society to shape ideas, opinions, values and behavior becomes greater. Societal discipline includes elements from proactive discipline and conflict discipline. Most of your time is spent talking with your child, helping her to develop the skills she needs to make good decisions. But you will also need to set limits related to societal influences and follow through on these non-negotiables you've established. So, how do you know which decisions are right for you and your child? You begin by learning about the principles and strategies of societal discipline.

Principles of societal discipline

Remember, a principle is a fundamental assumption or rule that guides your actions. Each of the three aspects of discipline have principles that point out how you can provide this kind of discipline.

Here are the principles of societal discipline....

✳ Awareness
✳ Commitment
✳ Honesty
✳ Communication
✳ Supervision

Awareness

I know, first hand, that parenting today is very hard. Not only must you think about the dynamics in your own family, but you must think about all the influences on your child outside your family. But I am still going to challenge you to raise awareness about the societal issues affecting your parenting. You can work so hard to nurture and teach your child but if you dismiss the influences of others on him, you miss many opportunities to impact the person he becomes. And you may be allowing others much more influence on your child than you realize. The idea that you have no control over the powerful society and its impact on your child is just not true. You can have a greater influence on your child than society does. It just boils down to how much you know about society's effect on your child. Knowledge is power. If you are aware of what your child is exposed to, you can be proactive in talking about it. You can also have a conflict discipline plan for the non-negotiable limits you set related to it.

Marcus

Eight-year-old Marcus loves video games. He talks about the characters in them as if they were real. Marcus doesn't have a video game system, but he knows a lot about them. His mother realizes that he knows a lot about them because when he goes to his friend's house that is all they do. While it is nice to see Marcus animated over something, his mother isn't sure that she likes how captivated he seems over video games. She decides to call his friend's mom and this is what she hears. "They all play these games. It's just the way boys socialize today. What harm can it do?"

For Marcus' mother, this conversation didn't add clarity to the situation it just added more confusion. She began to wonder, "Is this really the way boys socialize? What harm *can* it do?" After this conversation, Marcus' mother realized she didn't know enough about the impact of video games on Marcus. She decided that before she let him do something so often, she needed to understand more about it.

You know by now that clear boundaries positively impact your child. Having a clear and intact "fence" helps your child make good decisions. It is harder to close the gate on "the fence" after you've left it open for awhile, so I encourage you to raise awareness about the influences on your child before they have taken hold of your child. If Marcus' mother decides she doesn't want Marcus to play video games, it will be more difficult, yet not impossible, to get him stop.

Here are some tips for raising your awareness about societal influences on your child.

- Recognize that other adults and children will share their values and opinions about behavior through their words and actions.
- Think about the role models in your child's life and question the messages they impart.
- Find out about "what's hot" in the popular culture from clothes to shows.
- Form your own opinions about whether "what's hot" fits in with your value system.
- Develop a proactive plan that includes conflict discipline strategies for handling a particular influence.

Commitment

The second principle of societal discipline is commitment. In short, once you've raised your awareness, you've got to take a stand on providing this kind of discipline. When

Marcus' mother did her homework, she found that long hours playing video games had a significant impact on thinking, learning and social development.   With this new awareness, she had to do something about Marcus' fascination.   Making a commitment to modify, refine or change behavior isn't easy. It does require sacrifice on your part as a parent, but it is what the job requires. Helping Marcus understand his mother's concerns about the video games and making choices to spend his time differently was a difficult task for them.   So, here's a point worth making again...Try to raise your awareness and make a commitment about influences, before your child is fully entrenched in the activity or exposed to the influence.

At each developmental age, your child is likely to be exposed to new influences. The popular culture, other adults and other children give messages that exposure to these influences isn't problematic. But I believe that some of these influences are beyond your child's emotional capabilities at best and harmful to his development at worst.

Here is a list of influences to reflect on *before* your child reaches a developmental age or is exposed to the influence.

Infants...
- Exposure to television

Toddlers
- Exposure to television, particularly news or reality programming
- Violent or aggressive toys

Preschoolers
- Computer games
- Exposure to real weapons in your home or friends' homes
- Movies

School age children
- Video games
- Internet

Adolescents
- Dating
- Magazines
- Access to alcohol and drugs

This partial list of influences to your child isn't meant to overwhelm or frighten you. It is meant to raise your awareness about the potential issues facing you and your child before you are actually facing them. My recommendation to you, as you think about these influences, is to limit exposure whenever you can. Infants don't need to be exposed to television and twelve-year-olds don't need to date. Remember you are in the driver's seat when it comes to parenting your child through the rough waters of our current world. Your child needs you to take charge and help him make sense of the influences bombarding him on a daily basis. However, there will be times when limiting exposure isn't possible. Your toddler will be exposed to other boys who play with toy guns and your school age child will be exposed to the hype around certain movies. When exposure is inevitable, I want you to keep talking and keep setting limits. Resist the urge to relinquish your role to the popular culture. I know that confronting these challenges is like swimming against the tide, but it can be done. The most important thing to remember about making a commitment to guiding your child through our complicated world is this. If you don't take on societal discipline for your child...no one else will. Find the support you need in like-minded friends. Once you know he or she shares your values, use each other as sounding boards for the tough decisions each of you will have to make regarding discipline. Making the commitment isn't easy, but you and your child will benefit.

Honesty

When I recommend limited exposure to influences like television or inappropriate role models, by no means am I saying to shield your child from the realities of this world. Being honest with your child is critical to the parent/child relationship. Honesty builds trust and makes your child feel safe. You can't hide what is happening in your family and in the world from your child. Whether you tell your child or not, he knows what is going on in your family. He senses it from your tone of voice, your hushed words and your body language. He knows what is going on in the world, because if you don't tell him...someone else will.

One of my clients shared with me this sad story, just days after September 11, 2001. She had decided not to share the news about what happened with her three-year-old son, Todd. She had the television on in a room he wasn't in. She kept her emotions in check and tried to be up beat when she tucked him in at night. She continued her routine of dropping Todd off at childcare and going to work. But on the weekend, she was shocked at what she saw when she watched her son play. Todd used his blocks to build two towers and he used his toy plane to knock them down. This little boy had been exposed to the news at childcare. Both the television news and the other children shared this historic event with my client's son. And while I can understand my client's desire to keep her son from this horrific news, under the circumstances it was inevitable that he would be exposed to it. This is a perfect example of the need for honesty in societal discipline. This child did not need to sit in front of a television or be told about the tragedy in great detail. But his parents could have shared what happened in ways that fit his age. This situation was recovered when Todd's mother asked him to tell her what he was playing. Then she shared in an uncomplicated way what had really happened.

You will find that honesty becomes the cornerstone of your relationship with your child in societal discipline. You take the opportunity to tell your child about tough matters. You don't hide the news of a neighbor's death or a family member's alcoholism. You are the one to deliver the messages because you believe your child should hear it from you.

There are so many benefits to the principle of honesty in the parent/child relationship. Here is how honesty fits into societal discipline.

When you are honest with your child, he ...
- feels safe and secure because the information comes from you.

- knows that you will talk to him about tough subjects.
- knows that if you talk to him about tough subjects...he can talk to you.
- has information that is delivered in age-appropriate ways.
- receives information that has your values attached to it.
- has an opportunity to talk about how the information effects him.

Communication

Good communication is an important aspect of proactive discipline and societal discipline. But talking to your child about the influences from society doesn't mean you let go of your limits related to those influences. Societal discipline is a balance of being proactive and having a plan for conflict. In order to combat the power of the popular culture, you will need to spend time with your child talking about her ideas, opinions and values. You will need to validate how hard it is to resist the temptation to join the crowd. But just because you talk to your child about her desires and temptations doesn't mean you will back down on your non-negotiable rules.

Emily

Ten-year-old Emily has loved to dress up since she was a toddler. She enjoys wearing fashionable clothes and likes to spend time shopping with her mother. Recently, the battle lines have been drawn over which type of clothing is appropriate for a ten-year-old. Emily is drawn to clothes that are provocative for her age and Emily's mother is clear about what clothing she will and will not buy for her daughter. Emily's mother raises this issue with me. She shares, "I used to enjoy my time shopping with Emily. It was our time together. The closer we get to September, the more I dread it. Back to school shopping this year is going to be a nightmare."

What Emily's mother sees in this situation is impending conflict. What I see in this situation is an opportunity to teach. While Emily's mother might try to do everything in her power to avoid this issue with her daughter, I would actively take it on. Let me ask you this. Do you think Emily will suddenly let go of her interest in clothes? Do you think she will miraculously stop trying to negotiate for the clothes she likes the best? Is this issue going to go away as Emily gets older or get worse? I'm sure your common sense tells you that this situation is not going away; therefore the only thing to do is to take it on. Emily's mother told me that she was afraid to talk to Emily about this because she didn't want her to think the limits related to the clothes were negotiable. But remember, talking in proactive and societal discipline is necessary to align yourself with your child, to validate opinions and feelings and to set expectations. It is talking *in conflict* that makes your child think the limits are negotiable. Emily's mother actually needs to talk to Emily a lot about their differences of opinion about clothes. But that doesn't mean Emily will get what she wants. Her mother needs to respect her daughter's desire for the popular styles or the flashy clothes but she needs to explain why she isn't going to get them. Does Emily's mother do this when they are shopping? I hope by now you know that the answer is no. Emily's mother needs to have this conversation with her daughter when they aren't anywhere near a mall. If your child is like Emily, she will need to have this conversation more than once. If your child is trying to make sense of her desires while still accepting your limits, she may need to process this often. How often you might ask? The answer is as often as it takes to accept the limit and as long as the conversations take place without conflict. Imagine the issues you can talk about if you discuss issues without conflict. Because Emily's mother remained open to repeated conversations about this issue, she and her daughter had the chance to talk about values, body image and the influence of the retailers on what's popular. When you stay committed to your decisions and are honest with your child, you create strong communication with your child. If Emily's mother shows her daughter that she is willing to help her understand and accept these limits, Emily will know she can count on her mother for support in the future. At each developmental age, the issues that require this kind of communication get tougher; and the consequences get more serious.   This makes providing societal discipline very important.

When you communicate effectively in societal discipline, your child...
- has a place to share her ideas, opinions and feelings.
- learns that she is not alone in trying to make sense of the influences from society.
- learns that talking about issues and negotiating limits are not the same.
- trusts that you are someone she can count on to help her understand how society influences her opinions.

Supervision

Supervision is the act of overseeing what your child is doing to ensure that what he is engaged in is safe and acceptable. Because many families struggle with creating a balance between work and family and because of the powerful influences of the popular culture, supervision is a critical issue for today's families. At *every* developmental age, your child needs supervision related to the influences of the world we live in. I hear certain myths about supervision spread among parents at almost every workshop I give. I think these myths continue because frankly, supervision is hard. When I talk to parents about supervision, I try to dispel some common myths about this important principle of parenting. Here are five common myths related to supervision.

Myth #1...
Most of what my child is exposed to goes right over her head. When people are having adult conversations, she isn't even paying attention to what is being said.
Reality #1...
Everything your child hears goes right *into* her head. While I agree she may not be able to make sense of the adult conversations she hears or the images she sees, she is still taking it all in. If your body language conveys stress and anxiety, your child takes it in. If the conversations

are about issues she doesn't understand, she can become fearful. Remember, your child has enough work to do just growing and learning. Adult matters belong to adults, not to your child.

Myth #2...
My child should be able to have the same freedom to go places that I did when I was a kid.
Reality#2...
Your child should have the freedom to have fun and explore the world he lives in within clear and safe boundaries. Unfortunately, this might mean different freedoms from the ones you experienced as a child. The reality is that many of our communities have changed over the years, making the choices you make for your child more critical. Think about ways your child can enjoy the freedom of going to friends or riding his bike while still being looked out for and supervised.

Myth #3...
My school age child is capable of staying home alone after school. I work and this is the way it has to be.
Reality #3...
Depending on the age of your school age child, she *may not* be capable of staying home alone at all. Remember, the school age period is between the ages of 5 and 11. A five-year-old does not have critical thinking skills to handle the unexpected, therefore safety is a serious concern. Many eleven-year-olds have yet to acquire the necessary skills to handle emergencies. There are a number of low cost or no cost after school options that would be better suited to the school age child. Talk to your neighbors, church leaders or your child's teacher for ideas about how to safely plan for the after school hours.

Myth #4...
It's impossible to supervise my teenager, he is too independent and he doesn't want me around.
Reality#4...
It is *very possible* to supervise your teenager; you just have to be creative. Your adolescent is still learning to be independent and he needs you as his guide. I have heard more stories of how adolescents have gotten into situations

that they didn't think through and the reason they got in so deep was because they had too much unsupervised time on their hands. Proactively and mutually, develop plans for the time your adolescent spends alone. Know where he is going, with whom and how long he will be gone. Make it a high priority to supervise your adolescent; you will both be glad you did.

Myth #5...

It is important to know what your child is up to when she is school age but by the time she hits middle or high school her values are set and she will either get into or stay out of trouble, no matter what I do.

Reality#5...

This is perhaps the most disturbing of the myths about supervision. It implies that once your child hits the early adolescent period, your job is done. Nothing could be further from the truth. In fact, when your child enters middle school, I believe a very active period of parenting is just beginning. You have a great deal of influence over how your child learns about the world and over the choices she makes. The whole concept of societal discipline is based on the idea that you can teach your child how to think first and then make good decisions. Don't willingly hand your child over to the popular culture, walk her through it.

Throughout the chapters on how the approach works with particular ages, I will share societal strategies specific to supervision. But here are some general tips for providing supervision to your child, no matter her age.

- Discuss safe places and homes with your child. Let your child know where she can and cannot be.
- Know your child's friends and their families. A solid connection with friends and their parents is a wonderful way to keep your child safe.
- Create plans for checking in whether you are home or not. Even if you are working, having periodic "check ins" is a practical way of keeping in touch with your child.
- Drop in to where your child is. This strategy gives your child the message that he really needs to be where he says he will be.

- Supervise access to the Internet, television and other technology. These influences can jeopardize your child's safety just as much in the home as out.
- Don't leave your child of any age alone for long periods. Lots of time spent alone is an invitation for your child to get into situations that she is unprepared to handle, no matter how old she is.

The societal strategies

While you may agree that societal discipline is a critical aspect of Proactive Parenting, you may not know the specific and effective ways you can help your child. It isn't enough to just set a limit, you have to teach your child the skills he will need to accept your limits and still "fit in" with his friends. Proactive Parenting embraces this aspect of discipline. I believe you know what is right for your child. You just need a practical way to exert your more significant influence over your child.

Here are the societal strategies used in societal discipline.

- Learn about influences and their impact
- Explore feelings and desires related to "fitting in"
- Monitor influences
- Set limits on inappropriate influences
- Skill build and teach appropriate ways to handle societal influences

Learn about influences and their impact

The first step in providing societal discipline is to learn about societal influences and their impact. As a parent, you will be called upon to make many decisions about what your child should be exposed to. And the more information you have to make a proper decision for you and your child, the better. In a recent workshop, I shared why I thought a particular television program was inappropriate for middle school age children. Immediately, a woman said rather defensively, "You must be watching that show if you know what it is about." I responded by telling her that it is my job to know what societal influences my clients and their families are grappling with. But more importantly, just like her, I need to know what the popular trends are, learn about them and then make decisions about what is and is not appropriate for my own children. If I don't know anything about a certain program or recording artist, how will I be able to make the best decision about whether or not my children can be exposed to it?

Vaughn

Meliah is the mother of three children. Her oldest son is nine-year-old, Vaughn. Vaughn is a social boy who is eager to have a computer with access to the Internet. He brings up the subject daily with his mother. "Everyone has e-mail. Why can't I have instant messenger? Our family is the only family on the planet without a computer!" Meliah shares with me her concerns. "Lots of other parents tell me that Vaughn is going to need a computer for school work next year. But I'm reluctant to get a computer and go online. To tell you the truth, I don't know anything about computers so how will I know how to keep Vaughn safe?"

Meliah raises excellent questions. How will she be able to teach appropriately, supervise accordingly and discipline effectively if she knows nothing about this influence and its potential impact on her child? Meliah's first step in providing societal discipline around this issue was to learn about the influence and its impact. She shared with Vaughn that she knew that getting a computer and going online was definitely in her family's future. But before she could buy one and let Vaughn have access to it, she needed to learn more. Here are the steps Meliah took to feel more comfortable with this powerful influence, before she let her son have access to it.

Meliah...
- spent time at the local library learning how to use the computers available to the public.

- took a class through the adult education program in her town.
- talked to other parents about the struggles and benefits of having a computer in their homes.
- asked her son to help her research both the good and not so good aspects of having a computer in the home.
- talked to her son's friends and their parents about their family's rules related to computer use.
- read about the ways to keep her child safe when he is using the computer to interact with his friends.
- worked with Vaughn to develop family rules for using the computer and going online.

After Meliah did her homework on computers and their impact on families, she purchased a computer for her family. The degree to which conflict is a part of her family related to the computer is very low. Yes, Meliah put a lot of energy into learning about this influence and its impact, but she was able to then use proactive, conflict and societal discipline strategies that led to Vaughn's success in using the computer wisely. Remember, Proactive Parenting encourages you to use your energy skillfully, but of course, energy will still be required.

Explore feelings and desires related to "fitting in"

Whenever you make decisions about limiting exposure to negative societal influences, your child will have feelings about it. In societal discipline, it is critical to explore your child's feelings, validate her feelings and then help your child accept your decisions. If you want your child to accept your decisions, especially when it requires sacrifice on your child's part, then it is important to use this societal discipline strategy.

Paige

Eleven-year-old, Paige is entering middle school this fall. Paige's mother has learned from other parents that early in sixth grade, the parent/teacher organization hosts dressy dances. From all accounts, the dress code is rarely enforced which leads children to test the limits by wearing inappropriate attire. She also learned that a number of slow dances are played. Although it is August and school has yet to start, Paige's mother already knows that she will not be allowing Paige to attend these dances. She feels that the dressy dances are rushing an aspect of development that she would prefer to hold off on. However, she realizes that Paige will have feelings about not going to the dances and she wants to help Paige explore her feelings and still find ways to fit in with her friends. One summer day when she and Paige were taking a walk, Paige's mother shares her concerns about the dressy dances. It is during this time that she tells Paige how she feels about the dances and why she feels that they aren't right for her daughter right now. She also asks her daughter to tell her how she feels about not going to the dances. She lets Paige know, that while she won't be able to go to the dances she will work hard to find alternatives to the dance that seem fun to Paige. She says, "You may have some friends over that night for pizza and a sleepover. Or I can take you and your cousin out to a movie. I really want you to have fun with your friends and I think there are better ways for eleven-year-olds to do it than to go to a dance."

Although Paige had some difficulty hearing this information from her mother, there were aspects of this conversation that made it easier for her to accept the situation. Paige's mother shared her values, feelings and her decision about the dance before the dance is anywhere on the horizon. You too can help your child accept the limits you establish related to societal discipline.

Here are some tips for using the strategy, explore feelings and desires related to "fitting in".

- Talk to your child in advance about your feelings and values about certain social situations and limitations.
- Let your child know why certain social situations aren't right for her based on your understanding of her development and her temperament.

- Ask your child to share the difficulties associated with accepting your limits as it relates to fitting in with friends.
- Work together to find alternatives to certain social limits that both you and your child can be happy with.
- Let your child share her feelings as often as it takes her to understand and accept the limits you've imposed.
- Expect respect when you and your child are discussing feelings related to accepting limits and fitting in with friends.

Monitor influences

The word monitor means the action of watching over somebody to assure good behavior. The societal strategy of monitoring influences means you need to know what your child is reading, watching, doing and playing. I believe that everyone in our society has a responsibility to monitor influences on children. But the reality is that you are the most influential person that can do this important job for your child. Your child cares what you think and needs you to help him make sense of the images and messages he receives on a daily basis about behavior. Remember, whether or not your child can make sense of certain exposure to friends, toys, movies or television is based first on his development and then on his temperament.

Dante

Five-year-old Dante is an energetic and happy boy. His parents have been working with me to gain a better understanding of Dante's temperament because he has had some difficulty this year in preschool. Dante's teachers report that he is impulsive and often acts aggressively with other children especially if he is met with the unexpected. Dante's parents are concerned because his teachers say that Dante's behavior should be getting better as he gets older and yet it is, in fact, getting worse.

When I observed Dante at his preschool, I was able to see the behavior the teachers were concerned about. Dante, at age five was still engaging in behavior that was impulsive in nature. He often tried to get others attention by pushing, poking or grabbing. His ability to communicate his needs and desires verbally was under developed. After observing Dante in school, I met again with his parents. In an effort to put together a comprehensive behavioral plan for Dante and his family, I asked a number of questions about influences that may be contributing to Dante's behavior. Here is what I uncovered. Dante has two very close friends that are aggressive in getting their needs met and he spends many hours playing with them each week. He has unrestricted access to television and video games. His favorite program is wrestling and he watches it with his father every week. His parents have Dante enrolled in karate class once per week. Dante's parents do not restrict his movie viewing to those movies rated G. Dante's parents admit they get angry with Dante when he doesn't listen and they spank him to get his attention.

Now clearly when you see all the negative influences on Dante listed above, it becomes obvious that these influences must be contributing to his behavior. While Dante's parents and I came up with a plan that included much more than just monitoring influences, this strategy alone did positively impact Dante's behavior. Once Dante's parents understood the sum total of the influences on Dante's ability to use acceptable ways of getting his needs met, they were eager to take this strategy on. Together, we developed a plan that limited his time with the boys that also had issues with aggression. Dante's parents limited or eliminated exposure to television and movies with violent content. Dante's energy was channeled into baseball instead of karate. And with a proactive plan for discipline, Dante's parents no longer felt angry and upset enough with Dante to spank him. They learned new, more effective ways to encourage Dante to listen and behave in acceptable ways.

Set limits on inappropriate influences

If you are to set limits on inappropriate influences, the principles of awareness and commitment are essential. In other words, if you don't know what negatively influences your child, it will be next to impossible to set appropriate limits. You need clarity around inappropriate influences from society on your child, so that you can make the necessary commitment to keep these influences from your child. Do you find it hard just to set limits on the non-negotiables related to safety and respect? Many parents do. You might be certain that you don't want your child to drive your car until he has his license. But you might be ambivalent over what music he should listen to? The limits related to societal discipline are based on values. You decide what influences support or defeat what you are trying to teach your child. When you are firm about the influences you want to limit or eliminate in your child's life, you will be better able to set appropriate limits. When you set limits on inappropriate influences, you will be conveying your values to your child. Be prepared to talk to your child about your values and why you feel the need to limit exposure to certain influences. Do you feel strongly that you want your son to grow up and be respectful to women? If you have this value and the music he listens to at age twelve, is disrespectful to women, what must you do? As hard as it might be, you must set limits that support what you are trying to teach.

Oliver

At almost four, Oliver is not allowed to have toy guns or swords. His birthday party is Saturday, and his mother is concerned that he might get this type of toy as a gift. Here is how she prepared Oliver for the possibility. "Oliver, I have been thinking about what you might get from your friends at your party. Some of your friends might not know that we don't care for toy guns or swords. What should we do if you get this kind of toy?" Here is what Oliver thought he could do. "I could keep the toy so I wouldn't hurt my friend's feelings." To that his mother said, "I think it is great that you don't want to hurt your friend's feelings but we can't keep a toy like that, should you get one. We don't like gun toys because they remind us of the real thing and the real thing is used to hurt people. What we could do is say a polite thank you to your friend and then when the party is over we could return the toy for something else." She went further in helping Oliver accept the limit. "Let's practice opening a present that you don't like and still saying a polite thank you." After the party, Oliver looked disappointed. His mother asked him what was wrong. He said, "I didn't get any toy guns or swords." Oliver's mother said, "Why does that upset you, we would have had to take it back anyway?" Oliver said, "I know, I wanted to go to the toy store and see what else I could pick out."

In Proactive Parenting, setting limits implies follow through. Remember, you set limits in proactive discipline and you follow through with consequences in conflict discipline. In Oliver's story, he fully expected his mother to follow through on the limit she established, so much so that he accepted the situation before it even occurred. Predictability is a strong element of societal discipline. If you say your child can only go on the Internet when you are home...that is the limit. If you find that your child went on the Internet when you were not home, she loses the privilege to use it at all...that is the consequence. When you provide clear, firm limits with predicable follow through, your child learns that she is expected to take your limits seriously. She learns that she alone is responsible for the choices she makes. And she learns that the choices she makes have consequences to her and to others. In order for the learning to take place, you must set limits effectively. Here are some do's and don'ts for effective limit setting in societal discipline.

Do's and don'ts for setting limits effectively

Do...
• set limits in advance of conflict.

- talk to your child about your values and how certain influences either support or defeat how you are trying to parent.
- expect to talk to your child repeatedly, so that he may understand your point of view.
- share with your child, the consequences to actions should he choose to ignore the rules.
- be open to your child's point of view, without necessarily disregarding your limits.
- be direct and specific about the non-negotiable limits.
- be consistent in your limits and follow through.

Don't...
- talk about limits and expectations in conflict.
- follow through on limits inconsistently; let your no mean no.
- label the child; focus instead on the behavior.
- express your limits as a question...asking a question is not the same as setting a clear, firm limit.
- set limits randomly...make sure to think through the limits you choose to enforce.
- set a limit once and expect your child to remember it forever more.

Skill build and teach appropriate ways to handle societal influences

For societal discipline to be effective, your child must learn the necessary skills to accept your limits. Remember the "Just Say No" campaign for drug use prevention. It isn't as easy as that for today's child. It is important to learn about influences and explore feelings related to fitting in. It is critical to monitor and set limits on influences. But if you don't actively teach your child how to handle the powerful influences of society on his behavior, he is at a disadvantage. Like peer pressure, societal pressure is powerful in shaping behavior. Because of this, skill building is the most crucial aspect of societal discipline. Your child will need a repertoire of options for handling the typical situations of childhood and young adulthood. Have you ever said to your child when she is worried about a bully,

"Just walk away?" Or have you heard yourself say to your child about smoking, "Just stand up for what is right for you, don't smoke?" These are well-intentioned messages and they do begin a necessary dialogue between you and your child. But they simply aren't enough. If your child felt that dealing with the bully or the pressure to smoke was as easy as that, she would be all set. But she needs more skills than just that. She needs to know who the trusted adults are that she can go to. She needs the right language. She needs to know what she can say or do. She needs to role-play how she will handle a tough situation, so that she has the confidence in the real situation. Have you ever been on a diet and gone to a party with the intention of resisting dessert? You feel confident that you can stand firm on your decision, until you see the beautiful dessert buffet. Then the hostess repeatedly encourages you to just try a little something. She even starts piling food on your plate. Would you be able resist this pressure without lots of skill and practice? Why then do you assume your child can resist the pressures he faces? The pressures on him are just as great perhaps greater. And remember he doesn't have the life experience you have. Skill building to help your child handle the influences of the world he lives in is a very proactive aspect of societal discipline. It involves giving your child tools to use to resist the influences of the popular culture.

Sierra

Fifteen-year-old, Sierra is anxious for summer vacation. She has worked hard all year at school and in her extracurricular activities and she is eager for a break. The phone has already starting to ring off the hook with friends talking about what they will do and where they will go. Sierra's mother knows that "the fence" she has clearly established during the school year is going to have to look different, during summer. A couple of Sierra's friends are older than she and have access to a car. Sierra's mother asks her daughter to sit with her one afternoon to talk about the expectations around Sierra's social life this summer. She shares with her daughter that her number one concern is with her safety. She knows that alcohol may be part of the social scene this summer and she wants to know how Sierra will handle that. She specifically shares with her daughter her concerns about her ever getting into a car with someone who has been drinking. Sierra is candid with her mother and shares that it is getting harder and harder to say no to drinking. It is everywhere she goes. She even alarmingly shares that one friend in particular seems to have a real problem with drinking.

Because Sierra and her mother have been having proactive conversations for a long time about a lot of tough subjects, Sierra was not defensive about her mother's concerns. She in fact was looking for guidance in how to handle fitting in and staying true to her values while still maintaining her friendships. Sierra's mother could have said, "Just don't drink." But do you really think that would be enough to solve the problem that Sierra is really dealing with? During their discussion, Sierra and her mother talked about the circumstances that would make one strategy better than another. The whole idea of this skill building effort is to show Sierra that she has a variety of options available to get through any situation. Here are the skills and strategies Sierra's mother gave her to help her cope with this safety non-negotiable.

Sierra's mother...
- gave her examples of how to try to influence the group to do things and go places where the likelihood of drinking would be low.
- talked to her about what might make her daughter sense that the next activity would involve drinking, and then how to make an excuse to go home.
- invited Sierra's friends over to her house to socialize.
- shared with Sierra some of the excuses she could use when offered a drink, such as "I hate the taste of that or I don't feel good right now."
- offered to pick her daughter and her friends up anytime another teenager had been drinking and was then going to drive.
- encouraged her daughter to spend more time with a friend Sierra knew wasn't into drinking, so that they could support each other.

- offered to take Sierra and her friends to fun places where drinking wouldn't be an option and where supervision would be inherent.

These are just some of the strategies you too could come up with when you talk to your child about what skills and strategies he needs to handle a powerful influence like peer pressure to drink. Whether your child is younger or older, this kind of skill building will be a necessary part of your parenting today. Because there are many challenges facing the proactive parent, I will share specific strategies for handling these challenges in Chapter 10.

Nicole and Eve

Back to the amusement park. Remember how unprepared Nicole felt to make the right decision for Eve and her trip to the amusement park? Now that you know more about societal discipline, things can look quite different. So, what societal strategies did Nicole use to make the best decision for Eve? Here's what we came up with...

Learn about influences and their impact
- Tell Eve that you must have more information before you will be able to make a decision.
- Coach Eve on how to ask the right questions needed to make the decision.
- Offer to speak with her friend's parents if Eve feels uncomfortable getting the information.
- Find out who is going, when they will be home, how much supervision will be available, and any other information that will rule in or rule out the outing.

Explore feelings and desires related to "fitting in"
- Share with Eve the circumstances that would make the outing possible or not possible, before she calls her friend back.
- Encourage her to share her feelings about going to the amusement park.
- Ask her if she has any concerns about going, and feel free to share yours.

- Create a dialog, not a lecture, about Eve's friendship with this boy and what it means to her.
- Discuss how Eve will handle her feelings if you decide the outing isn't possible.
- Discuss with Eve how she will handle the unexpected should the outing take place. Be clear about your expectations for behavior.

Monitor influences
- Ideally, you get to know her friend by having him over before she takes any trip with him or his family.
  Note...if you aren't able to do this in advance, it might just be the deal breaker.
- Get to know Eve's new friend's parents. Talk to them about their expectations for their son's behavior.
- Look at the movies, television and magazines Eve is exposed to and at another time discuss the messages she is getting about having a boyfriend.

Set limits on inappropriate influences
- Make a commitment to say no to the trip if you feel uncomfortable with the supervision available or the circumstances of the outing.
- Limit or eliminate exposure to other influences that encourage or give Eve the message that having a boyfriend at age twelve is a must.

Skill build and teach appropriate ways to handle societal influences
- Give Eve the opportunity to share her unhappiness about not going on the trip. Be sure she knows that she must share her feelings respectfully.
- Offer another option to socialize, so that she sees your effort at compromise. You want her to understand that you respect her wanting to be social but were not comfortable with this trip.
- Give Eve the language she will need to decline the trip. Be sure to encourage her to be respectful of the other family and to you.
- Allow Eve another outlet for her feelings, besides talking to you, such as writing in a journal.

- Give Eve feedback on how she handled the situation. Try to focus at least 80% of your feedback on what she did well.

Nicole and Eve found out that the trip to the amusement park involved being dropped off at the park for several hours while her friend's parents visited with another family. Even Eve was able to see why her mother had concerns. The park was two hours from home and Nicole didn't really know either the boy or his family, making the outing impossible in her eyes. Tackling the tough situations and pressures your child faces is hard work. But the payoff to you and your child is that while keeping your child safe, you are teaching her your values and strengthening your relationship. A commitment to societal discipline allows you and your child to grow together towards an adult friendship rather than grow apart because you are increasingly in dispute over your different perspectives.

Chapter summary

Societal discipline is a critical aspect of parenting today. Your child needs your guidance and direction as he learns to live in our complex society. Its guiding principles are awareness, commitment, honesty, communication, and supervision. The societal strategies include learning about influences and their impact; exploring feelings while helping your child fit in; monitoring influences; setting limits on inappropriate influences and skill building.

When providing societal discipline the proactive parent remembers that...

- The best protection you can offer your child related to the popular culture is societal discipline.
- Societal discipline teaches your child to make good decisions in complex times.
- Societal discipline is about monitoring influences and having a plan for making difficult decisions.
- Societal discipline is about aligning yourself with your child.

- Societal discipline must be combined with a good proactive discipline plan.
- Societal discipline includes proactive and conflict discipline strategies.
- Societal discipline takes time...but reaps rewards.

Questions and Answers
Chapter 5

Turn The Tide

Societal Discipline

Q: Every time I try to have a conversation with my child about a negative influence, we end up in conflict. I know I'm not supposed to talk in conflict, so how do I get my point across?

A: You are right, talking in conflict isn't going teach your child what you hope. First, I would ask you to reflect on these situations and decide whether these are conversations or lectures. Remember, proactive conversations allow for your child's point of view. Second, if you really have something to share with your child, let her know that you will finish sharing your point of view but only when she is respectful and you can wait. Third, keep talking. After your child learns that this is how you will handle societal discipline, your approach will become predictable to her.

Q: I feel like the only parent who has trouble with certain trends and influences. Am I going to make my child a social outcast because I say no to everything?

A: I would never suggest an approach that would affect your child negatively socially. Societal discipline encourages you to help your child explore feelings related to accepting limits while still fitting in. And it encourages skill building so that your child can stay true to your values while still functioning effectively at home, at school and in the community. Societal discipline isn't just about setting limits on unacceptable influences; it is about finding compromise with your child in learning the skills he needs to accept your limits.

Q: I feel that the safest place for my child and his friends to be is at my home. But I am exhausted and sometimes resentful that no one else seems to supervise like I do. Do you have any suggestions for me in handling my feelings?

A: I do have some suggestions for you, but first let me commend you for your efforts. No doubt, it is hard to supervise the way your child needs you to, but it is clearly the right thing to do.

Here are just a few suggestions for you to put energy back in your precious jar.
- Get to know your child's friends' parents. Perhaps if you know them better you would feel more comfortable having your child spend some time elsewhere.
- Talk to your child about how to be respectful when friends are over especially regarding eating and cleaning up. Your child and his friends may be more helpful if the expectations are clear.
- Do something nice for yourself each day. Read the paper or take a walk. Every parent needs to put energy back in the precious jar so that giving to your child is genuine.

SIX

Make Waves

How To Apply Proactive Parenting

Abby, the mother of five-year-old Jillian, and eight-year-old, Thomas, stands up at a parenting workshop and asks, "Is anyone as tired as I am? My children argue with each other and me, all day long. I get resistance on everything I ask them to do. Does it ever get any easier?" The answers to Abby's questions are yes *and* no. Parenting takes time and energy, any way you look at it. But for Abby, the time she spends parenting is mired in the rut of constant conflict. In every situation where her children test the limits, she is trying to think on her feet. Without a plan, Abby is constantly putting energy into resistant children. In Proactive Parenting, time and energy is spent on planning ahead, teaching skills and mutual problem solving. Yes, you still spend time parenting but you will have positive results and see true progress.

The art of Proactive Parenting is combining proactive, conflict and societal discipline. In Chapter 3, you learned what proactive discipline is and how important being proactive is to how your child understands your expectations. In Chapter 4, you learned what conflict discipline is and how important it is to follow through on the expectations you have established. In Chapter 5, you learned what societal discipline is and how important it is to actively teach your child to cope with these influences. But how do you set the stage for what you expect of your child and then follow through on what you have established as non-negotiable? In this chapter, you will learn how to put the three types of discipline together. Let's look at a typical situation that highlights the importance of combining all three types of discipline.

Tricia has repeatedly told John, age eight, that he has to wear his helmet when he roller blades with his friend, Michael. John either forgets to wear it or insists that he doesn't need it; he won't fall. Tricia can't understand why he won't wear the helmet. She feels she has been proactive by telling him it's what she expects. Tricia has been proactive in telling John that the helmet is non-negotiable...he must wear it when he roller blades.   But Tricia hasn't been effectively following through.

John knows the rule, but thinks it is negotiable, since nothing ever happens when he doesn't wear the helmet. If John were to fall and hurt himself...a natural consequence, he might wear the helmet the next time.   Remember, in Chapter 4, you learned that sometimes the natural consequence is helpful in teaching the child the lesson. But in this situation, Tricia is trying to avoid injury that could result from a fall. She must be prepared to follow through so that John will learn that his actions have consequences. If Tricia established a non-negotiable rule, such as ...no helmet = no roller blading, John would be able to make a choice.   Wear the helmet and go to Michael's or don't wear the helmet and stay home.

Some children will make the right choice quickly and parenting will be easy. But if you have a child like that you probably wouldn't be reading this book. You're not alone. Most children will need to see the follow through in order to learn the lesson.

Tricia learned to follow through on this non-negotiable by starting with proactive discipline. The night before John was to go roller blading with Michael; she sat down with John. She stated clearly that she was going to enforce the helmet and roller blading rule. She said it didn't matter whether he forgot to wear it or just didn't want to wear it. It is a safety rule and it's important. She told John that tomorrow he needed to wear the helmet or not go with Michael. She said, "If you choose not to wear the helmet and I find that you have left anyway, I will have to get in the car and come and get you. I don't want to do that but that is how important this rule is." She asked John if he understood the rule and the consequences and he said he did. The next day he left the house without the helmet. This is not a surprise and it shouldn't make you angry.

Children do forget and will test the limits, especially if you have been inconsistent in your follow through in the past. John wants to know if Tricia really stands behind the rule she established the night before. So, here it was... Tricia's moment of truth. She had to start by putting proactive discipline and conflict discipline together. She got into the car and went to get John. John was embarrassed and upset when he got into the car to go home. Tricia told John that they could talk about it, when he was under control. When they arrived home they sat down at the kitchen table and discussed what happened. John said he just forgot and that he couldn't believe his mother embarrassed him that way in front of Michael. Tricia said that she didn't want to do it, but he knew the rule and the consequence, and he made a choice. Tricia told John that the next time he would have the opportunity to make a different decision. She ended the discussion by telling John that she loved him and just wanted to keep him safe. He grumbled that he wouldn't do it again. The next day John and Michael went roller blading and John wore the helmet. This situation illustrates the importance of putting proactive discipline and conflict discipline together. Parents often say that their children know the rules but don't follow them. This is because there is often no reason to follow them. In the situation with Tricia and John, Tricia had to be willing to follow through. And she will need to follow through each and every time John breaks the helmet and roller blading rule.

The Proactive Parenting approach is complete when you add societal discipline to the situation. It is critical to consider the other factors effecting John's situation such as his feelings about his friends and what the popular culture is saying. Did John not want to wear the helmet because it isn't cool to wear one? Does Michael wear a helmet? Is John's helmet too "babyish" for him? Is John the kind of child that just wants to resist your efforts to tell him what to do? During the conflict, you won't be thinking of these potential issues for John. That is why it is important to have the proactive conversation. As you are sharing your expectations, your child has the opportunity to share his concerns or problems. If Tricia found out that John's friends never wear helmets, she would have some insight into John's reluctance to wear his. Once you know what the issues are, you can think the situation through with new perspective. In some cases the rules can be modified and compromised. But in Tricia and John's situation abandoning this safety rule is not the right thing to do. So how can you use societal discipline to help John follow the helmet and roller blading rule? In this situation, you need to give John the skills he needs to wear the helmet although his friends may not. Begin by talking about the reasons behind the rule. Problem solve together how John can handle comments, teasing or criticism. Remember, if John has the skills and the language, he will use them. Be specific about what John's responses could be. Ask him to try to say these things out loud to get a feel for how the real conversation will go. An example of what John might say to Michael is, "If the bikers in the *Tour de France* wear helmets, so will I." This kind of discipline empowers your child. Remember, he needs a safe place to voice his concerns and to practice coping with standing firm among his friends. Ideally, you discuss the societal issues as part of proactive discipline, but any time you have these conversations is a step in the right direction. Just don't use the time you are in conflict to initiate this discussion. Considering the societal factors, in advance of the conflict, is the key to successful Proactive Parenting.

Once you have the lesson "in the bag," you can take it back out as a reminder. You can be proactive about using this lesson in future situations. If Tricia sees John leaving the house without the helmet, she should remind John what happened the last time he made that choice. Most children will respond to this kind of follow through and consistency. Some won't, and if your child is persistent, you will have to add logical consequences until the impact is great enough to influence the behavior. In Chapter 4, you learned about the concept called "raising the bar." Tricia would have to be prepared to provide a consequence with greater impact on John should he not respond to being picked up and driven home. That is why it is critical that you know your child's temperament when you provide consequences. Remember you want to provide consequences that will make an impact.

Practically parenting

After reading the previous chapters and thinking about the situation with Tricia and John you may be thinking, "I do some of what she is suggesting." And you are probably right! We rarely give ourselves the credit we deserve for parenting well. I find in my private practice, that families are often doing a lot right...just perhaps at the wrong time. Sometimes parents teach the best lessons when they are in conflict with their child. Though the words may be great, the timing is not. No one can hear about expectations when emotions are running high. The same conversation over breakfast is proactive and provides you and your child with a chance to talk.

So, do you want to know what aspects of Proactive Parenting you are already skilled at? Take the quiz...*Are you a Proactive Parent?* When you finish, you will know what you are already doing that benefits you and your family. You will also learn the areas you need to focus on to become more proactive and less reactive.

Are you a Proactive Parent?

Take this quiz to find out just how proactive you are in your parenting. You will be better able to focus your energies on learning how to be proactive if you explore the way you currently react to your child.

Answer the following questions by circling the number that best corresponds to your initial reaction. At the end, total up all the circled answers to see how proactive you are in your parenting.

1	2	3
Rarely	Sometimes	Often

1. I show respect to my child by listening when she speaks.

1   2   3

2. I encourage my child to express his feelings about rules.

1   2   3

3. I let my child make age-appropriate decisions.

1   2   3

4. I spend time with my child because I really enjoy her company.

1   2   3

5. I take responsibility for teaching my child how to solve problems and manage stress.

1   2   3

6. I expect my child to be responsible and cooperative.

1   2   <u>3</u>

7. I encourage my child to appreciate and share
his accomplishments.

1   2   <u>3</u>

8. I ask my child to share her thoughts, ideas and opinions.

1   2   <u>3</u>

9. I have a clear set of rules that everyone in the family
knows and understands.

1   2   <u>3</u>

10. I respond to problems in ways that are predictable and
consistent and not dependent on my mood.

1   <u>2</u>   3

11. I keep requests and commands simple and direct.

1   <u>2</u>   3

12. I am willing to hold firm to a request or expectation
that is important to me, even if other families don't
agree with me.

1   2   <u>3</u>

13. I tell my child in advance, what the consequences will
be for certain actions.

1   <u>2</u>   3

14. I follow through on the limits I've set, if my child
disobeys or manipulates the rules.

1   <u>2</u>   3

15. I make decisions counter to popular opinion when I
know they are right for my child.

                                      1   2   3

16. I anticipate situations in which my child might have
difficulty coping with the influences of others.

                                      1   2   3

17. I give my child concrete ways to say no to negative
influences.

                                      1   2   3

18. I routinely help my child develop the skills he needs
to deal with peer pressure.

                                      1   2   3

19. I express my love to my child every day by letting her
know she always has a place to share her feelings.

                                      1   2   3

20. I talk to my child about my values and why they are
important to me.

                                      1   2   3

  Now add up your total number of points and see how
proactive you are. Remember, even if you are a very
reactive parent, you can become proactive. This quiz is in-
tended to raise your awareness about the areas you need to
work on.

50-60 points   The Proactive Parent
  If you scored between 50 and 60 points, you are a
proactive parent. This means you see discipline as an
important aspect of everyday parenting. In good times

and bad, you teach your child the skills she needs to be successful in the world. Though you may have ups and downs in the parent/child relationship, your family life is generally harmonious. Keep up the good work, because every developmental phase will bring new challenges.

30-50 points   The Wavering Parent

If you scored between 30 and 50 points, you are a wavering parent. This means that sometimes you may be proactive yet other times reactive in parenting your child. My guess is that your child pushes the limits because your expectations may be inconsistent and boundaries are unclear. You can become more proactive by focusing on the aspects of your parenting that are reactive and committing yourself to using more Proactive Parenting strategies.

20-30 points   The Reactive Parent

If you scored between 20 and 30 points, you are a reactive parent. You may feel that your home is full of conflict and that family harmony is a myth. Take heart, even the most reactive parent can learn how to be a proactive parent. You've taken the first step by reading this book. You can begin to be less reactive and more proactive starting now. Some people see the benefits of Proactive Parenting very quickly, but remember change takes time, so be patient with yourself. Your child is worth the effort.

What kind of parent are you?

So how did you do? Are you a proactive parent, or are you on your way to being one?

The proactive parent

If you are a proactive parent, you combine proactive, conflict and societal discipline. You probably can relate to the approach presented in this book. Some people are naturals when it comes to parenting; and some of us had very good role models in our own parents. You are teaching your child the skills he needs to become capable, responsible and to be motivated from within. His ability to accept limits and act in acceptable ways will help him handle life's ups and downs. Remember, each time your child enters a new developmental phase, you will be faced with new parenting challenges and dilemmas, so continue to embrace Proactive Parenting. As your child gets older, the influences of society get stronger and stronger. He will need the skills he has developed as a younger child to make the more complicated decisions of adolescence and adulthood.

The wavering parent

You are not alone, most parents fall into this category. Often you have the right idea about what limits to set but you have trouble following through and combating the influences of society. While every parent is reactive occasionally in their parenting, you may be struggling a bit more with your emotions when your child behaves inappropriately. My guess is that your child may be pushing the limits because of your inconsistency. She may even be taking advantage of your inability to anticipate behavioral troublespots.   Other limits will be tested as a result of letting a smaller limit go unnoticed. You may form opinions about certain behaviors only after you see the ramifications of not dealing with them. Being proactive is something you will have to embrace as a new way of thinking about parenting. Learning to recognize the potential for situations to get beyond your child's capabilities is going to be your challenge. Review your answers on the quiz to identify the areas you need to work on as you commit to being less reactive and more proactive in your parenting.

The reactive parent

As a reactive parent, you are probably spending most of your time in conflict with your child. The emotions may run high in your family with no one quite sure how to stop the constant conflict. Whether change needs to focus on changing your style or learning how to work with you child's style, you can learn how to be a proactive parent. You've taken the first step just by reading this book and taking the quiz. You can begin to be less reactive and more proactive right now. Staying focused, having a plan and celebrating small successes will help you on your journey to becoming more proactive.

Take it again

Whether you are already proactive or struggling with your reactions to your child's behavior, try to revisit the quiz periodically. Start now to incorporate all three kinds of discipline into your parenting. Over time, you will see an improvement in the way your child responds to you. By taking the quiz periodically, it will confirm that you have made changes in the way you parent, and this will help you feel confident that you are on the right track.

The ASK Yourself Strategy

Now you know what you need to work on to become a more proactive parent. But are you confused about how to put it all together? Did the situation with Tricia and John make sense to you or do you need help understanding Tricia's plan? *The ASK Yourself Strategy* was designed to help you get started in an organized way. *The ASK Yourself Strategy* is a reflective strategy used in Proactive Parenting. It is an information-gathering tool that allows you to parent each child individually.

The strategy is effective in creating a proactive plan for teaching cooperation, responsibility and family values, as well as a plan for resolving conflict and monitoring the influences of society. *The ASK Yourself Strategy* helps you to combine proactive, conflict and societal discipline. It gets you started in thinking about parenting in a new way. As you use the strategy, you will gather the information you need to put Proactive Parenting into action. The age and development of your child as well as the situations he is expected to cope with change over time. Though your child's temperament isn't likely to change, I strongly believe you can teach your child the skills he needs to maximize the positive aspects of his temperament and minimize the less positive aspects. *The ASK Yourself Strategy* helps you to do just that. The strategy is useful in helping to influence behavior in a positive way, or when introducing a new skill you want your child to develop. Do you want your son to play a board game with his friends without ending up in tears; or do you want to teach your daughter to be more thoughtful of her sister? *The ASK Yourself Strategy* shows you how to apply Proactive Parenting in any situation.

The A in *The ASK Yourself Strategy* stands for Age and development of the child

Ask yourself: "Is my child capable, from a developmental perspective, of doing what is expected of him or of learning what I want him to learn?"

The S in *The ASK Yourself Strategy* stands for Situation

Ask yourself: "Is this the best possible situation for getting my child to cooperate, be responsible and accept limits? What is the popular culture's take on this situation? What is my position on this situation? What are my values related to this situation?"

The K in *The ASK Yourself Strategy* stands for Know the child

Ask yourself: "Given my child's temperament and the situation, are my expectations appropriate? Is there any aspect of my child's temperament that will make learning easier or harder?"

After you have gathered the information necessary to put the situation in perspective, you can develop a proactive plan that includes proactive, conflict and societal strategies. Here is an example of how the strategy works.

Peter

Peter is a twelve-year-old boy in his first year of middle school. When he comes home from school, he immediately calls his best friend to "hang out." When his mother asks him if he has homework he often says, "Not that much." Later in the evening, when his Mom and Dad offer to help him with his homework, he is short tempered, impatient and lashes out at their efforts to help. His mother notices that Peter is increasingly disorganized and leaves his projects until the last minute. Last night at nine o'clock, Peter realized that he needed poster board and markers for a project due the next day.

A. Age and development of the child.

Can twelve-year-old Peter handle after-school social time and homework without being disrespectful to his parents? From a developmental perspective, can you expect him to be able to carry out these activities respectfully? The answer is yes; you can expect Peter to be able to handle social time and his responsibilities for schoolwork without being disrespectful.

S. Situation

Is the situation set up for success related to cooperation and responsibility? Is something else going on with Peter that is making him feel overwhelmed? Is Peter faced with pressures to spend more time with friends and less time

on school? What are his parent's values around being
talked to disrespectfully? Is this an issue that is non-negotiable? The answer is complex. Peter has the need for
down time after school but then feels stressed and overwhelmed with getting his homework done at night. Peter
is taking the stress he feels, about balancing social time
and school responsibilities, out on his parents.

Transition to a new school, particularly middle
school, is challenging and will impact behavior. His
parents must decide if being respectful is non-negotiable regardless of the issues going on in his life.

K. Know the child

Given Peter's temperament, is the present routine a
good one? Think about his stamina, how does he generally manage stress? Does Peter take a bit longer to
adjust to new expectations? Does he persevere under
pressure or tend to give up? Is he generally able to communicate his feelings? All of what his parents know about
Peter's temperament will influence the proactive plan
that's developed.

The proactive plan

The ASK Yourself Strategy is the first step in developing
a proactive plan for managing this situation. Now that
Peter's age, development and temperament and how they
impact the situation have been assessed, his parents
have the information they need to develop a proactive
plan for modifying Peter's behavior. It is helpful to use
The ASK Yourself Strategy to put the situation in perspective. When you do, it makes it easier to develop a
proactive plan that includes proactive, conflict and societal strategies.

The proactive plan includes proactive strategies and
strategies for dealing with conflict and society. In chapters
3, 4 and 5, the proactive, conflict and societal strategies
were explored in detail. In this chapter, you will learn how
to put them all together, in real parenting situations.

Remember, just because you develop a proactive plan
doesn't mean you won't have to follow through on the non-

negotiables you have established. In fact, sometimes you should be eager to provide consequences for a particular behavior just to prove to your child that you will do what you say. I don't recommend providing consequences for no reason, but you should use the situations you are dealt, to put the approach into action. You need to be prepared that your child will test the limits. He will learn that rules are established for a reason, when he experiences the natural or logical consequences of his actions. Let's explore the proactive plan Peter's parents and I developed.

Proactive strategies

Here are the proactive strategies. Each was discussed in detail, in chapter 3.

- Have proactive conversations
- Set expectations and discuss consequences
- Explore other factors affecting behavior
- Provide emotional coaching and help with problem solving
- Spend time together

In the situation with Peter, you will begin by setting aside time to talk to Peter. Don't wait until you are arguing over homework to start sharing your expectations. Proactive conversations happen when you and your child really share your perspectives. While ideas and values may differ, proactive conversations and strategies are aimed at expressing expectations and problem solving. Some of the best proactive conversations take place over meals or at bedtime. Talk with Peter about his present after-school routine. Explain that it contributes to his being disrespectful to you later at night. Ask him if he is having any problems with friends, or at school. Make clear your expectations about respect. Tell Peter he needs to be respectful even if he is feeling overwhelmed. Get Peter involved in developing the new routine. His input will make it more likely that he will stick with the plan. Together, create a new plan that considers Peter's need to have down time as well as your desire for getting homework done when he is best able to do it. Help Peter break down the challenge into manageable pieces. When a child reaches the age of twelve he may appear more independent than he actually is. This is why it is so important to know your child. Coping with tasks may be more complicated for Peter than he lets on. Look at the amount of sleep he is getting. Because Peter is older, you may be underestimating how much sleep he needs to succeed. Remember, a child Peter's age should be aiming for about ten hours of sleep per night. Spend one-on-one time with Peter. If you want him to share his feelings and concerns with you, you will need to spend time with him talking about something other than the behavior you want modified. He is more likely to talk to you when you spend time with him regularly and he is relaxed.

You won't use all your proactive strategies at the same time. The process of modifying behavior takes time and is done in concert with other actions.

Conflict strategies

Here are the conflict strategies. Each is discussed in detail in Chapter 4.

- Establish authority
- Be direct and specific about the non-negotiables
- Remain calm
- Provide consequences
- Make an impact

Some strategies for managing conflict will be used during the proactive period and some during the conflict itself. During your proactive conversations with Peter, let him know you empathize with the transition he is going through but that disrespectful behavior is unacceptable.

Be concrete about the disrespectful words and behaviors you want to discourage. Communicate what the consequences will be if the disrespectful behavior continues. This is the most important aspect of conflict discipline. You must identify the consequence that will have an impact on your child. The consequences you choose for one child may not make impact on another child. If you want Peter to get the message, you must choose consequences that have an impact on Peter. It would be ideal if there were lists of consequences for particular actions and sometimes it seems that easy. But what has an impact on one child may not impact another at all. Whatever consequences you decide to use, you must clearly communicate them in advance and then you must be prepared to follow through. If you tell Peter that if he continues to be disrespectful he will no longer be able to "hang out" with his friends after school, then you must be prepared to enforce this consequence if he exhibits disrespectful behavior. He may test you to see if you will follow through, and you must communicate your resolve with action. Be sure the consequence has an impact and is one you will follow through with if need be. If Peter seems unaffected by the consequence you provided, then you didn't have an impact. You will need to use another consequence or "raise the bar" on dealing with disrespectful behavior. If the consequences don't have an impact, then the connection between actions and consequences did not take place.

Societal strategies

Here are the societal strategies. Each is discussed in detail in Chapter 5.

- Raise awareness about influences and their impact
- Explore feelings and desires related to "fitting in"
- Monitor influences
- Set limits on inappropriate influences
- Skill build and teach appropriate ways to handle societal influences

While proactive discipline and conflict discipline are distinctly different, societal discipline is an extension of proactive discipline. Some situations will have a component of societal discipline, like the situation with Peter, but some won't. It is important though to discuss it separate from conflict so that the concepts and strategies don't get overlooked.

When having a proactive conversation with Peter, it is important to open the discussion up to issues related to peer pressure. Is it "uncool" for a boy to be smart? If Peter focuses on schoolwork, does he get teased? These are just two of the issues that may be complicating Peter's situation. If you don't discuss them and help Peter to problem solve them, your plan will be ineffective. Look at the influences on Peter. Are the friends he is spending time with disinterested in school? Are the TV shows he is watching reinforcing a dislike for school? Monitoring influences is important if you are to understand the messages that Peter is getting and why these messages are affecting behavior. Once the negative influences are identified, you will have to set appropriate limits. Many parents get into conflict about setting limits on friendships, TV and other popular culture experiences. But remember, you are discussing and sharing expectations in advance of conflict. You are giving your child a chance to voice concerns, ask you for the reasons behind the rules and to participate in problem solving. It isn't enough to identify the negative societal influences and then set limits on them. You have to take the next step, which is to help your child accept the societal limits you impose. Peter will need you to help him develop the confidence he needs to take a stand and make his school work a priority. Give him options for dealing with the pressure that will come from his friends when he puts schoolwork ahead of "hanging out." Perhaps, Peter can do some of his homework before he even calls his friends. Perhaps, you can make dinner earlier as a way to end the "hang out" time and give Peter more time for schoolwork after dinner. You need to believe that if Peter has the right skills for dealing with this issue, he will use them. Obviously this kind of discipline is best done at early ages, but it is never too late to use societal discipline. In fact, the sooner you embrace it the better.

Precious time

Remember, putting it all together takes time. It may take you more time in the beginning to use *The ASK Yourself Strategy* but it will become second nature to you after you parent this way for a while. When you took the *Are you a Proactive Parent?* quiz, hopefully you were able to identify your strengths as well as the areas where you need help. Your goal should be to use the *The ASK Yourself Strategy* to help you focus your energies on the areas of Proactive Parenting you need to strengthen.

First things first

Parents often ask me, "What do I do when I'm in the heat of a situation and I don't have time to use *The ASK Yourself Strategy?* How can I be proactive if I'm already in conflict with my child?" This happens to every parent. A situation may have been going on for days before you finally reach your breaking point. Deal with the conflict first and then after the situation is under control, start to use your proactive strategies.

Mary, age five, and Anne, age ten, have been bickering every night for three nights. Mary wants a turn at sleeping on the top bunk and Anne refuses to let her. The first two nights their Dad ignored it but tonight he's had it! This is just one of the many situations that can take us by surprise emotionally. Their Dad said, "Why can't they get along? At their ages, why do I have to get involved with these conflicts?" If he wants the situation to change, he must be proactive in solving the problem. But first he needs to manage the immediate conflict situation. You know he will be listening to this every night if nothing is done. But, sharing what he expects now won't help the girls make other choices to solve this problem. He started by containing his emotions and keeping the situation in perspective. He intervened and stopped the conflict. After the situation cools down, he will have the chance to use *The ASK Yourself Strategy* and develop a proactive plan. The plan will include proactive conversations and problem solving. The plan may include societal strategies such as examining Anne's feelings about sharing a room with her sister who is five years younger than she is. Can you see how important it is to break the situation down into the three distinct pieces?

Let's look at another situation where conflict has arisen and must be managed before proactive strategies can be put into place.

Henry

Henry is a four-year-old with energy to burn. Throughout the day, he enjoys his toys in the playroom, in the living room and in the hall. At 6:00pm he is asked to begin cleaning up his toys before dinner. Henry is a very capable and attentive boy. He picks up a few blocks but when his Mom goes to make dinner, he starts playing again. Ten minutes later nothing is accomplished. When his Mom insists that Henry clean up this mess or else...! Henry throws himself on the floor crying. Dinner is burning, the baby starts crying and his Step-Dad walks through the back door.

A. Age and development of the child

Is Henry capable of the job he has been given? From a developmental perspective, can you expect a four-year-old to be able to clean up all the toys in each of these locations? The answer is yes and no. With concrete direction and supervision, a four-year-old can participate in the job of cleaning up a day's play. The key word being participate. The job of cleaning up "everything" is very abstract and overwhelming to a four-year-old.

S. Situation

Is the situation set up for success related to cooperation and responsibility? Is Henry able to do this type of chore when he is rested? Is too much going on at once? Does Henry sense that no one is engaged in what he is doing? The answer is complex. Giving chores to a hungry and tired child will never meet with the best results. At the end of the day, often parents have many responsibilities that make it difficult to engage in what a four-year-old is doing. Six o'clock is not the time to ask a four-year old child to do anything that requires reserve energy.

K. Know the child

Given Henry's temperament and the situation, is this an appropriate expectation? Can Henry follow multi-task directions or find the energy when he is tired to complete a complex job? Think about how Henry copes with being overwhelmed. It is important to know how Henry's temperament affects his ability to carry out expectations.

Proactive plan

In this situation, conflict needs to be managed first. The time to be proactive will be after the present situation is under control. Remember, proactive, conflict and societal discipline work together. It would be ideal if a parent could recognize a problem and then develop a proactive plan that starts with proactive discipline. But often it is a conflict situation that occurs repeatedly that gets a parent's attention and helps them recognize the need for a plan. Sometimes it is important to sacrifice the present situation in order to restore harmony in the family. Don't worry, the situation will probably occur again, but the next time you will be prepared. Here is the plan Henry's mother used in this situation.

Conflict strategies

Here they are again...the conflict strategies described in detail in Chapter 4.

- Establish authority
- Be direct and specific about the non-negotiables
- Remain calm
- Provide consequences
- Make an impact

In the situation with Henry, start by managing the current conflict. Establish authority by letting the situation go. End the struggle as soon as you realize you are in a no-win situation. Remember, it is unfair to hold him accountable, if this is the first time he has heard the expectations. You're the grown-up, and Henry is four. Take time later to examine whether or not your expectations are age-appropriate. You must remind yourself that you will have a chance to create a plan that will stop this from occurring again. In a direct and specific way, tell Henry that it is time to work together to clean up the toys. When the situation is as emotionally charged as it is now, keep your expectations of Henry relatively low. Your priority is to get through this conflict. Give him a small but manageable amount of the work. Once you've had a chance to develop a plan that includes appropriate strategies, then you can have different or higher expectations. Remain calm, yelling and getting physical are not going to help the situation. Remember, Henry is still a little boy and doesn't like feeling overwhelmed or at odds with you. If during the conflict, the situation gets further out of control and Henry violates a safety rule or is disrespectful, isolate him with a clear message about what you expect. Keep conversation to a minimum. Remember actions not words teach during conflict situations. Give Henry a chance to regain control, offering to help him if you can. Let Henry feel he has a genuine chance to start over. Give him some attention and affection. Be sure to let him know that everyone deserves a fresh start. Henry will want to try harder next time if he senses a real chance to start over.

Proactive strategies

Here they are again...the proactive strategies described in detail in Chapter 3.

- Have proactive conversations
- Set expectations and discuss consequences
- Explore other factors affecting behavior
- Provide emotional coaching and help with problem solving
- Spend time together

After the conflict is resolved, work together to clean up the toys. Role model cooperation. Later in the evening or the next morning, let Henry know that you have some new rules for playing with his toys. Do not wait until you are overwhelmed or upset to share these new expectations. You might decide to institute the following rules for Henry:

- Clean up as you go.
- Have a mid-day pick up.
- Create the "take one put one back rule" for games and toys.
- Make tidying up into a game. "Henry, you find all the red blocks and I'll pick up the books."
- Whatever rules you choose, you must communicate them to Henry in advance. This doesn't guarantee that he will always follow them but it does set the stage for how you will handle the inevitable conflict.
- When Henry complies with the rules, be sure to thank him for cooperating and for respecting rules. However, don't overly praise him for doing what is expected of him, it may sound like you're surprised he rose to the occasion.
- Have all the toys put away by four o'clock and allow bathes with toys, books and tapes for the late afternoon, early evening hours. These kinds of activities are calming and will help your child handle the evening transitions he must face with more reserve.

And finally, make dinner earlier. Most four-year-olds won't be on their best behavior by six o'clock. Once you have established the new rules, you must follow them. If Henry is to be expected to adhere to the new rules, he needs you to be consistent. Behavior won't be modified unless you are consistent.

Are there aspects of societal discipline in this situation? It will be important to examine the situation to see if there are, most situations have this element of discipline. For example, if Henry had a childcare provider that didn't have the same expectations that you do or if Henry spent time with your ex-husband on the weekend, then in fact adding societal strategies to your plan would be critical to Henry's success.

ASK Yourself...now

Start now on your journey to become a proactive parent. Think of a behavior or situation that you would like to influence in a positive way. Does your son resist cleaning his room? Does your daughter talk on the phone during dinner? Choose one concern and take the time now to use *The ASK Yourself Strategy.* In the beginning, you may use the tool often, but in time, the approach will become second nature to you and you will find that you look at each situation with the strategy already in mind. The tool can also be helpful if you are dealing with a particularly difficult situation or with a child who is particularly resistant to your efforts.

ASK Yourself Strategy Tool

This tool is helpful to the parent just starting to use Proactive Parenting or for use with particularly difficult behaviors or situations. Remember, the goal is to incorporate this kind of thinking into your everyday parenting. Here is how you begin.

1. **Describe the behavior or situation you would like to influence in a positive way?**

_____

_____

_____

_____

_____

2. **Begin to gather the information you need to develop a proactive plan.**

   The ASK Yourself Strategy
   A...Age and development of the child
   "Is my child capable, from a developmental perspective, of doing what I expect? Is my child capable of learning what I want to teach?"

_____

_____

_____

_____

_____

Note: Review Chapters 7, 8 or 9, depending on the age of your child, to be sure your expectations are age-appropriate.

S ...Situation
"Is this the best possible situation for getting my child to cooperate, be responsible and accept limits? What is the popular culture's take on this situation? What is my

position on this situation? What are my values related to
this situation?"

_____

_____

_____

_____

_____

_____

K...Know the child

"Given my child's temperament and the situation, are
my expectations appropriate? Can my child really cope
with my expectations? Is there any aspect of my child's
temperament that will make learning easier or harder?"

_____

_____

_____

_____

_____

Now that you have done 1 & 2...

3. Create a Proactive Plan.

*Note: It is important to describe in detail what you will
do and how you will do it. Don't forget to think about
when you will carry out each of the proactive, conflict
and societal strategies.*

Proactive Strategies

Have proactive conversations

_____

_____

Set expectations and discuss consequences

_____

_____

Explore other factors affecting behavior

Provide emotional coaching and
help with problem solving

Spend time together

Conflict Strategies

Establish authority

Be direct and specific about the non-negotiables

Remain calm

Provide consequences

Make an impact

Societal Strategies

Raise awareness about influences and their impact

_____

_____

Explore feelings and desires related to "fitting in"

_____

_____

Monitor influences

_____

Set limits on inappropriate influences

_____

_____

Skill build and teach appropriate ways
to handle societal influences

_____

_____

4. Carry out your plan and evaluate.

Note: It will be important to decide upon a time to revisit this issue and examine whether or not the plan is working or needs to be modified.

_____

_____

_____

Now you have a map!

I hope you took the time to use *The ASK Yourself Strategy* tool to create a plan for modifying a specific behavior in your child. A good map is only as good as the details it includes. The more details you include in your plan, the more effective you will be at modifying behavior. Keep in mind that each child, regardless of age, is an individual. The differences between two children of the same age will require different planning based on every situation and their individual temperaments. Let's take the age-old dilemma of taking a two-year-old to church. Greta is a feisty two-year-old who finds it very difficult to sit still for more than a minute or so. Matteo is also two but is able to play with one toy for a very long time. Which child will have an easier time in church, where the expectation is to sit and be quiet? You're right, it will be Matteo. Does this mean that Greta's parents shouldn't take her to church? Not necessarily, as long as they plan ahead and are prepared to step out back. Do you see how the children's ages are the same but their unique temperaments change the plan? Different situations can also change your plan? Perhaps Greta's parents would take her to the children's church service on Sunday but wouldn't think of taking her to Uncle Fred's funeral. I could go on and on about the differences among children and how this changes the parenting decisions we make. Use *The ASK Yourself Strategy* tool to help make the right decisions for your child.

Tips on developing a proactive plan

As you carry out your plan, it will be important to keep in mind some of the suggestions discussed throughout this book.

Here are some tips for developing an effective proactive plan for modifying behavior.

- Learn about development. As your child gets older, she is capable of being more responsible and independent.

The age and development of your child will affect the strategies and consequences you use to develop your child's skills.

- Anticipate situations your child may have difficulty with, and then plan for them.
- Know your child. Each child has a unique temperament and responds differently to stress, disagreements and misunderstandings. Have empathy for how hard it is to learn new skills.
- Use proactive, conflict and societal strategies together. Most situations require a combination of strategies. While every proactive conversation won't be met with conflict, every conflict situation can benefit from being proactive.
- Include your child in the planning. Ask for your child's input. Shared decision-making will yield more cooperation.
- Communicate your plan to everyone involved. It's impossible for your child or your spouse to know your expectations if you don't share them.
- When being proactive...talk. This is the time for you to share your ideas, values, and expectations, and it is the time for your child to share hers. Remember, a conversation is a dialogue not a lecture.
- When in conflict, don't talk...act. Actions, not words, teach in conflict situations.
- Don't unveil the plan in the middle of a conflict. During conflict, it is very difficult for your child to hear your concerns...be proactive.
- Spend time with your child. When you are trying to change your child's behavior, it is important to be sure he feels that you like him and want to be with him.
- Remember the 80/20 rule of feedback. In order to change behavior, people need 80% positive feedback and only 20% constructive feedback. Most of us do just the opposite.
- Express love to your child. Every parent/child relationship has conflict. And if you are to modify behavior then it is even more important to let your child know just how much you love him. The love you express goes a long way in creating family harmony.

Chapter summary

In this chapter, you read about how you can put Proactive Parenting into practice. You're ready to put it all together. I hope you took the time to take the quiz, "*Are you a Proactive Parent?*" It's a good first step toward identifying the ways in which you are proactive and perhaps, reactive in your parenting. I also urge you to use *The ASK Yourself Strategy* tool to gather information and create a proactive plan for a parenting dilemma you're dealing with in your own life. Now that you know how to put it all together, let's explore how Proactive Parenting works for children under 3 (Chapter 7), children 3 to 9 (Chapter 8), and children 10-18 (Chapter 9). Remember, development is a critical aspect of this approach and you must understand how your child thinks and learns in order to have age-appropriate expectations.

Questions and Answers
Chapter 6

Make Waves

How To Apply Proactive Parenting

Q: How can I be proactive, if I am in the middle of a conflict with my child?

A: The time to be proactive is before the conflict starts or after you have cooled down. Remember, sometimes you have to get a situation under control before you can start planning ahead for how you will handle it the next time.

Q: I know I am proactive...I tell my child repeatedly what my expectations are. Why isn't this working for me?

A: The key to the approach is to share your expectations with your child but not necessarily repeatedly. I wonder if you are following through on what you said you would do in the event your child doesn't follow the established rules. Remember, you talk during the proactive discipline, but actions not words, teach in conflict.

Q: My child is very resistant to anything I suggest. Am I doing something wrong?

A: Some children are resistant to consistency at first, but will get more comfortable with it the longer you are consistent. So stick to the plan you have developed. It is also important to spend time with your child talking or doing something unrelated to the behavior or situation you are hoping to modify.

Q: My two children are such opposites. I use the same consequences, and I don't get the same results. Does this approach only work with easy-to-parent children?

A: No, the approach works with every child. The key though is to choose consequences that make an impact on each individual child. What makes an impact on one child might not make an impact on another.

SEVEN

Get Their Feet Wet

How The Approach Works
With Children Under Three

Ethan, father of twenty-six-month old Holly and six-month-old Amy asks during a workshop, "Is it ever too early to start to discipline your child?" If you embrace the broad definition of discipline that I've discussed so far, the answer is no. It is never too early to discipline your child. Remember, discipline means to teach and learn. So, everything you say and do with your child is, in fact, teaching and learning. Proactive Parenting can begin when your child is very young. This is good training for both you and your child. The repetition with which you need to parent may be tiring but you never know when your child's understanding will "kick in." In this chapter, I will review how your infant or toddler thinks and learns. Using Proactive Parenting with a child under three has some nuances. I will also discuss, how to apply the principles of Proactive Parenting specifically to your child under three. I will do this first by examining the discipline principles with infants and toddlers in mind and then by using a case study for each age group.

The way you discipline a one-year-old who hits is different from the way you discipline a three-year-old who hits. When you understand the way your child sees the world, you will find it much easier to teach cooperation and acceptable ways of behaving. The strategies you use with a child under three will be geared toward her age, development, situation and temperament. So, let's review what you know about thinking and learning for a child under three.

Thinking and learning for infants and toddlers

From the time your child is born he is watching and interacting with the world and the people in it. When he is an infant until about the age of three, he is impulsively exploring his environment using all his senses. A child under three has yet to learn, consistently, that his actions affect the people around him. He will learn over time that his actions have consequences. In Chapter 1, I described how your child thinks and learns based on her developmental age. Remember, infants and toddlers are concrete thinkers. Your child knows it because he sees it. Says it because he heard it. And feels it because it is there. Your child's learning at this age is hands on; lots of explanation won't help you to teach your child too much. It will be more important for you to show your child through clear actions what you want him to do. Your child's *motis operandi* at this age is "I'll believe it when I see it."

Infants and toddlers are impulsive learners. By that, I mean your child will be motivated to act on an impulse or sudden desire to do or say something. This isn't necessarily a bad thing. It means your child is eager and motivated to learn. The only problem with this aspect of how a young child learns is that you must be one step ahead of him to keep him safe. Your child will learn about the world in different ways than an older child...he will act first and think later. Your child will explore the world with his eyes, ears, mouth, hands and feet. Learning is a whole body experience.

As your child moves from infant to toddler, her preferences, her sense of humor and her way of communicating what she wants have emerged and should be very clear to you now. Your child's temperament will clearly affect how she learns about her surroundings. Is she timid about new things and new people or is she a social butterfly? Does she persist when learning new things or does she give up too easily? Knowing about development and your child's temperament will help you immensely as you shape behavior in your child. In other words, it is important to know a lot about development and temperament to provide the right discipline for your infant or toddler. Look at the charts that review some important milestones in infant and toddler development that impact how you provide teaching and learning strategies to your child. It would also be a good idea to take the *Discovering Your Child's Style* quiz, if you haven't already. It is found in Chapter 2.

Developmental Milestones
That Impact Discipline
Infants and Toddlers

Note: All milestone information is approximate.
Your child will learn at his own pace and in his own time.
If you are concerned however, please contact your pediatrician
or child development expert.

Cognitive development...
refers to how your child thinks.

By age one, your child...

realizes things exist when out of sight.
understands simple directions.
uses five senses to learn.

By age two, your child...

can label objects.
thinks out loud.
develops short term memory.

By age three, your child...

begins to learn actions have consequences.
uses role playing to learn.
begins to learn self-control.

Developmental Milestones
That Impact Discipline
Infants and Toddlers

Note: All milestone information is approximate.
Your child will learn at his own pace and in his own time.
If you are concerned however, please contact your pediatrician
or child development expert.

Affective development...
refers to how your child feels.

By age one, your child...

is reluctant to change.
is sensitive to the word "no".
may exhibit separation anxiety.

By age two, your child...

demands to have his own way.
may be unhappy about routine changes.
has feelings not always expressed with
language.

By age three, your child...

can label a number of emotions.
can express feelings verbally.
follows rules if it suits her.

Developmental Milestones
That Impact Discipline
Infants and Toddlers

Note: All milestone information is approximate.
Your child will learn at his own pace and in his own time.
If you are concerned however, please contact your pediatrician
or child development expert.

Psychomotor development...
refers to how your child moves.

By age one, your child...

uses gestures to show desires.
can follow one command.
loves to explore his environment.

By age two, your child...

imitates to learn.
runs away to avoid discipline.
may get out of chairs, the crib or the carseat.

By age three, your child...

wants to do things by herself.
can help with self care.
uses fine and gross motor skills.

Proactive Parenting for infants and toddlers

In Chapters 3, 4 & 5, I've gone into detail about the principles that apply to each of the three types of discipline that make up Proactive Parenting. Now I would like to review the principles and comment briefly on how they apply to your child under three.

The principles of **proactive discipline**...

- **Anticipation** may be tricky if you are the parent of an infant because you may not yet be familiar with your child's development or temperament. Victoria, mother of three, says, "I feel that my first child was my greatest experiment. I learned my parenting through her. I wish it weren't so, but it's true." Like Victoria, all first time parents are "figuring it out" with their first child. This makes anticipating what your child will do a little more difficult. After all, with your first child you may have little experience with either typical development or your child's specific temperament.

- **Clarity** is the principle related to knowing your non-negotiable limits. Remember that you won't be able to enforce your limits if you are unclear about what they are. There are, of course, non-negotiable limits for infants and toddlers. Squirming on the changing table, throwing food, getting out of your car seat, and climbing the stairs alone are just a few non-negotiables I can think of. Take the time to come up with a short list of rules you are clear about. Only then will you be able to create a plan to ensure your child gets these messages.

- **Communication** is just as necessary when parenting the infant or toddler as it is for a child any age. However, giving your infant or toddler big explanations for why you are doing something or why she can't do something isn't what I am talking about. Your challenge is to communicate with words and actions the messages you want your child to receive. Simply make your words and actions match. As you take your son's hand you say, "We always hold hands when we are on the stairs." The time for longer conversations about expectations and consequences will come, but for now keep it brief and simple.

- **Role modeling** is a powerful way for your infant or toddler to learn. Positive role modeling should begin as soon as your child is born. Because your child is so dependent on you for her care, she uses you almost exclusively to learn the ways in which she can get her needs met. When you play a game with your baby, have you ever noticed that the more you laugh, the more your baby will laugh? But be careful, your child is always watching. Because your infant or toddler loves to imitate to learn, sometimes he might imitate something you didn't know you were teaching.

- **Respect** is an important principle in proactive discipline for your child regardless of her age. Role modeling respect, creating clear behavioral expectations, teaching your child appropriate ways of getting his needs met is, in short, creating a proper fence. All these aspects of proactive discipline show respect to your unique and wonderful child. Embracing respect as you parent is by far the most important principle of this whole parenting approach.

The principles of **conflict discipline**...

- **Action,** not talking is important when you are in conflict. You don't ask the toddler to give you the knife, you take it. You don't threaten to leave the restaurant, you leave. So simple are these examples that you might think "how hard can that be?" But you would be surprised to see how many parents negotiate behavior all day with their infants and toddlers. Take a few moments in the next week or so to watch other parents or even reflect on your own behavior. Do you ask your child questions like, "Do you want to go to bed now?" or Do you encourage your child to struggle with you by saying something like, "If you do that one more time, I'll..." Remember, action sends a stronger and less negotiable message to your child. And it is much easier to use this kind of action when your child is young.

- **Authority** is the principle of being in charge. If you are the parent of an infant or toddler, you probably don't have too much trouble with this principle. The younger your child is, the easier it is to see yourself as needing to be in charge of your child's behavior. Obviously, you need to be in charge of bedtime, mealtime and playtime. Unfortunately, this principle gets harder to put into practice as your child becomes more independent.
- **Consistency** is to parenting as location is to real estate. You simply must have it. Remember, consistency in conflict discipline relates to always acting on misbehavior but not necessarily acting on behavior in exactly the same way. Behavior can only be modified when positive behaviors are positively reinforced and negative behaviors are negatively reinforced. In fact, it is the consistency with which you parent now that lays the foundation for behavior in the future. If you get the skills "in the bag," the lessons are learned. For more on behavioral skill building and getting skills "in the bag," review Chapter 2.
- **Emotional Integrity** for the tired parent of an infant or a toddler is difficult. Your child is dependent on you physically and emotionally and let's face it, that is draining. Personally, I think parenting an infant or toddler is the most physically demanding. And when you're tired, it is harder to keep your cool. But it is so important to remain calm and centered as you parent your infant or toddler. Many of the issues that frustrate you have only to do with your child's desire to learn about the world she lives in and nothing to do with a need to drive you crazy. The best way to stay in control is to have age-appropriate expectations of your child and to take care of yourself. If you have an infant or toddler, it may be hard to find time to put energy back in your precious jar. Take a break by walking, reading or going out with friends. As long as you know your child is safely being cared for by someone else, meeting your personal needs may be just what you need to handle the everyday challenges of parenting a young child.
- **Predictability** is very important to the infant or toddler. More than any other developmental period, your child

wants predicable routines. Bedtimes, naptimes, mealtimes and playtimes routinely scheduled will help your child behave at his best. Sure you can change the routines from time to time, but know that you will have to pay a price. While you don't need to be rigid about schedules, it is important to know that structured routines help your child enormously to make sense of the world she lives in.

The principles of **societal discipline**...

- **Awareness** is the principle of knowing just what your infant or toddler is being exposed to outside your family. Your child could be exposed to the influences of childcare providers, family members or neighborhood children. Believe it or not, your infant or toddler's behavior could be affected by television he is passively watching. While clearly the influences your child is exposed to are greater as she gets older, she is still being influenced by the popular culture even now.
- **Commitment** toward eliminating or reducing exposure to negative influences is important starting right now. Your infant or toddler need not watch television especially news or reality programming. Caregivers who are aggressive either verbally or physically are not the best role models for your developing child. Make the commitment to know about and make decisions about the kind of influences you want your child exposed to or not.
- **Honesty** refers to being honest with your child about how you feel about certain influences. Since your child is so young, sometimes you can simply eliminate or reduce the influence you object to without your child even being aware of it. If you are unhappy with a childcare provider that smokes or uses physical punishment, you can switch providers. In other instances, it will be important to make a brief honest remark to your child as you act. For example, "We don't watch the TV while we eat", as you turn off the television.
- **Communication** in societal discipline refers to the honest and rich conversations you have with your child about the impact of society on behavior. This principle

of societal discipline will come more into play when your child becomes a preschool age child.

- **Supervision** is intense for the parent of an infant or toddler. It is very hands on and in the moment. The supervision of your child at this age is primarily about safety but it should also be about reinforcing positive behaviors and extinguishing negative behaviors. Remember, for more on behavioral skill building refer back to Chapter 2.

An infant case study

Now that I have discussed the fine points of the discipline principles for infants and toddlers, let's use *The ASK Yourself Strategy* to look at how the discipline strategies for a typical situation involving an infant would be affected.

Sleeping through the night

Madison is a seven-month-old infant who has always had difficulty settling down for her naps, much to her parents' dismay. She has trouble at night now too. She goes to bed at nine o'clock at night after a long and specific bedtime routine. She cries for about one half-hour but after Mom goes in two or three times, she settles down. She wakes at least twice per night. Mom and Dad are so tired that by the second awakening, one of them usually just takes her into their bed until morning.

A good night's sleep is something all parents of a young child daydream about. But when can you expect this momentous occasion to occur? The most notable experts on children and sleep offer opposing theories. So for many parents, teaching your child good sleep habits can feel like navigating an unfamiliar landscape with conflicting maps. Two of the leading experts on sleep are Dr. William Sears, who advocates sleeping with your child as an aspect of what is commonly called "attachment parenting," and Dr. Richard Ferber, who promotes a gradual and systematic process by which your child sleeps alone and learns to soothe himself back to sleep with less and less intervention from you. Pretty different approaches, don't you think? Given such contradictory expert advice, is it any wonder you feel confused? Proactive Parenting advocates an approach that encourages parents to choose one method and then stick with it. While sleep issues in your child are developmentally expected from time to time, you should be able to enjoy a good night's sleep most of the time. The mistake a parent may often make is to choose the Ferber method one night and the Sears method the next night, based on their own fatigue level. This inconsistency is confusing both to you and to your child. What matters most is that you choose and/or modify an approach that you believe in, and then stay with it. Consistency around bedtime routines is your strongest asset as a parent.

In the situation with Madison and her parents, they made it clear to me that they did not want her in their bed. This means that they were not willing to adopt "the family bed." It should be noted here that the American Academy of Pediatrics discourages sleep sharing because of the potential for infant suffocation. Because Madison's parents wanted her to be successful in falling asleep and staying asleep, I helped them to develop a proactive plan for sleeping through the night. To do this we began with *The ASK Yourself Strategy.*

A. Age and development of the child

It is important to note here that the first question to ask is always the following. Is the child developmentally on track for her age? If a child has a developmental delay then expectations should be geared toward developmental age not chronological age. So as we reflected on age appropriate expectations, here are some of the questions I encouraged Madison's parents to ask. Is Madison old enough to sleep through the night and nap successfully during the day? Can you expect Madison to calm herself when she is upset or tired? The answer to both of these questions is yes. Madison, at age seven months is at an age where she can begin to learn better self-regulation. Seven-month-old infants, if on the growth chart for height and weight, can successfully sleep through the night without feeding. However, learning healthy sleep habits is a process that will take time and a process that must be taught. Can you really expect a seven-month-old to go to bed with much less effort on the part of the parents? The answer is yes. Madison can learn, with the right bedtime routine and structure, how to soothe herself to sleep and stay there.

S. Situation

Is the bedtime situation structured in the best way possible for teaching new skills? Is Madison going to sleep when she is overtired or after she is overstimulated? Is the home environment consistent enough for her to develop healthier sleep patterns? Are there other transitions occurring in the family that would impact Madison's ability to learn? If multiple providers are caring for Madison, are they aware of what you are trying to teach? If not, how will this affect her ability to learn these calming skills? Since all babies have less reserve energy at the end of the day, is Madison going to have opportunities early in the day to practice self-calming? If any of these questions raise issues that would negatively impact learning, then they should be factored into the proactive plan for helping Madison become more successful at falling and staying asleep.

K. Know the child

Given Madison's temperament and the situation, are expectations appropriate? Remember what you learned about temperament in Chapter 2. The elements of temperament that may come into play here are the following. Is Madison active? Does she often have trouble settling down? Does Madison have difficulty adapting to change? Will she be persistent in getting you to come back into her room? Will she react intensely to whatever plan you try? Knowing Madison's temperament will help you to know whether learning these new skills will be easy or a bit more difficult. The most common myth I hear is when a parent says, "my child really doesn't need much sleep." This usually means your child is in the driver's seat at bedtime. Remember, Madison like any child can be taught to go to sleep more effortlessly, even if she is strong willed.

PROACTIVE PLAN

Using *The ASK Yourself Strategy* to gather information will make developing a proactive plan for Madison much easier. Armed with new insight, here is the plan Madison's parents and I developed.

Proactive strategies

Have proactive conversations
• Spend time as a couple discussing which aspects of the routine you want to keep and which you want to let go of. While proactive conversations typically happen between parent and child, in this example, you and your spouse have the proactive conversation about the proactive plan.

Set expectations and discuss consequences
• Put Madison to bed before she's fully asleep. The earlier she begins to learn to soothe herself, the better.
• Simplify the bedtime routine such as feeding, changing and reading one short story.
• Start the bedtime routine much earlier. Back up the actual bedtime by one-half hour until you get to the right bedtime. A seven-month-old requires about fourteen total hours of sleep, split between nighttime sleep and one or two naps to behave well and stay healthy.
• Remember nighttime and naptime should be a quiet time. Madison will learn the sleep expectations from you when sleep time is not playtime.
• Have a plan for conflict. Madison will resist the simplified plan until she is sure that you will be consistent.

Explore other factors affecting behavior
• Set aside a week free of baby-sitters or overnights elsewhere to do this. Expect that this change will take three or more nights depending on how persistent Madison is to change.
• Be sure you have the energy to be consistent and be sure that you don't have factors present that will negatively

impact your success. You should not try the new plan if Madison is sick, for example.

Provide emotional coaching and problem solving
- Watch your baby. Put whatever energy you have into watching how Madison already uses light, sound and movement to calm herself.
- Learn Madison's unique cries. Some cries mean, "I'm hungry." Some cries mean, "I want you to hold me." Learning what Madison is trying to communicate will help you to better meet her needs.
- Make sleep a priority for everyone. Get sleep when your baby sleeps...you need your energy to care for your baby.
- Be patient. These are complicated sleep associations that you are trying to change and it will take time.

Spend time together
- Be sure that the time you spend with Madison, away from bedtime, is loving and fun. You want her to get the message that you love her, but that at bedtime you are all business.
- Let Madison play in natural light, such as in front of a window. The moving trees and white light are wonderfully calming. You will be nearby but you will be letting her practice self-calming. A few minutes in front of the window in the morning is a good place to start.
- Let Madison practice calming herself early in the day. A little time goes a long way. Don't ever let your baby get "stressed." Remember, this is a process and will take time. Late afternoon and early evening are not the best times for her to practice because she will have the least amount of reserve energy.

Conflict strategies

Establish authority
- Make bedtime a serious time. Don't talk once sleep time has arrived.
- Don't rush to pick up your child if you hear her wake up. Sometimes she will use her voice, even if she is crying, to settle back to sleep after a partial awakening.

- Always rush to your child if the crying is unusually sudden, loud, or distressed.

Be direct and specific about non-negotiables

- Reassure Madison. On the first night you may go in her room, but don't talk. Just reassure her with a back rub or by putting her down. The talking you do would make Madison think that this new bedtime routine is negotiable.
- Increase the amount of time between going in to reassure. If you hear her cry getting softer, don't go in. She is actually learning how to do this and by going in you will be interrupting the learning.

Remain calm

- Control your own feelings of frustration. Your daughter is not doing this to frustrate you; she really doesn't know how to do this without your coaching.
- Support each other. As parents, you will need to reassure each other that this will be a change for the better. If following through on the plan gets too challenging, rely on each other for when to reexamine how the plan should be modified.

Provide consequences

- Make the action fit the message. If Madison is to go to sleep now, then going in at increased intervals to lay her down gives this message. She is an infant and this is not about punishment...it is about teaching her to rely on herself.
- Try soothing measures other than talking when your baby is crying. Imagine how confused she will be if you talk to her when she needs to have her position or diaper changed.

Make an impact

- Be prepared for Madison to be emotional. Making this kind of impact will be worth it. Madison needs the sleep she is missing and needs you to help her learn to fall asleep on her own.

- Be consistent. You must use the same process for middle of the night waking. Madison has learned that she doesn't need to fall asleep on her own, in the middle of the night, because you will come and get her.

Societal strategies

Learn about influences and their impact
- Think about the other influences that might add to the challenge. If care providers put Madison in for her naps and you take care of bedtime, it will be important for everyone to handle this in the same way.
- Teach caregivers exactly what you want them to do. The more consistency your child experiences, the quicker she will learn.

Explore feelings and desires related to "fitting in"
(This particular strategy does not apply because of the type of situation and because Madison is an infant.)

Monitor influences
- Keep social obligations to a minimum during the intense learning. It will be hard enough for the baby to be successful without the distractions of another environment. It doesn't mean you can't go anywhere, just keep sleep a priority.

Set limits on inappropriate influences
- Try to resist the urge to follow other people's timeline on sleep and naps. Madison will learn healthy sleep patterns in due time and with the right coaching. You need to do what is right for your family.
- Eliminate any television exposure before bedtime. Sometimes images "get stuck" in your child's head and real fears begin to surface as a result, making it hard to fall asleep.

Skill build and teach appropriate ways
to handle societal influences
- Make sure this is the right time to engage in this time consuming task. Being consistent and taking the time

to help your baby learn the necessary skills will take concentrated effort.
• Be patient. Teaching healthy sleep habits takes time but is well worth the effort.

Madison's parents used this plan to teach their daughter healthy sleep patterns. When I met with them two weeks later, Mom said, "Madison slept better after only two days following through with the plan. Now, when she wakes up or fusses, we just stick to the plan and she goes right to sleep." Understanding what your child is capable of from a developmental perspective and understanding your child's unique temperament helps you to create an individualized plan for maximizing sleep in your family. And every parent knows that maximizing sleep patterns benefits everyone! Being proactive in developing a family plan for sleep will secure good sleep patterns for all. The key to establishing healthy sleep patterns for your child is choosing an approach that suits your child and family, and then practicing the Three Cs of good sleep habits: consistency, consistency, consistency! Of course, once good patterns are established, you can be flexible on occasion. But keep in mind that every time you change the plan; your child must adjust. Your child's sleep pattern will be altered by vacations and late-night visits with friends, and her behavior the next day will remind you how wonderful a good routine can be. Think about the practical suggestions Madison's parents and I developed. You can incorporate some of these into your plan for achieving healthy sleep patterns in your family. Practice them regularly. After all, good sleep habits for your child begin with you.

A toddler case study

Now that I have discussed a typical infant situation, let's use *The ASK Yourself Strategy* to look at how the discipline strategies for a typical situation involving a toddler would be affected.

To go or not to go

Reggie is about to turn three and he is not yet toilet trained. All of his little friends are using the bathroom and his mom is starting to think it is time to start actively teaching Reggie to use the toilet. He is enrolled in preschool for September and the policy states that he can not go unless he is trained. His mom came to Proactive Parenting seeking advice about whether or not Reggie is ready to train.

Like every other aspect of parenting, toilet training your child is an active process. You can be proactive by making a few decisions in advance. Although there are many ways to teach a child to master the skills of using the toilet, the Proactive Parenting approach meets with the most success. Your child can become independent fairly quickly if he is ready when you begin. The physical signs of readiness to toilet train include dry diapers in the morning or after a nap and your child having a sense that he is "going". Emotional signs of readiness may include your child expressing a desire to use the toilet or have big boy underwear. Your child may take to toilet training in a variety of ways. Some learn quickly, some are successful with urination and not with bowel movements, and some want nothing to do with the process at all. Of all the practical tips, you may have heard or read about, being consistent in your efforts to teach your child and having a positive attitude are the keys to your child's success. In this situation, Reggie's parents and I agreed that we needed to know more about whether he was physically and emotionally ready to begin the toilet training process. Again, using *The ASK Yourself Strategy* helped us gather the information necessary to increase the likelihood of Reggie's success.

A. Age and development of the child

Is Reggie old enough to begin toilet training? Can you expect a child this age to use the bathroom independently? The answers to these questions have more to do with developmental readiness than with chronological age. And the answer may be yes or no. Reggie is certainly at an age where he can begin to learn how to use the toilet. However, if he shows no physical or emotional signs of being ready, the process will be complex and perhaps unsuccessful.

S. Situation

Ask yourself, "Am I ready for the challenge? The right attitude can make or break this process. Remember, Reggie will take his lead from his parents. Is the situation for training the best it can be for getting Reggie's cooperation, encouraging responsibility and accepting limits? Can Reggie learn what he needs to know to use the toilet? Are other transitions in your family being kept to a minimum? Just after having a new baby or during a move would be examples where the situation wouldn't be optimal for tackling toilet training. Summertime when your child has less clothing to contend with or on an extended home vacation would be times when training may go more smoothly.

K. Know the child

Given Reggie's temperament and the situation, are expectations appropriate? Is Reggie the kind of child that will eagerly participate or dramatically resist? Will he want to achieve this new skill or be hesitant? Will he take each accident to heart or go with the flow so to speak? Everything you know about Reggie's temperament will influence this proactive plan for toilet training.

PROACTIVE PLAN

After using *The ASK Yourself Strategy* to gather information about readiness, now we are ready to develop a proactive plan for Reggie's toilet training experience. Here is the plan Reggie's parents and I developed.

Proactive Strategies

Have proactive conversations
- Decide what words you will use to describe body parts and the process of elimination and be sure to teach them to Reggie. Remember, other people will hear the words you choose, so try to avoid using words that suggest that the process is dirty or embarrassing.
- Set the stage for your expectations for using the toilet. Engage Reggie in conversation and let him ask questions.

Set expectations and discuss consequences

- Think about whether you will allow your child to choose between a diaper and underwear. Or will you just go with underwear and contend with accidents. Since the process is about learning physical sensations, going with underwear and being matter of fact about accidents often teaches your child more quickly what it feels like to start and stop eliminating.
- Tell Reggie exactly when you will start toilet training. Make the countdown fun by using colorful stickers or a calendar.
- Be sure and let him know that accidents will happen. Tell him how you will handle this and why there is no need to get upset about them.

Explore other factors affecting behavior

- Take a seat, boys. It is easier for a boy to learn to use the toilet sitting down. Once he is well practiced at toileting, he can learn to urinate standing up.
- Limit fluids to regular amounts. Both increasing and decreasing the amount of liquids a child drinks will influence his regular pattern of elimination.
- Make sure through gentle conversation and through observable behavior that Reggie isn't fearful of using the toilet.

Provide emotional coaching and problem solving

- Go shopping for new underwear. Reggie will feel like he is part of the process if he can pick out his own big boy underwear.
- Purchase a potty-chair. While there are rings that adapt to your toilet, it is common for a child to be frightened that he may fall in the big toilet. Be sure the chair you choose can be emptied easily.
- Read a good book. There are several good books geared specifically toward boys or girls about learning to use the toilet.

Spend time together

- Have fun, especially since you will be spending extended periods at home in order to make the most of toilet training. Plan in advance what you and Reggie will do to make the best of staying put.

Conflict strategies

Establish authority

- Keep talking to a minimum. Treating the situation in a businesslike manner gives Reggie the message that you expect him to follow the bathroom rules.
- Be consistent. Switching between underwear and diapers can make the learning more difficult. Reggie needs to learn the feeling of controlling the sphincters that stop and start urination and bowel movements.

Be direct and specific about non-negotiables

- Be positive. When the day arrives to begin toilet training, be upbeat and supportive of what your child must learn. Let him know that accidents will happen and are part of learning how to use the toilet.
- Be direct and specific about what you expect Reggie to do. Keep negative remarks and excess excitement to a minimum; you want him to see this as a typical expectation for a "big boy."

Remain calm

- Remain calm. Remember, Reggie is still a little child. His feelings about toilet training may be mixed and he needs love and encouragement.
- Never force your child to use the toilet. He will quickly learn that this means more to you than to him. If he is in a negative developmental phase or trying to exert his control by not using the toilet, it may be a good idea to take a break and start again at a later time.

Provide consequences

- Let nature take its course. The natural consequence in toilet training is to let the accidents happen. It will be the physical sensation of stopping and starting to go that Reggie needs experience with.
- Be matter of fact about accidents. When an accident occurs just help him to get cleaned up and say something

like, "This is how you learn. Next time you feel that you have to go, let's run to the toilet." Toilet training is a process and set backs are inevitable.

Make an impact
- Let the natural consequences do the trick. Don't struggle or punish. Mild resistance on the part of your child is to be expected. But if you are constantly in a battle for control, your child may not be ready. You might want to reconsider toilet training at this time.

Societal strategies

Learn about influences and their impact
- Don't worry about Reggie's preschool start date. You should be training him because he is ready and not because of the preschool requirements.
- Accept the pace at which your child learns. It is normal for a child to be successful with urination and have more difficulty learning to control bowel movements. After all, these are different processes and each must be learned separately.

Explore feelings and desires related to "fitting in"
- Motivate Reggie by talking to him about his friends who have already learned to use the potty. Be sure to remind him of the friends who have yet to learn how to use the potty also.

Monitor influences
- Keep social obligations to a minimum during the intense learning. It will be hard enough for Reggie to remember everything he needs to be successful without the distractions of another environment such as public toilets.

Set limits on inappropriate influences
- Try to resist the urge to train Reggie on other people's timeline. Keep other adults and children from comparing or coaxing him to use the toilet. He will learn when he is ready and not because of the pressure from others.

**Skill build and teach appropriate ways
of handling societal influences**

- Be patient. While it seems like a major issue now, in time it will be a distant memory.
- If you decide the time is right, be prepared to focus on this developmental milestone in a loving and helpful manner. Your child needs your support to learn successfully.
- Set aside the time it will take. Dedicating three days in a row to teaching the necessary skills will allow Reggie to have success early. It will be hard for him to be consistent in telling you he has to go if you're in a busy mall or on a long drive.

With the proactive plan outlined here, Reggie and his parents had a positive toilet training experience. Reggie was using the toilet after a three day weekend, with only an occasional accident at night. At the end of two weeks, Reggie was independently using the toilet.

You can modify their plan to best fit your style of discipline and your specific family concerns. If you are a working parent who doesn't foresee being able to do this over an extended period, try starting on a three-day weekend. But be sure to review the readiness signs to be sure your toddler is really ready to learn. Your child can make a lot of progress in three days if she is truly ready. Talk to your childcare provider in advance about your plan to toilet train your child. Ask how the childcare agency handles toilet training. This is a common concern for working parents but remember, your childcare provider deals with this issue often and should be working with you on this skill development. Agree on a plan for your child in the childcare environment that supports your philosophy and action plan at home. For example, consider supplying your childcare provider with a similar potty chair and plenty of extra clothes. This will help your child feel "at home" while toilet training in childcare. Consistency once again will be more than half the battle, and well worth it for your child.

Chapter summary

In using Proactive Parenting for your infant or toddler, I recommend developmentally specific proactive, conflict and societal strategies. With proactive discipline, it is important of course to begin with age appropriate expectations. Only then, can you role model proper behavior. Keep in mind that as you use proactive discipline you should be paying particular attention to anticipation, supervision, redirection and distraction.

Conflict discipline is important for your infant or toddler. Don't ignore your non-negotiable limits. Remember by using small actions in conflict this kind of discipline will be easier than you might think. Remember to use the word "no" sparingly. I am much more in favor of small actions, repetition or brief isolation with a clear message.

Societal discipline, while clearly not the most significant type of discipline you will provide to your infant or toddler, is still something you should begin thinking about. Perhaps before reading this book you didn't think society impacted your young child at all. I hope that now you will look at the societal influences to your child in a new way and begin making the necessary commitment to take charge of these influences in a more proactive way.

When providing Proactive Parenting to the infant or toddler, the proactive parent remembers that...

* Learning about development and temperament begin the process of Proactive Parenting.
* Your infant or toddler requires all three types of discipline.
* Proactive Parenting with the child under the age of three is the easiest of all times to begin parenting this way.
* Planning strategies in advance for situations you know your child will have difficulty with is key.
* Proactive Parenting with the child under the age of three will set the stage for good decision-making in the future for both you and your child.

Questions and Answers
Chapter 7

Get Their Feet Wet

How The Approach Works With Children Under Three

Q: Proactive discipline seems to be about setting the stage for behavior in advance through proactive conversations. How can that kind of discipline be effective with an infant or toddler?

A: You're right, proactive discipline involves conversation but it assumes that the talking you do is age appropriate. For your infant or toddler, the talking you do will be brief, specific to what you want to teach and your words should match your actions. Keep in mind proactive discipline is also about proper role modeling, demonstrating respect for your child and anticipating situations where more planning is required. These aspects of proactive discipline are very important for your infant or toddler.

Q: I have a two-year-old who refuses to stay in the "time out" chair. How can I make this strategy work for me?

A: I am not an advocate of "time out" because often the child most in need of gaining self-control is the child least likely to get anything out of being placed in a chair and waiting for a timer to go off. Providing action in conflict discipline should be done right on the spot and moving a child to a "time out" location is rarely effective. If you would like to learn more about how to establish authority in conflict in more effective ways, refer to Chapter 4.

Q: I am a stay-at-home Mom and I never let my child watch television. Are there any societal issues related to my eighteen-month-old child that would require societal discipline?

A: While you may not have childcare or television to contend with, keep your eyes open for other influences that would require this type of teaching such as other playmates, other adults, toys and videos just to name a few. In order to parent in our complex society, you need specific strategies for teaching your child how society influences her behavior. This kind of discipline gives your child the skills she needs to make the right decisions even in everyday play situations.

EIGHT

Dive In

How The Approach Works
With Children Three To Nine

Grace and Kevin have been using the Proactive Parenting principles and strategies with their four children for six years. The children range in age from three to eight years old. "We knew we needed to do something different after our second son, Ian was born. He was harder to parent right from the start. Because Ian can be challenging, we have learned to anticipate where and when he will have difficulty and how to plan for his success. Now we approach all of our parenting decisions so differently. And to tell you the truth, all the children benefit from our proactive rather than reactive style."

Proactive Parenting is the most comprehensive approach you can use with children between the ages of three and nine. While preschool children and school age children have different abilities to learn, you can tailor Proactive Parenting to the specific developmental age of your child. After about age three, your child is capable of understanding that his actions have consequences. And because of this, at each stage of development, your expectations for behavior will need to be broadened to fit your child's expanding capabilities. In this chapter, I will review how your preschool or school age child thinks and learns. Using Proactive Parenting with a child between the ages of three and nine has some nuances. So, I will also discuss, how to apply the principles of Proactive Parenting specifically to your child age three to nine. I will do this first by examining the discipline principles you use with your child and then by using a case study for each age group.

The way you discipline a three-year-old who is disrespectful will be different from how you discipline a nine-year-old who is disrespectful. But when you focus on how your child thinks and learns, you will find it much easier to teach cooperation as well as acceptable ways of behaving. The strategies you use with your child will be geared toward her specific age, development, situation and temperament. So, let's review what you know about thinking and learning for a child between the ages of three and nine.

Thinking and learning for preschool and school age children

Your child by age three is beginning to understand that his actions have consequences. In comparison to the infant or toddler, your child is more consistently able to think before he acts. He can understand that you don't throw the ball in the living room because you might break the lamp. With guidance and support, your child will respond to your age appropriate expectations. As your child reaches age nine, the consistency with which she is able to think in advance of her actions is amazing. In Chapter 2, I described how your child thinks and learns based on her developmental age. Remember, cause and effect thinking is the hallmark of learning during this developmental period. Therefore, using Proactive Parenting with the preschool through school age child is aimed at teaching cause and effect. If you do *this...that* will happen.

As your child moves from preschooler to school age child, he is learning to connect and organize his feelings. As he builds his social network, he is developing a moral conscience. Using his unique style or temperament, learning takes place both in and out of his home. Your child's temperament will clearly affect how successful she is getting along at home, learning in school and making friends. Is she eager to go to school or does she complain of a stomachache every Monday? Does he cry when he hurts a friend's feelings or does he deny wrongdoing? Knowing about preschool and school age development as well as your child's unique temperament will be so helpful as you shape your child's behavior. I have developed charts that review some important milestones in preschool and school age development that have an impact on how you provide discipline for your child. Again, this would be a good time to take the *Discovering Your Child's Style* quiz, if you haven't done so already. It is found in Chapter 2.

Developmental Milestones
That Impact Discipline
Preschool and School Age Children

Note: All milestone information is approximate.
Your child will learn at his own pace and in his own time.
If you are concerned however, please contact your pediatrician
or child development expert.

Cognitive development...
refers to how your child thinks.

By age four, your child...

understands actions have consequences.
uses language to get her needs met.
has good memory skills.

By age six, your child...

has emerging reading and number skills.
can categorize information.
understands time.

By age eight, your child...

continues to learn concretely.
enjoys hands on learning.
explores his unique interests.

Developmental Milestones
That Impact Discipline
Preschool and School Age Children

Note: All milestone information is approximate.
Your child will learn at his own pace and in his own time.
If you are concerned however, please contact your pediatrician
or child development expert.

Affective development...
refers to how your child feels.

By age four, your child...

wants predictable routines.
knows how to get attention.
shows genuine concern for others.

By age six, your child...

wants others to "like him".
enjoys his social/academic success.
talks about his feelings.

By age eight, your child...

seeks approval from others.
begins to identify with a peer group.
prefers same sex friendships.

Developmental Milestones
That Impact Discipline
Preschool and School Age Children

Note: All milestone information is approximate.
Your child will learn at his own pace and in his own time.
If you are concerned however, please contact your pediatrician
or child development expert.

Psychomotor development...
refers to how your child moves.

By age four, your child...

is more independent with self-care.
loves physical play.
can sit for longer periods, if engaged.

By age six, your child...

is independent with self-care.
needs physical outlets.
has better fine motor... tying shoes/pencil grip.

By age eight, your child...

is in a slow period of growth.
is working on coordination skills.
is refining fine and gross motor skills.

Proactive Parenting for preschool and school age children

In Chapters 3, 4 & 5, I've gone into detail about the principles that apply to each of the three types of discipline that make up Proactive Parenting. Now I would like to review the principles and make brief comments on how they apply to your preschool or school age child.

The principles of **proactive discipline**...

- **Anticipation** and your child's success go hand in hand. When your child becomes a preschooler, his temperament is in full bloom. Now, you are able to anticipate how he will handle almost every situation. You may not know exactly what he will do but you know what kind of situations set him up for success or failure. You know your child better than anyone, so plan with that wonderful knowledge in mind. If you know that a warm bath after dinner ensures a smooth bedtime...then make time for bathtime. If you know that without a nap your child is difficult...then make time for naptime. Take the time to think about your day in advance, and plan ahead so that your child is able to be at his best.
- **Clarity** or the principle related to knowing your non-negotiable limits is important at every age. Keep in mind that at each developmental stage you will have new non-negotiables limits to relay to your child. As your child becomes more independent, you will have new expectations for her. Exactly what are the expectations for going to school, talking with teachers, going to a friend's house or playing outside? When you know what your expectations are, only then can you be certain that your child does too. Clarity around non-negotiable limits will be critical when it comes to following through in conflict discipline.
- **Communication** takes on a new depth in parenting the preschooler or school age child. Your proactive conversations can be a bit longer and can include time for your child to express her feelings about expectations. Be careful though, the preschool or school age child still needs conversations about expectations to be short and

sweet. And don't lecture; during proactive discipline, talking *with* your child not *at* your child is the goal. There are many good times in the life of your preschooler or school age child for proactive conversations. Mealtime, bedtime and driving time are great opportunities to discuss expectations, feelings about expectations and problem solving. Make the most of the time you already have to talk with your child.

• **Role modeling** during the preschool and school age period changes but is nonetheless significant. During this stage of moral development, your child is beginning to scrutinize your actions. "But Mommy you don't eat your vegetables" or "Why does Daddy get to stay home from church?" Remember that actions often speak louder than words. So, be sure that your actions match what you are saying to your child. The rules and expectations in your family have more weight if they apply to the whole family. And if they don't, be prepared to talk about why not.

• **Respect** like everything else is actively taught. The preschool and school age period is a great time to talk with your child about exactly which behaviors are respectful as well as those that are not. Teach your child that showing respect involves equal parts of...what you say and how you say it. Show your child how the same sentence said in two different ways conveys a very different message. Tone of voice and body language play a much larger role than words do in letting someone know how you feel. Talk about respect often but do so when your child is being respectful. She will be much more capable of learning about this valuable value.

The principles of **conflict discipline**...

• **Action** defines conflict discipline. The most common parenting mistake made during the preschool and school age period is reasoning with a child in conflict. Just because your child is now capable of more sophisticated language skills doesn't mean talking is always the best tactic. In fact, talking in conflict teaches your child that the limits are negotiable. Simple action in conflict is always the first order of business. If your child is not getting ready for school because he is distracted by television then shut off the TV. If your child plays roughly with the blocks then it is time to put them away. If your child is persistent, he will more than likely resist your simple actions but start simply anyway. Starting simple shows your child that you won't overreact to his resistance and it also allows you the opportunity to extend additional consequences if your child chooses to continue to misbehave. For more on how to "raise the bar" on providing consequences in conflict see Chapter 4.

- **Authority** should be established whenever your child disregards established limits. If you spend most of your time being proactive with your preschooler or school age child, you may find that you have to establish authority less and less often. Once your preschooler learns self-control, which is a major developmental milestone, you will enjoy a period when conflict is much reduced. The school age child demonstrates more consistent self-control, more independence and more creative problem solving. But if your child is more sensitive, more persistent, more intense or moody, her extremes of temperament may keep the two of you struggling. Be prepared to be the authority figure your child needs you to be regardless of how old she is.

- **Consistency** in following through on established limits is just as important to the preschool or school age child as it is for the infant or toddler. Remember, if you said, "never to hit" then you must be willing to convey the message that hitting will never be tolerated, every time your child hits. Being consistent, isn't about doing the *same thing* necessarily it is about doing *something* every time a non-negotiable limit is disregarded. Providing consistency is totally about your willingness to stand firm on the rules you have established. Be sure and take the time, out of conflict, to reevaluate your rules, though. While you may never have allowed your toddler to walk without holding your hand, now perhaps your preschooler can.

- **Emotional integrity** or the ability to keep your feelings and emotions in check as you teach your child acceptable ways of behaving should be getting easier now that your child is less dependent on you physically and is more independent emotionally. And if you have successfully learned how to follow through on the non-negotiable limits you've established, you need not lose your cool. Temperament comes into play here though, for your preschool or school age child may have figured out how to "push your hot buttons." If so, you will need to work harder than ever to stay in control in conflict. Remember yelling, giving commands at a distance and struggling over control are all counter productive and take from your "precious jar of energy". For more on protecting your precious jar of energy, see Chapter 4.

- **Predictability** is all about having a plan for discipline. Armed with a plan, you can preserve the energy you need to teach your child that her actions have consequences. While your preschool or school age child is enjoying newfound independence, he still needs predictable routines, limits and consequences. If you don't eat healthy food, you won't get treats. If you hurt your sister, you will need to play alone. The plan you create in advance of conflict allows you to keep your emotions under control in conflict. When your emotions are under control, you can follow through more effectively and more predictably.

The principles of **societal discipline**...

- **Awareness** raising about societal influences by now should be in full swing. Television, toys, video games, friends, coaches and teachers contribute to your child's identity. Popular culture tugs at every preschooler and has a tight grip by school age. The time has come to learn everything you can about what your child knows and is exposed to in the world he lives in. Find out about toys before you buy them. Find out about shows before he watches them. Don't let our complex society have a larger hand in raising your child than you do.

- **Commitment** to taking a stand on societal influences is of course hard, but oh so worth the energy. Violent toys sanction aggression. Disrespectful playmates role model disrespectful behavior. Making the commitment to eliminate or reduce exposure to unacceptable influences will never get any easier. In fact, if you don't start now i will get harder. Your preschooler or school age child still identifies more strongly with what you think is important than with her peers. Being ambivalent about what your beliefs are only leaves the door open for your child to test the boundaries of acceptable behavior. Think ahead, plan ahead and make the choices that are right for your child and your family.

- **Honesty** is, as they say, the best policy. Tell your child how you have raised your awareness about the day to day influences on her. Explain in simple yet understandable terms why he can't go to that movie or why you object to your neighbor's language. Your child lives among influences that he will form opinions about even if you don't put your spin on it. If parenting is all about teaching and learning, shouldn't you be a teacher? Your child should learn about values from you. There simply is no better filter for what is happening around your child than you are.

- **Communication** is the hallmark of societal discipline. Talking to your child about society and its impact on behavior should happen often and without lecturing. True dialogue about societal discipline should be an exchange between you and your child. Ask your son, why he thinks watching the news isn't the best thing for him to do. Tell your daughter how you felt when friends left you out as a child. In the preschool and school age period, the door to good healthy communication is usually already open. No matter what, you don't want to let that door close. The closer your child gets to adolescence, the harder it will be to push the door back open.

- **Supervision** starts to look a little different for your preschooler or school age child. But it definitely continues. Maybe your son can play successfully with his sister in the backyard but you should know exactly where he is and what he is doing. And for the mischievous child, maybe even sitting up on the deck would be too much freedom. You will need to learn how to create a delicate balance between your child's emerging independence and his need for a proper chaperone. While some parents recognize the continued importance of supervision for

age child, I worry about the school age
opular culture starts early to give us the
ages about spending time unsupervised.
taken, your school age child needs just as
rision as ever, you may just have to be more
creative in how you provide it.

A preschool age case study

Now that I have discussed the fine points of the discipline
principles for preschoolers and school age children, let's
use *The ASK Yourself Strategy* to look at how the discipline
strategies for a typical situation involving a preschooler
would be affected.

Self-control patrol

Lana is a five-year-old with a strong personality. She
has always had issues with tolerating frustration. Her
parents came to Proactive Parenting because Lana is
hitting children on the playground and after school.
Lana's parents thought that the behavior would get better
as Lana got older but it has not.

With recent studies showing long hours in child care
and too much television causing a child's behavior to
be more aggressive, Lana's parents were worried about
their child. While today's children are exposed to ever
increasing amounts of violence in our society, I assured
them that having a child who is aggressive is not inevitable. In fact, as a parent there is a lot you can do to
teach peaceful ways of resolving conflict. Many factors
impact whether or not your child will have aggressive
tendencies. The key is to understand why your child
may have problems with aggressive behavior so that the
strategies you choose will be most effective.

While never acceptable, it is developmentally expected
that a child two, three, and four will have more issues
with aggression than an older child. To some extent, your
child will struggle to communicate her needs to others
because of her emerging language skills. Your child may
also struggle with aggression because she has limited
experience resolving conflict. And while not always true,

more boys than girls have issues with aggression. Still, some experts argue that the way we play with boys may be more of a factor than gender alone; it is the age-old nature vs. nurture argument. The situation with Lana reminds us of the temperament factor. Remember, each child is born with a different set of strengths as well as different elements of temperament that need to be refined. If your child is more intense, more sensitive, or more persistent, this alone may lead to more issues tolerating frustration.

Your child learns so much from watching you. The way conflict is handled in your family will become the way in which your child will resolve conflict with siblings and friends. Whether too strict or too lenient, the way you provide discipline can be a factor in your child's aggressive behavior. The key to effective discipline is firm limit-setting and consistent follow through.

Don't forget the importance of sleep. Daytime behavior is a direct result of nighttime sleep. If aggressive behavior during the day is an issue, it may be helpful to increase periods of sleep and rest. For more information on sleep patterns, see Chapter 3. But I'd be remiss if I didn't mention the possibility of aggressive behavior being the result of a physical or neurological condition. Some health-related problems or chronic conditions can include an inability to handle frustration or anger. It is important to form a strong partnership with your child's pediatrician if you suspect physical reasons for your child's behavioral issues.

In addition to the factors that increase the likelihood of aggression in your child, there are also some influences that impact behavior. The kind of toys your child plays with can sanction aggressive behavior. Although a boy may use a stick as a gun, that is not the same as having an arsenal of toy weapons at his disposal. The television programs your child watches and the computer or video games she plays with clearly illustrate what behavior is considered acceptable. After all, if her favorite TV character hits a friend or shouts at her mother, why can't she hit and shout at you?

Your child will be influenced by her peers from a very early age. The behavior friends engage in and the consequences they receive will have a definite impact on your child. Regardless of the recent studies findings, you are your child's first and best teacher. The behavior you sanction and the actions you role model will go a long way in shaping your child's behavior, wherever she may go. If your child has experienced violence or someone close to her has, aggressive behavior may be her way of working out her feelings. Seek the help of a professional if you are concerned about how to help your child deal with her experience.

The good news however is that regardless of the factors influencing your child's aggression, the treatment of choice is developing a good behavioral plan. Let's look at the specific strategies Lana's parents used to decrease Lana's aggressive behavior. As always, we begin with *The ASK Yourself Strategy.*

A. Age and development of the child

Is it acceptable for a five-year-old to solve problems by hitting? The answer is no. In fact, while it may be developmentally expected that a younger child hits out of frustration, it is so important to let a child know that it is never an acceptable option for problem solving. Is Lana capable of using other more effective skills to solve problems? The answer is yes. Lana is capable of learning how to solve problems more effectively and in ways that are more age-appropriate, but someone must show her how.

S. Situation

Is Lana's everyday life a set up for success or a set up for frustration? Are the structures and routines she functions in going to teach cooperation and responsibility? What influences Lana's aggressive behavior? Is she exposed to aggression as a means of solving problems? Does she watch aggressive TV or play with other children who are aggressive? It will be very important that Lana's parents be willing to look at what might be influencing her behavior. Reexamine the limits that are placed on Lana's aggressive behavior. All of the situational factors must be looked at so that an individual plan can be created.

K. Know the child

Think about Lana's temperament...is she more susceptible to the influences around her because of her temperament? Is she more intense, more sensitive and more persistent than other children her age? Is she easily frustrated when things don't go as she expected? What are her strengths for problem solving or does she need lots of coaching to get those skills in her bag? All of what you know about Lana's temperament will influence the proactive plan you develop.

PROACTIVE PLAN

Using *The ASK Yourself Strategy* to reflect on the issue of aggression in this family is invaluable to developing a proactive plan for Lana. We begin by having compassion for how hard problem solving is for her. Here is the plan Lana's parents and I developed.

Proactive strategies

Have proactive conversations
- Talk to Lana about her feelings of frustration. Acknowledge the situations that pose the biggest challenge to her in getting along with other adults and children.
- Anticipate situations that are typically difficult for Lana. Talk to her about what is likely to happen and how she can be prepared for things that tend to take her by surprise.

Set expectations and discuss consequences
- Set firm limits in advance. This is the key to good discipline. It doesn't always mean she will behave accordingly, but it does set the stage for what is expected of her. Be sure to tell her the can do's and can't do's for playing with friends.
- Tell Lana exactly what you will do when she chooses aggressive ways of problem solving over the new, more effective ways you will teach her. "If you hit someone at the playground, first you will have to sit out for a minute and if you do it again, you will have to go home."

217

her factors affecting behavior

) bed. Daytime behavior is a direct result of ...giittime sleep. She may appear hyperactive or have a low tolerance for frustration when in fact she is just plain tired.

- Look at the children she is playing with. Do their elements of temperament clash with hers? Talk to her about how she reacts to her friends in play. Are there new ways of responding that will work better? If so, tell her what they are.

Provide emotional coaching and problem solving

- Role-play. Give Lana a chance to practice asking for a toy or waiting for a turn. Give her a typical situation that is hard for her, and act out different ways of behaving. Remember, tolerating frustration and disappointment are learned skills.
- Read books. Sharing a story with just the right story line can be a great way to share expectations and discuss challenging situations.
- Channel energy constructively. Lana may need to run around the backyard or do some jumping jacks before she can be expected to use her new ways of interacting with others. Her excess energy may be part of the issue and should be redirected.
- Give her creative outlets for expressing anger. Lana may need a constructive place to put her intense feelings. Perhaps a journal or a sketchbook where she can express herself would be helpful.

Spend time together

- Find a calm time to just play, read or snuggle with Lana. Don't underestimate how hard she is working to learn new ways of behaving. And remember, reward her efforts with love and attention, so that she feels valued and cared about instead of judged and critiqued.

Conflict strategies

Establish authority

- Be the authority that Lana needs when she is aggressive. It is important to recognize that it is in her best interest that you take control of situations that she can not.

- Role model effective conflict resolution. Lana is watching you and learning what is acceptable behavior when you're angry or frustrated.

Be direct and specific about non-negotiables
- Be clear and specific about the misbehavior. After the situation is under control, be sure you are clear about what she did that was unacceptable. Remember to wait until emotions are contained.

Remain calm
- Remain calm. It is fine to tell Lana that you are upset, but it is another to lose your temper. Remember, intense feelings whether hers or yours can be scary to her.
- Resist the urge to spank. If hitting or hurting is not acceptable as a way for Lana to solve her problems, it should not be role modeled to her.

Provide consequences
- Encourage Lana to breathe. Sometimes getting your child to take a deep breath breaks the connection between intense feelings and an inappropriate action.
- Separate Lana from others. Your child needs to get the message that inappropriate behavior has negative consequences. Removing your child from a difficult situation will help get her to focus on your message.

Make an impact
- Follow through. When you say you will leave the playground for hitting, then you must leave the playground when Lana hits another child. By following through, your child will learn that you mean what you say.

Societal strategies

Learn about influences and their impact
- Think about the influences affecting aggression. Which ones are adding to Lana's challenge to choose acceptable means of getting along with others? Are the influences other children, other adults, toys or television? You won't be able to set limits on these influences if you are unfamiliar with what is contributing to behavior.

Explore feelings and desires related to "fitting in"

- Validate Lana's feelings about how hard it is to develop social skills. She will be reluctant to learn effective social skills if you never acknowledge her struggles. Remember, in order for her to be ready to learn what to do next, she must have a chance to express her feelings.

Monitor influences

- Reevaluate your childcare situation. Is she over stimulated by being with thirty active children for many hours each day? While it may or may not be feasible to decrease your child's time in childcare, it is always worth considering. Perhaps minor adjustments could make a big difference. Only your family can decide what is right for you.
- Choose toys carefully. Toys that foster creativity, artistic expression, or just plain calm Lana down may be the best alternatives for this high-energy child.
- Limit TV. While there may be good programming on TV and in computer and video games, the child who tends to be aggressive would be better served with limited exposure to negative influences.

Set limits on inappropriate influences

- Reduce or limit exposure to influences that seem to increase Lana's aggressive behavior. Remember, you must first raise your awareness and then you must monitor influences that affect Lana. Finally, set limits on those influences that add to the problem.
- Choose friends thoughtfully. When your child is young, it will be easier to promote or discourage certain friendships. Finding a good fit will benefit you and your child.

Skill build and teach appropriate ways to handle societal influences

- Teach social skills. Parents are often surprised to find out that even a young child can benefit from an active approach to learning social skills. Lana has shown that she doesn't have the skills she needs to make and keep friends. So, give her positive and constructive feedback on what another child wants and needs.

After using this plan, Lana's parents found that simply raising their daughter's awareness about what else she could do when she was frustrated made a big difference. Her mother said, "It was so reassuring to see Lana use the ideas we gave her when she was playing with friends. I actually heard her say some of the things we said when we role played difficult situations."

The good news is that there is so much that you can do to teach your child how to get along in the world in calm and constructive ways. Showing your child that there are more effective ways of getting her needs met can be done by choosing just the right strategies. I believe that there are strategies to be used before your child loses her temper as well as strategies to use in the heat of the moment. But actively teaching your child new ways of solving old problems should take place out of conflict. Begin your teaching with proactive discipline, and soon your child will learn what works to successfully make and keep friends.

A school age case study

Now that I have discussed a typical preschool age situation, let's use *The ASK Yourself Strategy* to look at how the discipline strategies for a typical situation involving a school age child would be affected.

Strengthening the parent/teacher connection

Nick is an eight-year-old boy in third grade at his neighborhood elementary school. He is an active boy who loves sports and playing outdoors. During the summer, Nick participated in a number of sports and recreation camps. While last year he seemed happy about school, this year he is less enthusiastic about his educational experience. Each day after school, he changes his clothes and goes to an afterschool activity. After two weeks of school, Nick comes home and starts to scream, "I hate school! I am never going back to school again."

Back to school for many is a time of new clothes, new supplies and new attitudes. Once your child steps on that bus, you can breathe a sigh of relief...right? Not so, for the child who adjusts slowly to change or has increased academic pressures at school. You know your child better than anyone does. You can probably guess how your child will adjust to going to school. Whether it is your child's first preschool experience, a new grade in elementary school or entering middle or high school, each child will experience a period of adjustment. Keep in mind that each year, the teacher, the expectations for classwork, homework, and behavior are usually new. And for many, the school, the transportation, the classmates, the mealtimes, the schedule and routines may be new, too.

Based on your child's temperament and how he has made transitions in the past, you can expect that he will adjust in one of the following ways. He may be eager to go to school and adjust quickly to the expectations. He may be eager to go to school, but once there adjust slowly because what he expected is different from what he is experiencing. Or he may be hesitant to go to school and once there adjusts slowly to the requirements of being in school. While you may be hoping that your child is eager to go and adjusts quickly, most parents can expect one of the last two scenarios. Given all that your child must adjust to, is it any wonder that he may be apprehensive before school starts and that his adjustment may take as long as a month or two? Teachers anticipate that this period of adjustment will be harder on some than on others. Often, they don't see their class "in a groove" until the end of October. Still, there are things you can do as a parent that will encourage a smooth adjustment. Today, the role you play in your child's school success is more important than you might imagine. Although your child spends weekdays at school, he stills spends more time at home with you. As I've said before, you are your child's first and best teacher. Experiences you can provide everyday will make the transition back to school a smoother one. The proactive plan we develop will include some back to basic tips that will be invaluable in facilitating learning and making school success certain.

Let's look at the specific strategies Nick's parents used to ensure a smooth transition to school for Nick. Again, we begin with *The ASK Yourself Strategy*.

A. Age and development of the child.

Are Nick's outbursts after school to be expected given his age? The answer is no, when you look at development alone. An eight-year-old child typically has some coping strategies for handling adjustment even if it is stressful. Can eight-year-old Nick handle after-school social time, homework and all the new expectations of the new school year? From a developmental perspective, you should be able to expect him to carry out these activities. Given the fact that Nick is clearly having trouble, it will be important to assess his situation and temperament.

S. Situation

Are the routines before and after school clear and predictable for Nick? Is Nick exposed to routines that encourage cooperation and responsibility? Are the back to school routines you've established appropriate for his temperament? Nick may be taking the stress he feels about all the new expectations at school out on you. Remember, transition to a new school or even a new grade, will have an impact on his behavior. Nick will be better prepared to make these transitions at school if he can successfully make them at home.

K. Know the child

Given Nick's temperament, is his present routine going to meet with success? Has he always found adapting to new people and things challenging? Is this more or less the way he has adjusted to school years in the past? Think about his stamina, how he generally manages stress. Does he have the ability to communicate his feelings? All of what you know about Nick's temperament will influence the proactive plan you develop.

PROACTIVE PLAN

After using *The ASK Yourself Strategy* to gather information about Nick's development, situation, and temperament, we are ready to develop a proactive plan for adjusting more effectively to school. Here is the plan Nick's parents and I developed.

Proactive Strategies

Have proactive conversations
- Talk with Nick about what is going on at school. Remember, if you ask, "How was school?" you're not likely to get more than "fine" for an answer. Instead, try asking your child, "What was the best thing that happened today and what was the worst thing that happened today?"
- Talk with Nick about his feelings about school. Do this on the weekend so that he feels less pressured or overwhelmed. Explain that it is normal to take some time to get used to the new expectations.

Set expectations and discuss consequences
- Be concrete about the disrespectful words and behaviors you want to stop. Communicate what the consequences will be if the disrespectful behavior continues.

Explore other factors affecting behavior
- Look at the amount of sleep Nick is getting. Because he is older, you may be underestimating how much sleep he needs to perform to his potential.
- Provide balanced nutrition and enjoy regular exercise. These basics are important for school success. Reports show that American children are less fit and more overweight than just ten years ago. Whether you take a walk or play while raking leaves, proper nutrition combined with regular physical activity develops healthy muscles and channels excess energy.
- Ask Nick's teacher about his learning style. As your child progresses to the older grades, academic expectations get tougher. Nick may be finding school harder and is therefore less interested in school. His teacher will

be able to help you assess whether or not his school struggles are typical or out of the realm of normal.

Provide emotional coaching and problem solving

- Create new after school routines that consider this new adjustment. Perhaps a full day of school and the new expectations require other aspects of Nick's life to be less intense.
- Help Nick break the challenges he is experiencing down into manageable pieces. Regardless of how he has adapted to other transitions in the past, his behavior is telling you he needs some coaching for this adjustment.
- Get Nick involved in developing strategies for making the adjustment easier. His input will make it more likely that he will try the strategies at school and at home.
- Read as a family. Exciting research confirms that reading every day enhances your child's development and his ability to learn. Reading together will create positive feelings about reading and school and can be some of the closest moments you and your child share.

Spend time together

- Spend time with Nick. If you want him to talk to you, you will need to spend time with him without an agenda. He is more likely to talk to you about his feelings and concerns when he is relaxed.
- Volunteer in ways that fit with your family and work responsibilities. Working parents often struggle with the idea of volunteering, yet there are ways to assist the teacher outside of the classroom. Helping prepare materials or collecting items needed for a project are ways to contribute without being in the classroom and still forge a home-school connection. This home-school connection will give you an invaluable way of getting feedback about how Nick is doing.

Conflict strategies

Establish authority

- Step in with authority when Nick gets overwhelmed. While his stress is real, his outbursts must be met with boundaries.

Be direct and specific about non-negotiables

- Be direct and specific about what you expect Nick to do when he is losing his cool. Keep negative remarks and excess excitement to a minimum; remember it is hard for him to handle his feelings of being overwhelmed by school.

Remain calm

- Be calm and positive. When the moment comes when Nick loses his cool, with a gentle hand on his shoulder, remind him of what you expect. Keep talking to a minimum so that he can use his own skills and strategies for calming down. Later, let him know that slip-ups do happen and are part of learning how to handle change.

Provide consequences

- Be prepared to provide a consequence to the disrespectful behavior. Nick may test you to see if you will follow through. If you want him to get the message to use self-control, you must communicate this with your actions by consistently following through. For more on choosing the RITE consequences, see Chapter 4.

Make an impact

- Make impact. If Nick seems unaffected by the consequences you provide than you didn't make impact. If you didn't make impact then the connection between actions and consequences did not take place.

Societal strategies

Learn about influences and their impact

- Resist the urge to overschedule Nick in enrichment activities. School is work for your child and he needs some unstructured time to play.
- Find out about Nick's friendships at school. Is he playing with children that are a good or not so good fit for him? Is he being picked on at school or witnessing social behavior that is upsetting to him? What happens in your child's school life does affect his ability to have self-control.

- Strengthen your connection with your child's teacher. It will be important to work as partners to make Nick's transition a smoother one. Especially if there are learning issues associated with his intense feelings of dislike for school.

Explore feelings and desires related to "fitting in"
- Empathize with Nick. Let him know that while you understand transition is hard for him, he needs to find acceptable ways of handling it...and you will help him.
- Encourage unstructured play. Your child doesn't require expensive classes and lengthy programs. Let him play with friends he already knows. This is a nice way to give Nick time to be carefree. When he is ready, he will do the necessary work to form new friendships. Your child may need some guidance to just step out the back door and play, especially if he usually plays in structured settings.

Monitor influences
- Don't over schedule activities. Remember, managing school alone will be hard for Nick. Adjusting to the changes at school is a lot for him to contend with, without having to adjust to a busy schedule of additional activities. Your child may really enjoy coming home from school and having some unstructured time with you or his neighborhood friends.
- Talk to the teacher routinely. Strengthening the parent-teacher connection is worth your efforts. You and your child's teacher are partners in your child's education. Communicating in times of peace will lay the foundation for working together on any more challenging issues that present themselves throughout the school year.

Set limits on inappropriate influences
- Modify or limit the influences. Whenever possible take charge of the influences contributing to Nick's feelings of being overwhelmed.
- Decrease any non-essential expectations. Keeping other routines and schedules simple during the back to school period is a good idea for a boy who adapts slowly to change.

Skill build and teach appropriate ways
of handling societal influences

- Help Nick develop the skills he needs to cope with these new expectations. While the behavior he is presently exhibiting is typical for the slow to adapt child, you can teach him how to better deal with his concerns. Role-play how to have self-control in challenging situations.
- Balance taking a break with getting homework done. Nick will require some time to relax after school. Try to make certain that he has this period of time to refuel. But don't let the time get away from you. Your child will be better able to concentrate and complete assigned tasks if homework is done before dinner.

If you struggle with a child who adapts like Nick, being proactive before your child goes to school may be the best way to support your reluctant child. With the proactive plan Nick's parents and I developed, Nick was comfortable in no time. Even his teacher shared how much more relaxed Nick was at school after everyone came together on his behalf.

In this next school year, make a new commitment to get back to basics. Be enthusiastic and positive about school. Your child takes her cues from you. If you are having "separation anxiety," she will pick up on it. Visit the school or the playground of the school your child will be attending. Your child will benefit from seeing and becoming comfortable with at least part of the grounds in advance. Invite a friend over to play. If you know a child in your child's class, this is a great way to encourage friendship and build support.

Adopt routines that mimic school routines. Eating at times similar to the school schedule and moving bedtime back to an earlier hour will go a long way toward helping your child adapt. Let your child become involved in choosing between two acceptable outfits or choosing the healthy snacks you buy. Encouraging responsibility and initiative will contribute to school success. Read a good book. Let your child know that every child has to make the summer-to-school transition. This will be comforting as well as encourage your child to discuss her feelings. Get involved in school. Research shows that your child's success in school is directly related to your involvement.

Chapter summary

In using Proactive Parenting for your preschool or school age child, again I recommend using developmentally specific proactive, conflict and societal strategies. With proactive discipline, it is important to recognize your child's increased ability to have meaningful, teaching, coaching conversations. Our best parenting work takes place out of conflict. Keep in mind that as you use proactive discipline with the preschool and school age child, you should be paying particular attention to sharing not lecturing, and skill building not punishing.

Conflict discipline continues to be important for your preschool and school age child. Be clear about your non-negotiable limits and share them often with your child. Your child consistently understands cause and effect now. Use this to your advantage.

Societal discipline is becoming clearly a very significant type of discipline you will need to provide for your preschool or school age child. His friendships with adults and children will become more and more important to him as he journeys through this developmental period. Make a commitment to know what he is exposed to, talk a lot and help him begin to learn how to make his own decisions.

When providing Proactive Parenting to the preschool and school age child, the proactive parent remembers that...

* Learning about development and temperament is critical to the success of Proactive Parenting.
* Your preschool age or school age child requires all three types of discipline.
* Proactive Parenting with the child between the age of three and nine is the most effective way to teach cause and effect learning.
* Planning strategies in advance for situations you know your child will have difficulty with is key.
* Proactive Parenting with the child between the ages of three and nine will set the stage for good decision-making in the future for both you and your child.

Questions and Answers
Chapter 8

Dive In

*How The Approach Works With Children
Three To Nine*

Q: My son is four and he resists my limits. I must admit that I feel unclear about what the limits ought to be now that my child is older. It seemed so easy when he was younger to know what the limits were. Any suggestions?

A: At each developmental period it is important to step back a moment and redefine what your non-negotiable limits are. Once you have made decisions about where and when your child can have an increased sense of independence, it will be easier for you to communicate this to your child. The three chapters on how the approach works with children of different ages should help you. Be proactive and read ahead so you know in advance what you will be up against.

Q: My children are five and seven-years-old. I don't find this age particularly challenging. Am I missing something?

A: Many experts agree that of all the developmental periods, school age is the most stable. In other words, children have a lot of skills but not a lot of challenges. While it is an easier period than some, I think school age children can sometimes get lost in the shuffle. And the pressures once faced by older children are certainly trickling down. You aren't doing anything wrong if you find it easy, but be attuned to the impact of others on your children. And by all means keep the door to communication with your children open.

Q: I feel like I spend most of my parenting time talking and problem solving about my child's friendships. Why is this so consuming and why does my child need so much help?

A: Working on social skills is by far the biggest challenge in this developmental period. Congratulations to you for spending so much time on this kind of teaching and coaching. It is likely your child's temperament that makes this harder for her. Keep up the good work; this is exactly the proactive way to be handling this learning.

NINE

Pack Their Bags

How The Approach Works
With Children Ten To Eighteen

Julianne says she wouldn't get up in the morning if she believed what her friends are saying about parenting today's adolescent. While she and her twelve-year-old daughter Vanessa struggle over typical issues such as clothing and friendships, she just isn't having the same experience as other mothers she talks with. Popular culture messages would have you believe that adolescents are difficult, disrespectful mini-adults with constantly raging hormones. This is absolutely not true! When you use a parenting approach comprised of strategies that respect your child's development, temperament and the tough challenges she faces as a teenager in today's complex society, her adolescence can be an exciting, productive and wonderful time for both of you.

Remember, your adolescent is facing enormous pressure at school and with friends that you probably faced when you were much older. The world expects a lot from adolescents physically, cognitively, emotionally and socially. Because this is a period of great change in growth and development, using Proactive Parenting is essential. In this chapter, I will review how your adolescent thinks and learns. Using Proactive Parenting with a child between the ages of ten and eighteen has some nuances. The issues and concerns for younger adolescents and older adolescents are different. So, I will discuss, how to apply the principles of Proactive

Parenting specifically to younger and older adolescents. I will do this first by examining the discipline principles you use with your child and then by using a case study for each age group.

Thinking and learning for younger and older adolescents

So, why are there so many myths, jokes and fears about today's adolescent? Well to begin, your adolescent is in a critical phase of development that involves moving from child to adult. This is a developmental period when your child is very self-focused. During this time, your adolescent is going through three important processes. I call it the "*I Age*". Here are the three I's.

- **Independence**...Your adolescent is yearning for a newfound independence, yet our society gives both parents and adolescents dangerous messages about independence. Your adolescent is not capable of making adult decisions. While he can think in more abstract ways, he is still learning how to make decisions that are age-appropriate, safe and well thought out. Don't just "dump" him into adolescence, guide him through it. He still requires structure and routines for free time along with lots of adult interaction and supervision.
- **Individuation**...Your child is exploring his individuality. Does he see himself as smart, artistic, athletic, political, or musical? What are his strengths, interests, goals and plans for the future? This period of exploring "*who you are*" is an essential process of becoming a capable adult. Yet trying to figure it out can be very hard for many adolescents.
- **Identification**...or the process of describing yourself in relationship to others, shifts from parents to the peer group during adolescence. But remember what you do and what you say still carries the greatest weight regardless of your child's developmental age and temperament. Sure, there are times when your child may seem to prefer talking to anyone else but you. But

don't be fooled, the role you play in his life is important to him. The structure you provide, the limits that you set and your ideas and opinions matter to him.

While parenting your adolescent can be complex, it can also be very rewarding. Your child is becoming an adult and needs all the guidance, coaching and loving support you have to offer. Don't listen to the messages others give you about your adolescent not wanting you involved in his life. Your child cares about what his friends think but he also cares deeply about what you think. He wants you involved in what interests and excites him but perhaps in new ways than before. He wants you to talk *with him* not *at him*. He will respect what you have to say as long as you respect his ideas, opinions and feelings, too.

I have developed charts similar to the ones in Chapters 7 & 8. They review some important milestones in adolescent development that have an impact on how you provide discipline for your child. As I recommended in Chapter 7 and 8, this would be a good time to take the *Discovering Your Child's Style* quiz, if you haven't done so already. It is found in Chapter 2.

Developmental Milestones
That Impact Discipline
Younger and Older Adolescents

Note: All milestone information is approximate.
Your child will learn at his own pace and in his own time.
If you are concerned however, please contact your pediatrician
or child development expert.

Cognitive development...
refers to how your child thinks.

By age twelve, your child...

uses cause and effect thinking.
has emerging time management skills.
can think reflectively.

By age fourteen, your child...

has emerging abstract thinking.
can handle multiple tasks.
has subject preferences.

By age sixteen, your child...

can think abstractly.
can plan for future events.
can consider a variety of opinions.

Developmental Milestones
That Impact Discipline
Younger and Older Adolescents

Note: All milestone information is approximate.
Your child will learn at his own pace and in his own time.
If you are concerned however, please contact your pediatrician
or child development expert.

Affective development...
refers to how your child feels.

By age twelve, your child...

chooses friends based on shared interests.
may have interest in opposite sex friendships.
may be more focused on friendship than
school work.

By age fourteen, your child...

has identified peer groups.
may conform to group norms.
has interest in dating relationships.

By age sixteen, your child...

wants to make independent decisions.
wants privacy.
expresses thoughts clearly and directly.

Developmental Milestones
That Impact Discipline
Younger and Older Adolescents

Note: All milestone information is approximate.
Your child will learn at his own pace and in his own time.
If you are concerned however, please contact your pediatrician
or child development expert.

Psychomotor development...
refers to how your child moves.

By age twelve, your child...

has started the period of puberty.
is less coordinated because of changes.
can complete routine chores.

By age fourteen, your child...

is fully in puberty.
has self-care as a priority.
is capable of complex tasks like cooking.

By age sixteen, your child...

has emerging driving skills.
is capable of complex tasks like laundry.
can work at a job.

Proactive Parenting for younger and older adolescents

In Chapters 3, 4 & 5, I've gone into detail about the principles that apply to each of the three types of discipline that make up Proactive Parenting. Now I would like to review the principles and make brief comments on how they apply to adolescents.

The principles of **proactive discipline**...

- **Anticipation** continues to be important as you plan for the kinds of discussions and limits you will have for your adolescent. By this time, you know your child's temperament pretty well so this will help you as you try to predict where your issues may lie. But for many parents, the change in the way their adolescent is able to think is what makes anticipating issues a bit harder than in the past. Adolescents aren't as unpredictable as some would have you believe. Review adolescent development and be prepared to alter your style to fit what development experts already know about your adolescent's emerging thinking patterns.
- **Clarity** about your child's new and expanding opportunities for independence has never been so important. As you allow your adolescent more freedoms, such as staying after school, going to the movies or driving a car, you must be very clear about what the rules and expectations are for behavior. Think about what your non-negotiables are in relation to the places your child goes and the people he spends time with. Don't wait until your child gets into trouble to establish the rules. Remember, if you haven't been clear about what you expect then how can you hold your child accountable for rules that have never been shared?
- **Communication** with your adolescent needs to be constant in order for you to bring your child safely to adulthood. The mistake you may be making though, is to only talk about rules, values and potential consequences to misbehavior. Of course, you need to talk to your adolescent about those things. But first you must establish routine, non-threatening communication

about other things so that your adolescent will want to talk to you. Remember, for communication to be effective with your adolescent, now that she is capable of abstract thinking, it must be two-way. That means you need to have a dialogue or conversation not a lecture. Start talking about things you have in common or issues that don't tend to be difficult for the two of you. Once productive, fun conversations have taken place it will be easier to have some of the tougher ones.

- **Role modeling** good adult choices and behavior is more important in this period than you might think. The popular culture may be telling you that your adolescent wants nothing to do with you, but as you know by now, I completely disagree. As your adolescent works through the process of identification that I talked about earlier, he is keeping his eyes on you. He is figuring himself out by comparing his ideas and opinions to the choices and decisions he sees you making. While he may rebel or say he would never make your choices, be patient. The power of what role modeling teaches is enormous. Can you see by looking at the good and not so good choices you've made in your life, what you may have learned by watching your own parents? Maybe you made decisions similar to those your parents made or perhaps made decisions in complete contrast to those your parents made. Regardless, what they role modeled, for you, had power.

- **Respect** between you and your adolescent is another two-way street. If you want your adolescent to respect you then you must teach respect, expect respect and respect your child in return. If you are just embracing the idea of teaching and expecting respect now that your child is in adolescence, it will be more difficult. Truly the sooner you start to teach this value, the better. But it is never too late. Remember, the visual of the fence I introduced to you in Chapter 3? As your child gets older, I want you to imagine the backyard that the fence contains getting bigger. But the fence does not go away! The respectful way to create boundaries for your adolescent is to let the backyard get bigger as your child can show her ability to handle greater responsibility. But don't remove the fence entirely because your adolescent still needs structure and boundaries to feel safe and secure as well as to make good choices.

The principles of **conflict discipline**...

- **Action** in conflict is still the best way to deliver your messages to your adolescent. Like everything in Proactive Parenting it is best to have prepared your child in advance for the actions you will take in conflict. In proactive discipline, you have told your child what to expect from you and in conflict discipline, you must show your child that there are consequences to making choices that disregard the rules. If you tell your child he can't go to a friend's house unless a parent is home, then what should happen when your child goes there and there is no parent at home? The action to me is clear...you must go to get your child. If you *tell him* the rule and he makes a choice to disregard it...then you must be willing to *show him* the consequences of that decision. Talking in conflict never delivers the message as powerfully as action.
- **Authority** and respect for it, is a lost concept for many of today's adolescents. Adults should not shy away from letting adolescents know the boundaries related to certain actions. You can be your child's friend and confidant in proactive and societal discipline but in conflict it must be clear that you are in charge. When you are in conflict with your child regardless of her age, you must be willing to step in and show your child where the "fence" is.
- **Consistency** with regards to behavioral expectations is just as important for adolescents as it is for a child any age. If you are going to enforce rules about computer time or an evening curfew, then you must be willing to follow through. Remember that your limits are only as good as your follow through. Your adolescent gets the "tell me" message in proactive discipline. He gets the "show me" message in conflict discipline. Messages about expectations will be only as strong as your ability to follow through. Temperament plays a big role in how much consistency is required though. Did you take the *Discovering your Child's Style* quiz in Chapter 2? If your

child has either the Dynamic or Situational style, you should know that your child will need you to be very consistent in your ability to follow through on limits you've established.

- **Emotional integrity** as you parent your adolescent is so important for overall family harmony. Conversations belong in proactive and societal discipline. And action belongs in conflict discipline. Yelling and arguing are never productive and can sometimes be quite harmful. Hurtful things said in the heat of the moment can never be taken back. When you have a plan for discipline that pulls apart when to talk and when to act, you should feel more in control of your own emotions. The need to engage in ineffective communication usually comes when you're out of ideas and options for problem solving. Let your child know, in advance, that you will only talk if everyone remains calm and respectful. If you are faced with a situation that you haven't had a chance to think through, tell your adolescent that you need time to think about it. Reflecting, planning and anticipating will again help you to keep your emotions in check as you communicate rules and expectations to your adolescent.

- **Predictability** is the principle in conflict discipline that ensures that your child will make good decisions even when you aren't with her. If you have been and continue to be consistent with your follow through related to non-negotiable limits you've established, then your child is prepared for the consequences of the choices she makes. When you respond to your child in ways that are predictable, then the idea that your rules have weight becomes something your child can trust. Your adolescent becomes internally motivated to do the right thing. She behaves because she is able to think situations through before she makes decisions.

The principles of **societal discipline**....

- **Awareness** about what your child is doing both inside and outside your home has never been more important. Now that your adolescent is completing schoolwork and making friends more independently, do you feel like you're less aware of what interests him? Many parents of adolescents cite this distance as a contributing factor to the decrease they see in communication with their child. And it is true, it is impossible to talk to your child if you really have no idea what her life is like. Watch her favorite TV programs, pick up one of her magazines and listen to her music. If you want to have anything to talk to her about, you have to share some aspects of her life.

- **Commitment** to setting limits on harmful influences can only be done if you know what your child is exposed to. How can you tell your son what is objectionable about MTV if you've never seen it before? So the first step is raising your awareness and your next step is to take a stand on what you will and won't allow your child to see and do. Once again, the earlier in adolescence that you do this the better. Typically an eleven-year-old is going to have less difficulty accepting "your fence" on these matters than a seventeen-year-old does. And as your adolescent matures, you should be allowing more freedoms. Making the backyard bigger is okay, but keep the dialogue open so that you can attach your values to those influences from the popular culture.

- **Honesty** is another one of those two-way streets that are critical to parenting your adolescent. And if you want it from her, she will most certainly expect it from you. Virtually every subject should be *discussible*. While it is still important to take into consideration how your child handles sensitive information, it is never the wrong choice to be honest. Factor in your child's temperament and share information in small doses but share information nonetheless. If you don't discuss the tough subjects, I assure you someone else will. And as I've said before, you can't do the teaching and coaching that is necessary to give her the skills to handle the tough pressures in adolescence if you and your child aren't honest. Today's adolescent is savvier than you think; she already knows more about sex, drugs and violence than you ever knew at her age. Why not talk to her and let her get positive messages that are stronger than any messages she can get from the popular culture? Let her know through honest, open, two-way communication that there is nothing off limits for the two of you to discuss.

- **Communication** is only as good as the amount of positive energy you put into it. Lots of positive effort = much better communication. Do you have a friend or a boss that talks negatively? Does he or she find something wrong with everything and never seems to like anything you do? It's hard to spend any time with that person isn't it? I know I have very little desire to spend time with negative people. How does your adolescent see you? Is most, if not all, of your communication negative and done in conflict? Limiting your conversation to what you don't want your adolescent to do and who you don't want him to hang around with will surely close the door to communication. An important principle of societal discipline for the adolescent is to spend your time communicating *out of conflict*. Talking to your child may be hard at first but it will be worth any effort you expend. Look at the times you already spend with your adolescent. I once saw an advertisement encouraging communication between adolescents and their parents. It said to think of the car as a chat room. Talk about the music you do like and talk about the friends you find funny and interesting. When you find positive things to talk about with your child, she will enjoy talking to you. Once you and your daughter are connected, talking about the more difficult matters will be much easier to do.
- **Supervision** for the adolescent is less direct but still *very necessary*. With all the communication technology available, there is virtually no reason to wonder about where your child is and with whom. Enlist the help of other parents to set ground rules for how and where your adolescent will spend time. I am giving you permission right now to supervise your child in ways that may seem overprotective to him or to other adults. Keeping your child safe is your responsibility and don't let others talk you out of what your instincts tell you to do. With clear expectations, your adolescents *will* accept the freedom you offer with certain conditions attached. "You can go to the movies with friends while I shop at the mall." Or "You may choose to go the dance, if I am a chaperone or you may choose to have your friends come here to watch a movie." Compromise, communicate and be clear about

how you will balance your child's emerging independence with your need to keep him safe.

A younger adolescent case study

Now that I have discussed the fine points of the discipline principles for younger and older adolescents, let's use *The ASK Yourself Strategy* to look at how the discipline strategies for a typical situation involving a younger adolescent would be affected.

Back talk

Mia is a twelve-year-old with a strong personality. Her parents come to Proactive Parenting because they are concerned about Mia's attitude and disrespectful behavior in school and at home. While her teachers say she is negative and disinterested at school, at home she is downright argumentative. Her father says during our visit, "I could have told you adolescence was going to be hard for Mia and for us...she has always been a strong willed, independent girl. The only difference now is that there are so many more situations that she pushes us about and we can't seem to talk to her about anything."

Although young adolescents sometimes look and act like young adults, they still need your guidance in managing school life and thinking about the future. Mia's parents can be the most powerful guides in their adolescent's journey toward making good choices, if they take an active role in talking to her now. Here are some key thoughts I'd like you to consider as you reflect on this particular case study.

- The first is to acknowledge that adolescence is a developmental period of great change. These years include rapid cognitive, physical and emotional growth and development. While an adolescent might appear confident, strong willed, independent, and opinionated, she may be feeling confused, awkward, embarrassed, left out, self-conscious and stressed.

- The second key thought I'd like you to consider is that conflict provides a valuable opportunity for learning, yet teaching during conflict is not enough. Conversations in times of peace go much further in forming a respectful parent/adolescent relationship. Remember to talk to your child rather than lecture or preach and be sure to do it when she isn't doing anything you object to.
- And here is the third and very critical key thought...You can make things better or you can make things worse as you parent during these tumultuous times. If you talk only in conflict you are engaging and reinforcing the argumentative behavior. Making distinctions between when you will talk and under what circumstances will be an important part of any proactive plan for managing disrespectful behavior.

Let's look at the proactive plan Mia's parents and I developed to make communication between them better.

A. Age and development of the child

Is it acceptable for a twelve-year-old to be disrespectful and talk back to her parents? Is a bad attitude to be expected because Mia is now an adolescent...and do you have to put up with it? The answer to both questions is no. Mia is capable of using other more effective skills to communicate her feelings. She is capable of learning how to share her ideas, feelings and opinions in ways that are more acceptable to those around her, but someone should teach her how.

S. Situation

Are there any situational factors affecting Mia's ability to be cooperative and responsible? What contributes to Mia's disrespectful behavior? Does she have more difficulty when she is stressed or anxious? Do others respect her ideas and feelings? Does she have age-appropriate input to decisions that affect her? It will be very important for Mia's parents to be willing to look at what might be contributing to Mia's behavior. What limits are placed on Mia's behavior? What are the consequences to her when she is disrespectful? Is the only talking that takes place in this family, during conflict? All of the situational factors must be examined so that an individual plan can be created.

K. Know the child

Think about Mia's temperament...is she more susceptible to the influences around her? Mia's father said he predicted that adolescence would be difficult for Mia. Why? Does her persistence get in the way of her accepting limits? Is she more intense, more sensitive or less able to adapt to change than other adolescents or family members? Does Mia's family have expectations of her that are fulfilling a prophesy about her being difficult? Remember, all of what Mia's family already knows about her temperament will influence the proactive plan that is developed.

PROACTIVE PLAN

Once *The ASK Yourself Strategy* has been used to gather important information about Mia and her family; we are ready to develop a proactive plan for talking more effectively with her. Here is the plan Mia's parents and I developed.

Proactive strategies

Have proactive conversations
- Start talking to Mia about the communication patterns you find respectful as well as those that you find disrespectful. It may be difficult at first but making this clear from the start is an important step in building positive communication with Mia.
- Hold family meetings. During family dinners, set the ground rules for talking in your family. Make it clear that talking will only occur, from here on in, when everyone is calm and under control. The point is to set the stage for expectations by talking in advance of conflict.
- Use vicarious experience to teach. Talk to her about situations that other adolescents found themselves in and the consequences that resulted from the choices

they made. In this way, you can share your expectations but you aren't directing your opinions toward Mia.

- Give Mia positive feedback. She needs to know when she is talking with you in ways that are acceptable. It doesn't mean she has to agree with you, it just means she must get her point across respectfully.

Set expectations and discuss consequences

- Anticipate situations that are typically difficult for Mia. Communicate in advance what you expect her to do in these challenging situations.
- Set firm and clear limits in advance. It is important during this time that you allow Mia the opportunity to share her point of view. This doesn't mean you have to change your non-negotiables. It simply means that you listen to her point of view and allow her the chance to be heard. This is often, when done well, the time your adolescent sees you as a person willing to compromise. This doesn't always mean your child will behave accordingly, but it does set the stage for what is expected of her.

Explore other factors affecting behavior

- Look at how much sleep Mia is getting. Adolescents typically go to bed too late and either get up too early or too late in the morning. A regular sleep pattern is the best intervention for the child who is more intense and persistent.
- Learn about Mia's friendships. It is critical that you know her friends and their families. Whether positive or negative, friendships may be contributing to Mia's attitude toward school and family.
- Measure Mia's stress level. As adolescents approach middle and high school, expectations soar academically and socially. Helping her to manage her stress will go a long way to helping her adopt the best attitude.

Provide emotional coaching and problem solving

- Encourage Mia to express her feelings...artistically or in writing. Adolescence is a time of great change and she may benefit from expressing herself in ways other than through talking.

- Role play challenging situations. Give Mia both the language to use in difficult situations as well as ways to get out of challenging situations.
- Encourage healthy connections. The more positively connected an adolescent is, the more others are looking out for her best interest. Mia will have increased opportunities to be involved in productive activities the more she is connected.

Spend time together
- Remind her of her past and talk to her about her future. In developing her identity, it is important for her to talk about both.
- Spend time together. Work to develop a common interest. This time and interest you share will go a long way to reducing conflict. It is harder to be easily agitated by someone after you have spent special time with them.

Conflict strategies

Establish authority
- Be the authority that Mia needs. It is important to recognize that it is in Mia's best interest that you take control of situations that she can not. Demonstrate a can do attitude. It's fine to share with Mia what she can't do...but are you sharing with her what she can do? Make the effort to point out the available acceptable choices that Mia has to pick from.
- Don't engage in a power struggle with words. Remind her that you will only discuss *negotiable* issues when she is calm and under control. Non-negotiable limits aren't up for discussion.

Be direct and specific about non-negotiables
- Be clear and specific about misbehavior. After the situation is under control, be sure you are clear about what she did that was unacceptable. Remember to wait until emotions are contained.
- Choose your battles. Some conflict between parent and adolescent just doesn't matter in the spectrum of things.

Don't let your ego or your desire to feel respected make issues seem bigger than they are.

- Remove yourself from a difficult situation. Mia needs to get the message that a disrespectful attitude will not be reinforced. This small action in conflict will help her to focus on your message.

Remain calm

- Remain calm. It is fine to tell her you're upset, but it is another to lose your temper. Remember, you lose your credibility when you get out of control.
- Role model effective conflict resolution. Mia is watching you and learning what is acceptable behavior when you're angry or frustrated.

Provide consequences

- Follow through. If you said you wouldn't renegotiate the rules when certain circumstances arise, then don't. By following through, Mia will learn that you mean what you say.

Make an impact

- Be sure to make an impact. If the consequences you impose don't influence Mia's behavior, then you haven't found the right ones. Review how to choose the RITE consequences. You will find this information in Chapter 4.
- Consider family or community service. She will have plenty of time to think about the inappropriate choices she made while she is raking the yard or cleaning the bathroom. This strategy is more effective than being sent to her room. My guess is that her room may be a pretty nice place to be.

Societal strategies

Learn about influences and their impact

- Know Mia's interests. It is important to keep current on the movies, books and TV she enjoys. Not only is it important for you to know what is influencing your daughter but it will help you to set limits on inappropriate influences. Remember, it also makes for creating conversation.

- Get to know her friends. Again, you will only know what she is up against in the popular culture if you have a complete picture of what and to whom she is exposed.
- Strengthen the parent/teacher connection. Get to know her teachers, make conferences and stay connected. While this gets more difficult in middle and high school, you will learn a lot about Mia through her interactions at school.

Explore feelings and desires related to "fitting in"
- Talk with Mia about how she feels about peer pressure. Not only must you talk about how it feels to make the same choices as friends but it may be even more important to talk about how it feels to make unpopular choices.
- Give Mia a number of options for appearing to fit in while remaining true to her values and those of your family.

Monitor influences
- Monitor TV, Internet and phone access. Keep the phone and computer in visible central locations. Staying on top of these connections will keep her safe and will allow for conversation about these influences.
- Always know where Mia is. Keeping her busy with productive activities and being present and involved are the keys to good adolescent supervision.

Set limits on inappropriate influences
- Continue to provide Mia with age-appropriate structure and boundaries. Too much freedom and too little supervision may put Mia in situations beyond her emotional capabilities. And remember, you must take on the limit setting related to societal influences because no one else will.

**Skill build and teach appropriate ways
to handle societal influences**
- Get Mia involved in a cause. Whether it is volunteering at an animal shelter or participating in the environmental

clean up in your town; Mia's passionate nature can be channeled into something productive and meaningful both to her and to others.

• Involve Mia in complex problem solving situations. Her emerging reasoning skills will be invaluable as you coach her to develop new social and emotional skills.

With patience and a positive attitude, Mia's parents have created a respectful and open dialogue with their intense and persistent daughter. Now Mia enjoys spending time with her parents talking about the challenges of adolescence. Recently, she said to her parents, "I like it better now that we talk without yelling. I didn't like how I used to feel when I was home."

The good news is that there is so much that you can do to teach your child how to get along in the world in calm and constructive ways. Showing your child that there are more effective ways of getting her needs met can be done by choosing just the right strategies. I believe that there are strategies to be used before your child loses her temper as well as strategies to use in the heat of the moment. But actively teaching your child new ways of solving old problems should take place out of conflict. Begin your teaching by creating a proper fence. With appropriate expectations of your young adolescent, you too can have the family harmony Mia's family now enjoys. It doesn't mean all conflict is gone, but it does mean that disagreements are handled respectfully, non-negotiables are clear and limits have follow through.

An older adolescent case study

Now that I have discussed how the Proactive Parenting strategies apply to a situation involving a younger adolescent, let's use *The ASK Yourself Strategy* to look at how the discipline strategies for a typical situation involving an older adolescent would be affected.

Not drinking and not driving

Harry is a sixteen-year-old boy who loves sports and school. His mother says, "I feel funny even coming to Proactive Parenting because Harry is a great kid and we have rarely had issues. I don't even think Harry drinks, but I am really worried about alcohol issues now that he and his friends are all getting their drivers licenses." Harry's mother has a very legitimate concern even though Harry has always been a "good kid." Across the United States, alcohol and other substances are readily available to any adolescent who wants to try them. And the peer pressure to try and chronically use alcohol is high. Add in the statistics on new drivers, substances and accidents and Harry's mother would be remiss if she didn't create a proactive plan for Harry.

As your adolescent gets older, he will make more of his own decisions about what to do and how to behave. Whether or not the door to communication is open between you and your child, adolescents are making decisions about using alcohol, marijuana and cigarettes. This door to communication is naturally open when your child is young. Can you remember when every thought your child had slipped easily out of his mouth the minute it entered his mind? Unfortunately, the door to communication gets closed when your conversations aren't open, constant or respectful. Talking with your child is essential to his learning how to make good decisions especially when you aren't there.

The keys to keeping this door to communication open between you and your adolescent is to talk early and often. Leave no subject off limits. The rule I have with my own children is that I will talk about any subject as long as the conversation stays respectful. Set your ground rules for talking in advance. Talk in the car, over breakfast or on a walk...but keep talking. Remember, your adolescent wants a conversation not a lecture. Feel free to share your opinions but be sure to listen to his. Once communication between you and your adolescent is constant and open, only then can you teach good decision-making.

Let's look at the specific strategies Harry's mother used to address the peer pressure to drink and drive. Again, we begin with *The ASK Yourself Strategy.*

A. Age and development of the child.

Is it acceptable for Harry to drink alcohol? Of course, the answer is no. There are laws prohibiting underage drinking for very good reasons. Whether or not adolescents drive after they have been drinking, alcohol impairs thinking, feeling and decision-making. Research shows that the short-term effects make it completely unsafe for him to drive. And the research also shows that the earlier an adolescent engages in chronic misuse of alcohol, the higher the likelihood that he will have issues with alcohol as an adult.

S. Situation

Will Harry be exposed to alcohol and drugs in school or in your community? Is he likely to have a friend who misuses alcohol? Unfortunately, the statistics on drinking in the United States tell us the answer to these questions is yes. But can Harry be given the tools he needs to resist peer pressure and make good decisions about drinking and driving? The answer is absolutely! It will be very important for Harry's mother to be willing to look at what might contribute to Harry's temptation to drink with his friends. All of the situational factors must be examined so that an individual plan can be created that will help Harry resist the peer pressure to drink.

K. Know the child

Think about Harry's temperament...is he more susceptible to the influences around him? Harry's mother said, "He is a great kid and we rarely have issues." Here is where I reminded her about the *Discovering your Child's Style* quiz. Does Harry have the Agreeable or Compliant style? We often think that the adolescent with the Dynamic or Situational style will have the most difficulty with peer pressure. But regardless of your child's style, when it comes to peer pressure, temptation is a big problem, especially if your adolescent is too agreeable. Being too agreeable puts Harry at risk when it comes to resisting the pressures to drink and drive. Remember, all of what

Harry's mother already knows about his temperament will influence the proactive plan that is developed.

PROACTIVE PLAN

After using *The ASK Yourself Strategy* to gather information about Harry's development, situation, and temperament, we are ready to develop a proactive plan for teaching Harry to make good decisions about alcohol and driving. Here is the plan Harry's mother and I developed.

Proactive strategies

Have proactive conversations
- Talk to Harry on a regular basis about how to resist peer pressure to drink. Point out the strengths he already has in making sound decisions and offer to help him with the parts of decision making he still needs to learn.
- Listen to Harry's opinions and feelings. You can have a conversation with him about the temptation to drink without giving him permission to do so. If you lecture him, he will be less likely to hear your important messages.
- Always remind Harry of your expectations about either driving or riding with drivers who have been drinking. Do this before he leaves the house. Never assume he knows how you feel. Reminding him in advance of a night out is more powerful than you realize.

Set expectations and discuss consequences
- Make it extremely clear that you don't want Harry to drink. Stay away from soft limits like, "I hope you won't drink" or "You're not going to drink, right?" Harry needs you to be crystal clear. "Don't drink and drive."
- Talk with Harry about the consequences of making bad decisions. Give him information in writing or on the web especially about taking risks with alcohol and driving. Other more objective sources may give your concerns credibility.

Explore other factors affecting behavior
- Be sure to recognize when Harry's resistance to peer pressure will be lower. At times when he is tired or

stressed out by school and friendships, his ability to resist the pressures to drink may be higher.

Provide emotional coaching and problem solving

- Develop a plan for resisting peer pressure and for keeping Harry and his friends safe. Give Harry options for what to do should he find himself in a situation where his friends have made the decision to drink.
- Be sure Harry has outlets for his emotions related to peer pressure. Whether he exercises, writes in a journal or listens to music, it is important to have active ways to relieve stress other than using alcohol.

Spend time together

- Be available to spend time with Harry just listening to how hard it is to make good decisions when his friends might not.
- Create an atmosphere of fun in your family. Harry will want to stay close to you if your family truly enjoys being together. Make your home a place where Harry and his friends can hang out and be themselves.

Conflict strategies

Establish authority

- Stay awake and be there when Harry gets home. Let him know you are aware of when he comes home and the condition he arrives home in. Parental presence is a powerful deterrent.

Be direct and specific about non-negotiables

- Make it clear that any drinking that takes place is unacceptable. But don't have a conversation in the heat of the moment. The ability to discuss the situation rationally will be impaired by any use of alcohol and your emotions.

Remain calm

- Keep your emotions under control. Remind Harry that you will not argue over your non-negotiable limits related to drinking. If you find Harry has been drinking, don't discuss your rules then. Talking with him when he is under the influence of alcohol, won't get you anywhere.

Provide consequences
- Revoke Harry's privileges. If Harry has been found to have been drinking, his use of the car should stop. And his ability to come and go should be seriously reconsidered and limited.

Make an impact
- Choose consequences that affect Harry. While it is best to work overtime in proactive and societal discipline to increase the chances that Harry won't cross the line and take that first drink, if he does, you simply must provide consequences that impact him so that he thinks long and hard about doing it again.

Societal strategies

Learn about influences and their impact
- Educate yourself about what Harry is exposed to. Connect with his friends, his friend's families, coaches and teachers. Being connected puts you in touch with information you need to keep Harry safe.
- Look for everyday opportunities to talk about the impact of drinking on the lives of those who abuse it. Remember, to converse not lecture.

Explore feelings and desires related to "fitting in"
- Ask Harry about the situations that make resisting peer pressure more difficult. Get a conversation started by asking a question like, "Is it more difficult when you hang out with certain friends or in certain places like a party?"
- Offer Harry options for hanging out that you can both be comfortable with, like having friends to your house or taking friends to a ball game. Talk about these options *before* he makes plans.

Monitor influences

- Ask Harry to keep you informed of where he is and who he is spending time with. Open your home to Harry and his friends. Make your home the place to be so that you will know where he is and what he is up to.
- Set a good example...Harry will notice the decisions you make about using alcohol. It doesn't mean you can't drink, but watch how much you do and when you do. Because role modeling teaches so much, never drink and drive.

Set limits on inappropriate influences

- Let Harry know the rules for where he can go and under what circumstances. If you let him know in advance what places and situations are off limits, you can help him accept your limits.
- Say no to certain social situations. If you know there will be limited if any supervision at a sleepover, don't let Harry go. You *can* decrease the likelihood that Harry will be in the wrong place at the wrong time.

Skill build and teach appropriate ways of handling societal influences

- Let Harry practice realistic ways of saying no like, "I don't want a drink, I'm driving." Or, "I have a game in the morning and if I get caught drinking, I'm off the team." Offer to let him use you as an excuse for not making certain decisions.
- Give Harry positive feedback for making good decisions in stressful situations like, "I think you were smart to choose having friends over tonight rather than go to the party. The drinking issue just doesn't come up here."
- Encourage Harry to look at his decisions, trying to learn from his experiences. Give him real feedback like, "It must be so hard to resist the urge to drink, but the way you use your sense of humor really seems to help you. I think you are doing a great job, doing what's right for you."

With a good plan and a strong commitment on his mother's part, sixteen-year-old Harry doesn't drink and drive. You truly can help your child make good decisions.

While you can help your adolescent the most by talking about decision making before decisions are made, be aware that not every adolescent or even adult makes the right decisions all the time. In fact, showing your child how to handle bad decisions is an important opportunity for learning. Listening to him, without judgment, makes it more likely that he will come to you for help and learn from his mistakes. The research shows that when you talk to your adolescent about making good decisions about alcohol and other substances, he will be more likely to resist the peer pressure to smoke, drink or take drugs.

Chapter summary

In using Proactive Parenting for your younger or older adolescent, again I recommend using developmentally specific proactive, conflict and societal strategies. With proactive discipline, it is important to spend time talking with your child more about what he is doing right than what he is doing wrong. Keeping that door to communication open requires effort on your part. Yet, the benefits you will receive from being truly part of your child's life are invaluable.

Conflict discipline is always important though it can be more difficult in adolescence. The key to providing it is to establish ground rules for respectful problem solving. While respecting your child's ability for abstract thought, don't lose sight of the need to continue to demonstrate cause and effect. Your child's actions surely have consequences and whether good or bad, some of the choices she makes now will have consequences that will last a lifetime. Be clear about your non-negotiable limits and share them often with your child.

Societal discipline will be the most significant kind of discipline you provide to your adolescent. The degree to which you understand your child's life, set limits on negative or destructive influences and help him to make sense of the world he lives in will directly affect his ability to grow up healthy both physically and emotionally. Make a commitment to provide this kind of discipline, because if you don't, no one else will.

When providing Proactive Parenting to the younger and older adolescent, the proactive parent remembers that...

❋ Learning about development and temperament is critical to the success of Proactive Parenting.
❋ Your younger and older adolescent requires all three types of discipline.
❋ Proactive Parenting with the child between the age of ten and eighteen is the most effective way to teach good decision making.
❋ Planning strategies in advance for situations you know your child will have difficulty with is key.
❋ Proactive Parenting with the child between the ages of ten and eighteen will bring your child safely through adolescence and into adulthood.

Questions and Answers
Chapter 9

Pack Their Bags

How The Approach Works With Children Ten To Eighteen

Q: My son simply won't listen to me when I try to talk to him about important matters. Do you have any suggestions for the parent of a teenager reluctant to talk?

A: I'd love to know more about why he is reluctant, but I can give you some of my thoughts. Ask yourself the following questions and you will get a better sense of what might be getting in the way of talking effectively with your son.

* Do you talk *at*, not *with* your son?
* Do you only talk to him when you have important negative or serious messages to deliver?
* Do you disregard his opinions, feelings and ideas when he does talk to you?
* Do you talk about the same subjects often and for too long?

If you answered yes to any of these questions, your communication style may be getting in your way. The art and science of talking to anyone, never mind an adolescent, involves two-way, that is back and forth conversation. Try to change just one or two of the ways you talk with your son and you are bound to see a difference in how he opens up to you.

Q: You don't mention "grounding" an adolescent in your approach. Do you think it is a good strategy for providing a consequence in conflict discipline?

A: I don't mention "grounding" in my approach because like "time out" I don't believe it is effective. Remember, in conflict discipline the consequences you provide are respectful, infraction based, timely and effective. When an adolescent is sent to his room for an undetermined amount of time, she doesn't see a direct connection between what she did and its effect on her and others. And for today's adolescent, being housebound isn't such a terrible thing. With cable TV, phone and Internet privileges, staying home seems pretty fun to me.

Q: When I bring up sensitive subjects to my adolescent such as seeing certain movies or how I feel about smoking, aren't I just putting ideas into her head? Because she knows how I feel doesn't this just encourage her to rebel against me?

A: Trust me, you can't put anything into her head that the media and her friends haven't already put there. In fact, if you know your child tends to push your limits or rebel against you, even more reason you should be talking often about your ideas, opinions and feelings. But be sure to listen to hers. Your adolescent wants you to hear her point of view. Remember, this respect you extend to her doesn't mean you change the rules, it simply means you validate her difference of opinion.

TEN

Keep Your Head Above Water

Challenges To The Proactive Parent

You've read the book, you've taken the quizzes and you've even created a proactive plan or two. You feel like you've learned how to become more proactive in your parenting, so it's smooth sailing from here on out, right? I wish I could say it is that easy. But unfortunately, there are many challenges facing you as you try to be a proactive parent in today's society. You may be juggling the demands of work and family life, trying to nurture relationships, contending with pervasive media messages that undermine family values and learning about the unique needs of your child. Is it any wonder that parents get discouraged at times? Oh sure, we all get discouraged from time to time as we struggle against the powerful current of our fast paced, overwhelming culture. But the true measure of our success in life won't be measured by what cars we drove or the homes we lived in...it will be measured by the love we give and receive. If you've gotten this far in reading *The Promise of Proactive Parenting: Sea Change,* you know I believe you can have a positive parenting experience. Yes, it is hard work. Yes, it takes time. But you can change the world one child at a time.

A sea change is defined as a substantial transformation. My hope in writing this book has been to create a sea change in you, your child and the world your child lives in. Proactive Parenting is aimed at refining your style so that you can be the best coach and teacher for your child, giving him the skills he needs to be more effective in his life. Don't you believe that if your children and my children are more effective in the world, that the world will truly be a better place? I do!

So, that is why the last chapter of this book is dedicated to showing you how to keep your head above water as you contend with the challenges of raising your child today.

Facing the challenges to the proactive parent

Did your parents ever refuse to let you go to a sleepover or to a certain movie and did you respond by saying, "But everybody else is doing it." This was an attempt to get your parents to loosen the reigns a bit. However, today when your child says, "Everybody else is doing it." ... everybody else probably is! The effect of other families not having "fences," will clearly impact your ability to be effective with your child. Sometimes you will need to respond to your child's request for more independence and sometimes you will have to make those tough decisions that make parenting the hardest job there is. The first step in facing any challenges placed before you, though, is to recognize them. Once your awareness is raised about these obstacles to parenting, you will be better able to make the best age-appropriate decisions for your child.

In this chapter, I will examine five challenges that I believe have a huge impact on parenting today. I will present the challenge and then I will give you some tips and strategies for being proactive in dealing with the challenge as you parent.

Here are five challenges to be discussed in this chapter.

1. Balancing work and family
2. Parenting together...whether you're together or not
3. Parenting your child with special needs
4. Making sense of media messages
5. Raising your child in a materialistic society

Balancing work and family

While there are a lot of opinions out there on how to balance work and family, there simply isn't a single right way to juggle the demands of each. Yet, there are ways to prioritize and manage time in ways that bring about the best results. As a parenting expert, I'm sure you've guessed that I believe raising a physically and emotionally healthy child takes precedence over all else. Though I, too, struggle with putting in the vast hours it takes to parent well while at the same time putting in the necessary time and energy to grow a successful business. The lyrics from one of my mother's favorite songs, sums up the work and family balance issue for me. "Regrets...I've had a few but then again too few to mention." At the end of this journey, I want to say that I never regretted the love, energy and yes, time I put in to raising my children. I once heard a father say, "On my death bed, I know I won't look back and regret that I didn't spend more time at work. And I don't want to look back and say, I regret that I didn't spend enough time with my children."

So, what does this parenting expert think about the challenges of balancing work and family? I am going to share with you my key beliefs about work family balance. You may or may not agree with them, but a wide variety of research supports these beliefs. And then I will give you tips and strategies for the balancing act that I have found helpful both in my work and in my home.

My beliefs

* Parents need to take primary responsibility for parenting. Which as you know by now, I believe parenting is an active process of teaching and learning that takes a significant amount of time. Does this mean one parent shouldn't work? Ideally, one or the other parent should be present the majority of time but of course, either or both can work. The idea is for work life to revolve around family life not the other way around.
* Making sacrifices professionally is definitely preferable to making sacrifices when it comes to parenting. If your

goal is to raise a child capable of making good decisions in tough times, someone has to put the necessary work into shaping learning and decision making. Can both parents work 50 hours per week and still raise an effective child? I'm sure it's possible but only if you delegate your parenting to someone who is loving, capable, structured and willing to shape values, set limits, expect cooperation and responsibility for about twenty years. The person most likely to have these qualifications is you!

- Your child needs positive female and male role models, regardless of gender or family make up. Both men and women play important roles in the teaching and learning your child requires for healthy relationships.

Strategies for balancing work and family

Given the fact that a lot of us need to work for financial or professional reasons, how do we make it all come together?

Here are some tips and strategies for achieving the right balance.

- Keep schedules simple, especially when your child is spending time with you. Your child doesn't need a myriad of structured activities...he just wants to be with you.
- Keep the transitions your child is expected to make each day to a minimum. Changing locations and care providers often each day is very difficult especially for a younger child. A child who has an intense temperament or adapts poorly to change will need fewer transitions as well.
- Prepare for the week in advance. Doing as much as possible the night before or on Sunday will make the crunch times easier to handle. Imagine how helpful it will be to set yourself up for success.
- Don't expect a lot of your child at the end of the day. Think of late afternoon or evening as time to wind down not up.

- Start routines earlier and make them simpler. And keep your expectations low. Your child doesn't necessarily need a bath every night or an elaborate dinner.
- Plan meals ahead or go simple. If you're looking for the benefits of eating together as a family, make that special dinner on the weekend.
- Don't be afraid to set limits or follow through even if your time with your child is limited. Your child will behave better in the long run if boundaries are clear and if consequences to misbehavior are predictable and consistent.
- Have a homework helper so that homework doesn't have to wait until you get home or begin after dinner. More than likely, your child is ready to relax at that time not begin challenging assignments. Again, this is especially true the younger the child.
- Make bedtime sacred. Although you want to spend time with your child, believe it or not, it is more important for behavior and school performance for her to get to bed early.
- Reevaluate work. Reflect on each child's age and temperament, you may need to reconsider work hours, location and childcare. Remember, your active parenting years are shorter than you think. A note of caution here though. Don't believe the myth that says wait until your child hits middle school or high school, then you can work all you want. Adolescents need their parents so very much. Your years to fully explore your professional options will come when the nest is empty.

Your child wants to be parented by you. If you keep your family in focus, it truly will all come together. Leave your mind open to all potential possibilities...remember there isn't one right way, there are many right ways.

Parenting together...whether you're together or not

A fundamental skill for powerful parenting is your ability to set clear, direct and specific limits. Limits should be easy for your child to follow. But it's hard to always know what your non-negotiable limits for behavior should be, so wouldn't you think that parenting *with* someone else would make it easier? Not so, according to many of the parents I work with in consultation. While most parents agree that parenting together is important, many say that blending two parenting styles makes setting limits even harder. Factor in that a significant number of parents are no longer living together or are even remarried, and imagine how hard it is to parent together. However, whether you are together with your child's other parent or not, your child is in the middle. Deciphering inconsistent messages about expectations for behavior is going to be very difficult for your child. Delivering consistent and predictable messages about behavior is the responsibility of both parents whether they are together or not.

The styles

In Chapter 6, I describe three different parenting styles. They are the reactive style, the wavering style and the pro-active style. Here are the nuances of each.

If either or both of you have the reactive style of parenting you may feel that you are spending most of your parenting time in conflict with your child. Although you may have clear limits, you tend to react to your child's misbehavior in angry or frustrated ways. Emotions may run high in your family with no one quite sure how to stop the constant conflict. Peaceful times seem few and far between. Often, behavioral skill building doesn't take place, but testing of boundaries and limits does. This style of parenting encourages your child to either avoid or provoke your reactions and teaches your child how to negotiate limits.

If either or both you have the wavering style of parenting, you may have limits but you may be inconsistent about following through on them. Do you do a lot of talking and not a lot of acting when it comes to conflict discipline? The inconsistencies of this style actually encourage a child to push the limits and boundaries. Remember, a child will test the boundaries of the fence in order to find them, not to change them. A child may even take advantage of his parents' inability to present a united front when it comes to rules and expectations. When you waver in your limit setting and follow through, your child learns that sometimes you mean what you say but often you don't.

If you have the proactive style of parenting, you have firm unmistakable limits that are clearly conveyed to your child. This style of parenting fosters age-appropriate independent decision-making by your child. When misbehavior occurs, words are followed by appropriate action. Your parenting is like having a backyard surrounded by a sturdy fence. Your child can choose to run or swing or slide but the boundaries of his yard are clear. You are teaching your child the skills he needs to become capable, responsible and to be motivated from within. His ability to accept limits and act in acceptable ways will help him handle life's ups and downs.

Strategies for parenting together

Typically, one parent may have one style while the other has a different style. The styles you and your partner have will either facilitate working together or not. Are you both reactive? Is one person reactive while the other parent wavers? Working together to blend your styles is where the real work of parenting together lies. Open communication and a commitment to doing so on behalf of your child is the key. Here are some strategies for blending styles that will make it easier for you to be proactive as you parent together.

- Know your styles. This would be a good time to take the *Are you a Proactive Parent?* quiz, found in Chapter 6, if you haven't already done so. Remember, to talk about your styles when neither of you is upset about a parenting dilemma.
- Think about what steps each of you can take to adopt a more proactive style. Use the results of your quiz to focus your energies on being more proactive.
- Make the time to routinely discuss what each of you is doing to blend the best of your styles. Your goal is to

present to your child more unity around non-negotiable limit setting.

- Review what your limits really are. It will be impossible to convey them to your child if you are unclear about which rules are non-negotiable.
- Decide, in advance and away from your child, how you will handle discipline issues that you don't agree on. Don't let your child know that he has the power to start arguments between you.
- Offer support. Create a signal between you and your partner that conveys you need help when you are in conflict with your child.
- Take a break. If one parent is in conflict with the child and the other disagrees with what is happening, take time out to discuss the plan. Tell your child you will get back to her when the two of you have decided how to handle the problem.
- Get professional help. If you feel unable to blend your styles on your own, enlist the help of someone trained to help you. Role modeling healthy conflict resolution for your child is very important.

Respecting each other as you present a united front is the key to parenting together. Take the time to reflect on what brought you together in the first place. Especially when times are tough remember, the respect you show each other is the respect your child is learning to have for you.

Parenting your child with special needs

Should I provide the same discipline to my child with special needs that I do for my other child? If you have a child with special needs, you may be asking yourself that question quite often. Special needs are defined as any physical disability, learning disability or chronic illness with symptoms that may be mild, moderate or severe. Since the Proactive Parenting approach teaches you to factor into your parenting the specific development and temperament of each child, the approach for the child with special needs is no different than it is for any other child. In fact, a behavioral approach to teaching and learning such as Proactive Parenting is the approach of choice for the child with special needs. Let me illustrate my point here. Remember, the bell curve from Chapter 2? You can use that bell curve to represent the continuum of development and temperament for any child.

Figure I

The Bell Curve of Temperament
Continuum of distractibility for three children

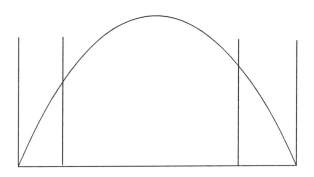

Mackenzie   Greg   Meg

 Mackenzie is a child who is sometimes distracted and sometimes not. This is considered normal variation for distractibility.

 Greg is a child who is more distracted than is typical. This level of distractibility is still considered within normal limits.

 Meg is a child who is more distracted than is typical and it interferes with her ability to function. This level of distractibility is outside the realm of normal.

Let's look at the element of temperament called distractibility. In Figure I, you can see that the three children represented have varying levels of distractibility. Mackenzie is only distracted in situations that you would expect him to be. Greg is often more distracted than Mackenzie but still within the normal range for this element of temperament. But Meg is clearly distracted to the point that her inability to focus affects her schoolwork, friendships and ability to follow important directions. When an element of temperament is exaggerated to the point that it falls outside the bell curve, it is considered out of the realm of normal and may be a disorder. In Meg's case it is called Attention Deficit Disorder.

The best way to help Greg and Meg use strategies to focus better is to institute a good behavioral plan. The goal of using a good behavioral plan like Proactive Parenting is to move both children back on that bell curve towards the middle. Do you see that while only one child would be considered to have special needs, the plan for both would be the same? Now of course, the behavioral coaching Meg's parents will have to do will be more significant than the coaching Greg's or even Mackenzie's parents would have to do but the approach remains the same. You see, a child with special needs really does require discipline plans similar to the type you provide to a typically developing child. In fact, there are no special methods aimed at discipline for the child with special needs. Your child may simply require more consistent discipline because of all she must cope with related to her special needs.

Meds or no meds

A note about medication here. While a child with special needs will always require a behavioral plan, he may or may not need medications. The decision to use medication in conjunction with a good behavioral plan is best discussed with a trained medical professional. If you're considering medication, keep these important points in mind.

- Never use medication alone to manage behavior. Your child still needs strategies to cope with being too sensitive, too anxious or too distracted.
- Consider putting a good behavioral plan into place before you begin medication. If you are able to successfully move a child back in the direction of normal on the bell curve than perhaps medications are not necessary.
- Ask your health care professional to prescribe medication after you have instituted a good behavioral plan but have been unsuccessful in moving your child back in the direction of normal on the bell curve.
- Become comfortable with your decision. If your child needed a medication for a rash or asthma, you wouldn't hesitate to administer it. If you can truly say that you have instituted a good behavioral plan and followed through on it consistently, but have seen little change in your child's behavior, know that you have made your decision thoughtfully.

Strategies for parenting your child with special needs

With 10-20% of America's children coping with some type of chronic condition, you are not alone in trying to parent using sensitive, practical and proactive discipline strategies. While all families struggle with similar discipline issues, your parenting may be complicated by feelings of lack of control over the illness or condition and empathy for all your child must cope with.

Here are some important strategies to keep in mind as you think about discipline for your child with special needs.
- Learn about your child's condition. The more you know about your child's particular illness or learning disability the better prepared you will be to provide effective discipline.
- Celebrate your child's strengths. With so much focus on what your child may not be able to do, you never want to lose sight of the wonderful gifts and talents your child does have "in the bag."

- Anticipate the situations in which your child may have difficulty. Does your child typically have difficulty socially or academically? If so, use the knowledge you have about these themes to plan ahead.
- Develop a plan. Having a clear plan for handling challenging situations will help you to follow through on the limits you establish. For example, the child who is easily distracted will be more likely to succeed with a specific homework plan.
- Accept your feelings. While you might feel empathy for what your child must contend with, relaxing the rules will have a negative affect on the role you play in shaping your child's behavior.
- Strengthen the parent/teacher connection. You and your child's teacher must act as partners in providing discipline to your child. This partnership will go along way in helping your child understand what is expected of her.
- Know your rights. Certain federal and state laws may make provisions for you to receive certain services in the community or at school. While not every child with special needs can receive special education services, your child with special needs may be eligible for modifications to the curriculum that make participating in school a bit easier.
- Increase your supervision of your child. For a child with behavioral issues related to a particular condition, it may be important to actually watch over her more intently. This will allow you to role model appropriate behavior as well as intervene on inappropriate behavior more readily.
- Use lots of small action cueing and repetition. Remember, your child will need more consistency and predictability to get those skills "in the bag."
- Ask for help. It can be hard to provide discipline to a child with a chronic illness or disability. Your pediatrician, parenting professional or even other parents may be able to offer you the tips and support you need to parent well.
- Take care of yourself. Caring for a child with special needs requires more of you. Finding periods of time

where you can refill your precious jar of energy will be important.

If you are a parent of a child with special needs, you might hope that there is a magic approach to discipline. But there isn't. Fortunately, facing your discipline issues is more straightforward than you may think. The answer lies in learning Proactive Parenting well and using it more.

Making sense of the media

Television, print advertising and the Internet are major forces in the popular culture. Your child is exposed to more information and savvy promotion than just one generation ago. Whether on television, in print or on the Internet, your child is exposed to thousands of media messages each day. Advertisers are targeting your child with billions of advertising dollars. Television programming and movies set trends for clothing, language and music at lightning speed. And as a direct result of this bombardment of messages aimed at your child, you have new challenges in parenting. The reason I chose to include making sense of media messages as a challenge to the proactive parent is to raise your awareness about this profound influence on your child. Exposure to anything for large amounts of time on a routine basis shapes behavior and teaches values. There are benefits that come from responsible use of media. Your child has access to richer and more varied types of information that impacts knowledge and development than ever before. Because of the technology of television and the Internet, positive people use the media to influence social change and to do good things for others. And television, movies and the Internet can be a lot of fun for your child, his friends and your family.

Yet, I'm sure you've heard the down side. Exposure to negative messages and opportunistic people impact your child as well. The power of the media when used irresponsibly is frightening. Both positive and negative messages can influence what your child thinks she must have and do. It is impossible to extract these messages once they have been taken in. Without any discussion, your child will adopt attitudes, behaviors and values based on these messages.

The impact of these messages aimed at your child will have a different effect based on your child's age. A young child, while still exposed to media messages and societal trends will be affected in different ways than an older child. If your child is preschool age or younger he is forming perceptions and attitudes about the world and is therefore influenced in a more unconscious way by such things as the Internet and television. Your young child is highly influenced by the way the media influences what you say and do. Remember, what you role model is very important to how your child learns.

Your older child is more profoundly influenced by media messages. She is likely to look to her friends for acceptance and reassurance because fitting in matters a great deal. And so, the way her friends interpret media messages will have additional power over her behavior and opinions.

Strategies for making sense of media messages

So, powerful media messages are everywhere, "what can I do about it" you wonder? The only weapon against this kind of conditioning is to discuss the messages your child receives. Helping your child to recognize the power of media messages, setting limits on inappropriate in-fluences and helping your child to accept your limits is a huge piece of parenting toward this challenge. Do you really know what messages your child is being exposed to? Are you aware of the impact these messages are having on his behavior? Violence, sexuality and negative images of women, aging and the family itself are just some of the messages that may undermine your parenting. How do you make sense of these mighty messages your child is exposed to?

Here are some strategies for making sense of media messages.

- Talk to your child often about the media messages he is exposed to. Keeping the door to communication open is your best defense against the influence of negative messages.
- Point out positive use of media. Not all media messages are negative, be sure to mention the constructive and socially conscious ones.
- Watch television or go online with your child. Showing your child what is acceptable is the first step to clarifying expectations. And watching a favorite show and talking about the characters' triumphs and tribulations is fun.
- Teach your child how to watch. Examine and discuss with your child exactly what the messages are. What do they mean to her and how does your family agree or disagree? Media literacy is a way to place filters on the inevitable messages your child will be exposed to.
- Keep computers and televisions in central locations, so that monitoring use is easier for you and safer for your child.
- Role model reasonable exposure to media. If you don't want your child online and watching television constantly than you should set a good example.
- Set clear limits about the family rules for use of television and the Internet, both in and out of your home. Make these rules clear to your child and revisit them often.
- Problem solve together, the possible dilemmas associated with easy access to so much information and the powerful messages that come with it.
- Monitor limits and provide consequences. If you tell your child not to watch a certain movie or read a certain magazine, then there must be a consequence for doing so. Remember, your limits are only as good as your follow through.
- Encourage other activities such as reading, writing, sporting activities or hobbies. There are so many other productive ways for children to spend their time.
- Strive for balance between simplicity and technology. Schedule family fun activities that don't involve media. You will be amazed at what you find out about your child if you have an opportunity to talk.

- Use the media to your advantage. Go online to movie or television review sites, so that you know exactly what you can say, "yes" or "no" to.

The older your child gets, the more fully entrenched in the popular culture she will become. And the concerns you have about television, magazines, movies and the Internet will become front and center. Whether your child is in preschool or high school, your parenting must be aimed at shaping your child's interpretation of media messages. As a proactive parent, you can be an influential guide for your child as she interfaces with the popular culture.

Raising your child in a materialistic society

One of the biggest challenges facing you today is raising your child in a materialistic society. It doesn't matter how much money you have or what your cultural background is, your child is inundated with messages from the popular culture that happiness comes from having the right things. Do you ever feel the need to have the latest style jeans or most advanced cell phone? Have you ever participated in the quest for just the right car or in the latest collectible craze? It's hard to resist the temptation created by exposure to advertising and savvy promotion...isn't it? It is becoming harder and harder to distinguish between what you need and what you want. If you find it a challenge to resist the persuasive popular culture messages, can you imagine what a challenge it is for your child?

Everyone talks about how busy life is and how limited time is. Work and family balance topped the list of challenges to the proactive parent found in this chapter. Do you find yourself feeling guilty about the time you spend away from your child? In an effort to make up for being away, it might be tempting to try and show your child how much he is loved by buying him things. Unfortunately, *presents* and *presence* are not interchangeable concepts. Taking the time to clarify your values and taking steps to communicate those values to your child may be taking second place to having the right things and being in the right activities.

Like so many parents are you looking for opportunities to express your concerns to your child about materialism? Do you want to learn the concrete strategies you can use to combat the influences of this sophisticated and complex popular culture on your child? If you create the dialogues necessary to clarify values and you learn practical strategies for raising your child in a materialistic society...you can change the dynamic of materialism in your family. By now you know that I believe that societal change can be measured one family at a time.

Strategies for raising your child in a materialistic society

Regardless of the struggles you face in raising your child in a materialistic society, you can take an active role in combating these powerful influences. Here are a number of strategies that may help.

- Raise your awareness about exposure to materialistic ideas and behavior. The first step in coping with the influences of the society at large is to understand what the influences are and how they affect you and your child.
- Listen to your child's real concerns and feelings. Faced with more advertising and peer pressure than ever, your child will be influenced by materialism. Actively listening to your child's concerns is critical if you want her to talk to you about the tough choices she has to make.
- Role model good choices about buying and acquiring material things. You are your child's first and best teacher and the choices you make will directly affect your child.
- Clarify your personal ideas and beliefs related to your unique family situation. In order to role model the "right values", you need to know what they are for you.
- Teach your child how to wait for what he wants. Delaying gratification is so important in a society where everything can change at the touch of a button or the click of a mouse. Simple strategies such as working on the hardest homework first or waiting a day to make that impulsive

purchase can teach your child the benefits that come from waiting.

- Give your child the skills she needs to stay true to her values. It is not enough to "just say no." Your child needs concrete strategies for resisting the urge to focus on material possessions. Give her the language and show her the actions she can take to make the right choices.

- Limit television and discuss programs and commercials. With the amount of advertising dollars aimed at your child, you may feel defenseless against the media machine. But a simple strategy is to limit your child's exposure to the efforts to get him to be the ultimate consumer.

- Teach media literacy. Show your child how to look at advertising and discuss the techniques advertisers use to get him to buy the latest product. Your child will soon become skilled at seeing the tactics advertisers use to manipulate him.

- Set limits and follow through. Unfortunately, no matter how proactive you are about teaching values, the day will come when you will need to set limits on negative influences. Following through on the limits that are established is critical if behavior is to be shaped.

- Teach your child how to give of herself without giving with things. Making holiday gifts or cooking for a sick neighbor are beautiful ways of showing your child that giving has more to do with what a person does than what material goods she has to offer.

- Engage in community service and charitable giving. Teaching social responsibility is a very important aspect of development. Learning that one is part of a bigger community and that others benefit from our kindness and generosity is a beautiful gift you can give your child.

- Create family rituals. Family rituals give your child a sense of belonging. In many ways, rituals give your child something different than what he gets from his peer group. Family rituals and traditions have incredible lasting power.

- Teach gratitude. Taking the focus off of "what I don't have" and placing it on "what I do have" is important for you and your child. Learning to be thankful and appreciative is a process that takes time, encouragement and patience.

- Teach your child about money, through chores and allowance. Actively teaching your child what money is and what money does provides an opportunity to teach fiscal responsibility. Chores and allowance can be effective ways of making concrete the abstract qualities of money.
- Help your child learn about responsible spending. Give your child the chance to save money toward a purchase. This experience will teach responsibility and delayed gratification and will lay the foundation for future spending. Your child will learn that the pleasure of impulsive buying is short lived.
- Keep your own spending within limits. Making choices about what spending is appropriate for your family is personal but important. If your child is to learn to appreciate what she has, acquiring things shouldn't come too easily.
- Simplify. Being in the right after school activity or having another toy will not bring happiness. Simplifying life can decrease stress and give back some precious time you can use to spend together.

Show your child how to seek pleasure in things that don't cost money. Take walks, play on the school playground or go to the library. These are simple and no cost ways of enjoying time together. The best way to diminish exposure to materialism is to spend time with your child. What your child truly wants from you is time not things. The years of childhood are fleeting...take the time to make memories and shape values now.

Creating a Sea Change

Learning to be proactive is an active process. You've taken a big step in reading this book and using new tools and strategies as you parent. Be patient with yourself, creating positive change in you and your child will take time. Remember, it is a journey not a race. So, where do we go from here?

- Love the child you've got. While I hope you've become more able to describe your child's most challenging aspects of temperament, I also hope that you see your child's greatest strengths. Celebrate them!
- Trust that you know your child better than anyone. While you will never be able to change the way your child is hard wired, you certainly can smooth out the rough edges and teach him skills to be more effective in his relationships with others.
- Keep learning about how to be proactive in your parenting. If you wanted to learn a new language, you wouldn't go to just one workshop or read one book. You would recognize the need for ongoing exposure to what you needed to learn to be able to speak the language.
- Parent peacefully with your child's other parent. The story of your child's life is unfolding and he loves you both regardless of what is or isn't in your own bags. Make certain your child sees the love and respect you expect from him in the way you treat each other.
- Set a good example. Never forget the profound power of what you are teaching your child through what you do and say. The teaching you do both actively and passively through your words and deeds will have a lasting effect on your child long after you are gone.
- Nurture and protect your child from exposure to the seamy side of life. The time your child has to be a child is getting shorter and shorter. Let your child enjoy being a kid for as long as possible.
- Have reasonable expectations of your child. In our fast paced world you might forget that indeed your child is a child. Many a challenging day can be traced back to too many errands and transitions and too little play and rest.
- Lean on your neighbor. Talk with other parents; get connected to your church or your child's school. We are all in this together and it is important that we share our common triumphs and struggles. It really does "take a village."
- Remember there is no other job in the world as important as raising healthy, cooperative, capable, responsible children.

Dive in, make waves, keep your head above water....but do what it takes to love, enjoy and teach your child what she needs to live a rich and productive life. Shape her life so that she leaves the world a better place because she has lived.

Questions and Answers
Chapter 10

Keep Your Head Above Water

Challenges To The Proactive Parent

Q: I sometimes resent the fact that I spend eighty percent of my energy on only one of my children. Aren't my other two children getting short changed because I spend so much of my time creating fences for one?

A: When you parent toward temperament you must parent with the strongest temperament in mind. But I want you to trust that while one of your children really needs strong fences in order to behave his best, your other children are benefiting from what you are teaching him. Some children learn best concretely and actively. By that I mean it has to happen to him in order to get the learning "in the bag." But other children learn best by watching others. By that I mean they learn vicariously. I assure you, all of your children are learning about expectations and follow through, just perhaps in their own unique ways.

Q: I feel like I am in the minority when it comes to what I will and won't allow my child to be exposed to. It's lonely being the only parent who doesn't let my son watch violent movies or let my daughter hang out at the mall. Should I doubt my judgment when it comes to the impact these things will have on them? Am I being overprotective?

A: Unfortunately, if you feel like you are in the minority on these opinions you are probably right on. Just because a lot of parents have the same thinking about some of your issues doesn't make them right and you wrong. Are you protecting your children from unhealthy influences? Yes. Are you overprotective? I don't think so. If you don't provide the proper fence about societal influences, do you think anyone else will? Keep trusting your instincts when it comes to what you think your children can handle. But to feel less lonely, surround yourself and get connected to those parents who like you are doing the right things for their families even if they are viewed as unpopular.

Q: With all the choices available to parents related to work, travel and leisure time, is it really practical to parent in this comprehensive way?

A: If your goal is to raise a respectful, capable child who is successful interacting with friends and family then this is what it takes. Sacrifice is surely involved in giving what is necessary to nurture any relationship but especially the one between you and your child. It may seem like a lot of work now, but with practice it will become second nature and you will love the changes you see in your family.

Index

Proactive Parenting Order Form

Telephone Orders...Call Proactive Parenting at 781-545-6585. Have your credit card ready.

Web Orders...Go to www.eproactiveparenting.com and click on order now. Have your credit card ready.

Postal Orders...Mail this form and payment to:
Proactive Parenting
Post Office Box 846
Scituate, MA 02066

Sales Tax: Please add 5% for total products shipped to Massachusetts addresses.

Shipping: Please add $4.00 for up to two products to handle the cost of mailing.

Name_____

Address_____

City_____ State_____

Zip Code_____

Telephone_____

E-mail_____

Payment type __Check __Credit card (Specify type_____)

Credit Card Number_____

Name on Card_____

Expiration Date_____

Lynne Reeves Griffin is available to speak in your community. Call Proactive Parenting at 781-545-6585 for information about fees and services.

Printed in the United States
16652LVS00002B/49-510